Heirs to the Princes

Heirs to the Princes
The Welsh Administrative Elite, from the Edwardian Conquest to the Black Death

David Stephenson

UNIVERSITY OF WALES PRESS
2025

© David Stephenson, 2025

All rights reserved. No part of this book may be reproduced in any material form (including photocopying or storing it in any medium by electronic means and whether or not transiently or incidentally to some other use of this publication) without the written permission of the copyright owner. Applications for the copyright owner's written permission to reproduce any part of this publication should be addressed to the University of Wales Press, University Registry, King Edward VII Avenue, Cardiff CF10 3NS

www.uwp.co.uk

British Library CIP Data
A catalogue record for this book is available from the British Library

ISBN 978-1-83772-276-1
eISBN 978-1-83772-277-8

The right of David Stephenson to be identified as author of this work has been asserted in accordance with sections 77 and 79 of the Copyright, Designs and Patents Act 1988.

For GPSR enquiries please contact:
Easy Access System Europe Oü, 16879218
Mustamäe tee 50, 10621, Tallinn, Estonia. *gpsr.requests@easproject.com*

Typeset by Geethik Technologies
Printed by CPI Antony Rowe, Melksham

For Sylvia

Contents

Preface	ix
Acknowledgements	xiii
Maps	xv
Introduction	xxiii

Chapter 1	Edward I's Developing Policy in Wales: The 'Charm Offensive'	1
Chapter 2	The New Elite	19
Chapter 3	'The Men of Position: Those Who Can Be a Help or a Hindrance'. A Biographical Gazetteer Arranged by Region	59
Chapter 4	Reflections on the Survey of the New Elite and the 'Men of Position'	105
Chapter 5	Things Fall Apart	127

Notes	155
Bibliography	183
Index	191

Preface

Perhaps the best way to introduce this volume is to provide an assortment of leitmotifs for the fourteenth century in Wales, as presented by some of the leading historians of the past century. R. R. Davies:

> The difference between English and Welsh in fourteenth-century Wales was in part – and we need not mince our words here – that between conqueror and conquered, between a foreign governmental and commercial elite and an unprivileged native society, between settlers and natives. It was a contrast which permeated many aspects of Welsh life of the period – those of office-holding in church and state, of the redistribution of land in favour of a settler caste, of urban privileges and marketing prohibitions.[1]

A little later in the same work, however, Davies acknowledged at least some of the complexity of the situation:

> It is a distortion of the history of Wales in the fourteenth century to classify men into collaborators or nationalists; for most of them the choice never presented itself in those crude terms. They were, or rather most of them were, Welshmen living in a society where the distinctions between Welsh and English were, at various levels, profoundly important; but where the adjustments of daily life frequently blurred and emasculated those distinctions.[2]

A. D. Carr:

> The activities of the descendants of Ithel Fychan show how communities in late medieval Wales were still dominated by their traditional leaders. The careers of Ithel ap Cynwrig Sais and Rhys ap Roppert reflect a world in which king, prince or marcher lord might propose but where local leaders certainly disposed. The period between the Edwardian conquest and the outbreak of the Glyn Dŵr revolt is sometimes seen as a time when the Welsh were oppressed by alien officials. Men like Cynwrig and Rhys are a reminder that this belief over-simplifies a complex political and social milieu.[3]

Glyn Roberts:

> It has long been known that one of the remarkable features of the reigns of Edward I and Edward II was the emergence of a Welsh official class in Gwynedd and the royal possessions in south Wales – a class which showed remarkable loyalty to Edward II in his struggles with a dissident baronage.[4]

J. Beverley Smith:

> Edward II drew particularly valuable support from among the men of the principality of Wales, and the action of these royal adherents in undermining the position of the king's baronial adversaries has a bearing upon the whole history of the reign ... Edward I had in his service numerous Welshmen in whom he could place his trust. These men were drawn from two spheres of political influence. There were some who belonged to Welsh families which had long associations of service with the marcher lineages, notably those of Bohun and Mortimer. Others were men of the principality of Wales whose predecessors had in many cases been prominent members of the households of the Welsh princes of northern and southern Wales.[5]

It is evident therefore that some of the most distinguished historians of Wales have pointed, in different ways, to the complex dynamics of Welsh society and politics from the later years of Edward I through to the age of the Black Death and the early stages of the Hundred Years' War. But the phenomenon of the rise of a Welsh administrative and military elite in a period all too often regarded simply as one dominated by a story of misery and oppression at the hands of alien conquerors, has remained in significant measure under-researched. Those Welsh magnates who succeeded in achieving leadership across the greater part of Wales have proved to be an elusive group, as have the factors which led to the readiness of many ambitious figures to achieve dominance in Wales not by integration into royal and Marcher rule but by its violent elimination and replacement. To improve our understanding of these matters is the object of the present book.

Acknowledgements

The following words of thanks are not at all the usual sort. This book has been produced against a background of traumatic circumstances. After discussions with Dr Llion Wigley of University of Wales Press, I set to work on it at the start of 2022. Some months later, after ten years of holding cancer at bay, my wife Jan sadly died and her funeral was followed by my suffering a serious fall down a flight of stairs in my home, which saw me hospitalised with various bones broken, and a diagnosis of hitherto unknown but severe diabetes. I was only discharged from hospital when my friend Rhydian Brittain offered me a room in his house, and use of his book-room and internet access. There I was given extraordinary care by his son Simon, which accelerated my recovery and enabled me to return to academic work. I was able to work on a number of chapters for publication in multi-authored volumes, and to restart work for this one. All went well for some months, but in late September of 2023, just a few days after I received the formal contract for this book, the small house that serves as my library and office suffered a major fire. The house has needed total internal rebuilding; but almost miraculously the books survived because they were so closely packed on shelves that they were slow to burn, and because the Llanidloes fire brigade were astonishingly quick to get to the house and so expert at getting the fire under control. It was at this point that the Brittain family, Rhydian, Simon and his wife Wendy, once again proved crucial, by giving me the use of a very large room in which I could store some thousands of books. I must also thank the great team responsible for rebuilding, rewiring and redecorating the house for making it all as painless as possible, and those friends who helped to carry the books from a smoke-blackened near ruin to safety.

In the writing of this book some of my debts are not new ones: over the years and in a number of books and papers I have been lucky to be able to think and to write following the massive efforts of some truly great scholars whose work has illuminated so many aspects of medieval Wales. In the case of the present volume, I have been privileged to learn from, if not always to agree with, the work of Tony Carr, Rees Davies, Ralph Griffiths, Glyn Roberts and Beverley Smith. Other debts will be apparent from the bibliography and the notes. Encouragement has also come from my on-line classes on thirteenth- and fourteenth-century Wales. Some members of those classes are far from amateurs, but have published valuable commentaries themselves, and will, I hope, go on to write still more. With close to a hundred members, I cannot notice everyone by name but must record particular thanks for their input to Gideon Brough, Judith Cuddihey, Esther Colby, John Davies, John Fleming, Stella and Charles Gratrix, Philip Hume, Kirsten Lawton-Smith, Mo Lloyd, Gail and John Peacock, David Pilling, Julian Ravest, Nicola Roberts, Andy Shell, Andrew Smith. and Mel Walters. Once again, I have been able to benefit from the skills and patience of so many at University of Wales Press, notably Llion Wigley (Senior Commissioning Editor), Dafydd Jones (Editor of the Press), Steven Goundrey (Production Manager) and Heather Palomino for her copy-editing. The splendid regional maps were drawn by Craig Asquith.

There is one further acknowledgement, which explains the dedication. Over the last year and more Sylvia Bestwick has supported and sustained me with care, encouragement and companionship to a degree which I could not have anticipated and had not thought possible.

THE NORTHERN MARCH AND FLINTSHIRE

THE SOUTHERN PRINCIPALITY AND APPURTENANT LORDHSIPS

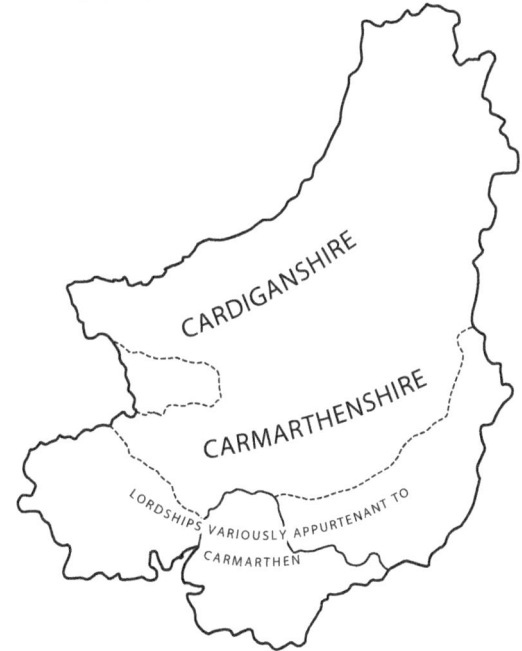

THE SOUTH WESTERN MARCH

Introduction

*The collapse of the traditional order:
the end of the Age of the Princes*

The twelfth and thirteenth centuries in Wales have not unjustly been described as the age of the princes. Rulers such as Madog ap Maredudd (d. 1160) in Powys, the Lord Rhys (d. 1197) in Deheubarth, and Llywelyn ab Iorwerth (d. 1240) and Llywelyn ap Gruffudd (d. 1282) in Gwynedd were rulers, often of much of Wales beyond the bounds of their patrimonial lands, who may be counted amongst the state-builders of medieval Europe. But after the Welsh wars of Edward I there remained little of the great heritage of Welsh kingship.[1] There were, of course, descendants of the princes and other rulers who survived the disasters of 1277 and 1282–3, but they were able to carry only a patchy and enfeebled echo of the tradition of the princely rulers into the period that followed the death in December 1282 of Llywelyn ap Gruffudd, prince of Wales, and his brother Dafydd who claimed for a few months the same position until his capture and execution in 1283. By the end of 1283, the surviving Welsh lords of princely descent and continuing significance were few: Rhys ap Maredudd, lord of Dryslwyn in Ystrad Tywi had stood by Edward I in 1277 and 1282–3, and had been rewarded accordingly. The same situation applied in the case of Gruffudd ap Gwenwynwyn of Powys, perhaps the most powerful of Prince Llywelyn's Welsh opponents. He not only maintained control of his lordship of southern Powys but extended that territory by the acquisition of the lordship of Mechain. But Rhys ap Maredudd rose in rebellion in 1287, was captured in 1291 and executed in 1292. He left no heir at liberty. Gruffudd ap Gwenwynwyn died in 1286 and was succeeded as lord of Powys by his eldest son Owain, who in turn died in 1293, leaving a child heir, Gruffudd who died in 1309. Gruffudd's sister Hawise became the heiress to the lordship of Powys, and was rapidly married off to John Charlton, a Shropshire gentleman and a courtier of Edward II. Owain ap Gruffudd's brother Llywelyn, who had succeeded to some of the lands of Powys according to the terms of a family compact of 1278 redrawn in 1291, died in 1295 without a male heir; some of his territories passed as dower lands into the hands of his widow, Sybil, to be held for her life, while the remainder reverted to the estate of Owain ap Gruffudd's heir, Gruffudd. Thus, the two great Welsh lordships of Dryslwyn and Pool passed into other hands, one by escheat to the Crown, and the other by marriage.

Some lesser survivors managed to hold on to restricted realms. Such was the case with the 'barons' who held small baronies or lordships in the land of Edeirnion in the upper Dee region, or those in the adjacent land of Dinmael. These baronies, parts of the county of Merioneth and the lordship of Denbigh respectively, were held mainly by descendants of Owain Brogyntyn ap Madog ap Maredudd, the twelfth- and early thirteenth-century minor lord of part of Powys. As a result of a tradition of partition of the baronies amongst numerous co-heirs they became more and more fragmented, and their holders were reduced over time to the status of impoverished minor gentry. One line of the barons of Edeirnion had a rather brighter future. These were the descendants of Gruffudd Fychan (d. 1289), a son of Gruffudd ap Madog of northern Powys. Gruffudd Fychan had been lord of the commote of Iâl and of Glyndyfrdwy in Edeirnion, in the years after 1277, but support for Prince Llywelyn in 1282 meant that he lost Iâl, and was lucky to hang on to Glyndyfrdwy. At first he was denied even the title of baron, being simply a tenant at will (i.e. without any security of tenure) of the king. His son Madog, however, was recognised as a hereditary tenant (by barony) of Glyndyfrdwy and managed to add half of the commote of Cynllaith to the family lands. The family emerged as prominent figures in the region

Introduction

of the Berwyn mountains, with part of their lands (Glyndyfrdwy) on the western side of the Berwyn and the other part (Cynllaith Owain) on the eastern side. They were connected by marriage to the important family of Lestrange, in which context Gruffudd ap Madog ap Gruffudd Fychan appears as keeper of the manor of Ellesmere, which had been granted to his brother-in-law Eubolo Lestrange. Another marriage, that of Gruffudd Fychan (II) ap Gruffudd ap Madog to Elen, daughter of Thomas ap Llywelyn ab Owain, one of the few fourteenth-century representatives of the dynasty of the Lord Rhys, brought together the descendants of the dynasties of Powys and of Deheubarth. Gruffudd Fychan II may not have controlled huge lands, but his family tree, and that of his wife brought together much of the dynastic histories of Wales. By the later years of the fourteenth century, the current head of the family could be pictured by the poet Iolo Goch as the very epitome of the successful Welsh squire. His name was Owain Glyn Dŵr. Owain could trace his lineage back to the rulers of Powys and of Deheubarth, and he was to become famous throughout England and Wales.[2] Elen, the wife of Gruffudd Fychan II, was also of royal blood. She was a daughter of Thomas ap Llywelyn, a son of Llywelyn ab Owain ap Maredudd, who hung on to a commote and a half in southern Ceredigion in the aftermath of 1282–3. He had been a minor in the war of 1282–3, and this may explain why he escaped the imprisonment which befell his kinsmen.

The marriage alliance between Gruffudd Fychan II and Elen ferch Thomas was far from a matter of chance. It reveals how few were the dynastic options available to families who wished to preserve the royal bloodlines of the old dynasties. Of the male representatives of such dynasties, several had been deprived in the aftermath of 1282–3 of all but a few scraps of land, and had been easily led or pushed into rebellion, like Madog ap Llywelyn, of the Meirionnydd branch of the ruling house of Gwynedd, descended from Cynan ab Owain Gwynedd. Madog ap Llywelyn failed to make good his claim to Meirionnydd, but he held lands on Anglesey, reportedly granted to him by Prince Llywelyn ap Gruffudd. His bloodline ensured that he led, or was placed at the head of, the Gwynedd rising of 1294–5, but he was eventually captured and spent his remaining years as a prisoner in the Tower of London. His sons managed to secure possession of the family lands in Anglesey, and in one case became a king's esquire. Maelgwn ap Rhys Fychan of Ceredigion, his father Rhys Fychan ap Rhys ap Maelgwn, and his kinsmen Gruffudd and Cynan, sons of Maredudd ab Owain, were captured after they had persisted in rebellion against the English king, whether in 1283, 1294–5, or rather later, like Llywelyn ap Gruffudd, son of the last Welsh lord of Senghennydd in the land of Morganwg, who was driven into rebellion in 1316. One other prominent rebel, associated with Dafydd ap Gruffudd in 1283, and leader of the Glamorgan rising of 1294–5 as well as the treasonous conspiracy of Thomas Turberville in 1295, was Morgan ap Maredudd, descendant of the Lord Rhys, and of the lords of Gwynllwg. Morgan showed a marked, and decidedly suspicious, ability to distance himself from other rebels, and was subsequently rewarded and employed by Edward I and Edward II.

Another, rather more prosaic, exception to this pattern of rebellion followed by either execution or imprisonment was the lord of Mawddwy. Mawddwy, which was obtained by William de la Pole, a son of Gruffudd ap Gwenwynwyn, was a mesne lordship held from his brother Owain, and William's descendants, careful not to be associated with the dangerous tendencies to rebellion or conspiracy, held it for several generations, without ever becoming particularly well-known or powerful beyond western Powys.

One more princeling who survived the wars of 1277–83 (because he lived in England and did not participate in them) was Prince Llywelyn's youngest brother, Rhodri ap Gruffudd. Rhodri posed no threat to either Llywelyn or to Edward I, and that was in significant measure the key to his survival. But he was the ancestor of the charismatic Owain Lawgoch who began to raise claims to the principality of Wales in the mid-fourteenth century, and benefited from the sympathy and even the help of the French government. His importance as a 'problem' for the English was underscored when they paid him the compliment of organising his assassination in 1378.

Introduction

There were only a few exceptions to this story of frustration and consequent rebellion and failure, followed by violent death or by imprisonment. And yet the old lines of former ruling dynasties were not entirely extinguished, and some of them survived to become members of what was, in effect, a new social order of leadership in post-Conquest Welsh society. Members of this new aristocracy, who came to the fore in the decades after the conquest, and particularly those who formed its small but highly influential elite, were often able to trace descent from former ruling houses. It seems that such descent was still a significant aid to worldly advancement, though, as we shall see, it was but one element in the recipe for worldly success.

The background to a new order in Wales

It is of course possible to depict developments in Wales after the 'Conquest' of 1283, or perhaps after the suppression of the rebellions of 1295, simply in terms of the construction of an English supremacy. Marcher lords of overwhelmingly English origins were restored to lands that had been seized or seriously threatened by Llywelyn ap Gruffudd. In the lands, primarily in West and North-West Wales, that were taken into Crown hands, the senior posts like those of the Justices of North Wales and of South/West Wales and the Chamberlain of North Wales were monopolised by English officials; below these officers the territories of what became the northern and southern principalities were dominated by county sheriffs. Initially none of these officials was Welsh. Much the same can be said of the military commanders, the castellans of the new castles in the Crown lands which Edward I had ordered to be built, such as Flint, Rhuddlan, Conwy, Caernarfon, Beaumaris, Harlech, Aberystwyth, and Builth.

But such a picture is perhaps simplistic: some of the officers just noticed might discharge their duties through deputies, and over time these tended increasingly to include Welshmen. To be an English official in the principality lands could be a dangerous occupation, as witnessed by the killing of Geoffrey Clement, deputy-justiciar of south Wales, and Roger Puleston, sheriff of Anglesey, in the course of the risings of 1294. The king gradually had to acknowledge that it was better to rule Wales through Welsh officials. At the lower levels of administration this was simply a matter of common sense. The Welsh community had to be regulated by officials who could communicate in Welsh – that is those who were of Welsh birth. And, therefore, it was inevitable that Welshmen should dominate the lower structures of governance within Wales: the *rhingylliaid* and other 'grass-roots' officers all bear witness to this sort of practical political discrimination.

But the twelfth and thirteenth centuries had also witnessed the growth of a much more complex and sophisticated administration in Wales, so that within both Marcher lordships and the lands of the Welsh princes and greater lords there had emerged a class of senior officials who were adept at exercising diplomatic, financial and military duties, while supervising specialist staff such as lawyers, physicians and castle builders. Senior administrative officials with broad competence had grown up in Welsh principalities and lordships, and in Marcher lordships, particularly in the thirteenth century. They had risen not just administratively, but also socially: members of this developing ministerial aristocracy were on occasion rewarded with lands to be held by privileged tenures, and some, a highly privileged and ambitious few, married into the ranks of the Welsh families of royal descent, while others found wives in the families of the lords of the March. It is to the development in the thirteenth century of the ministerial elite that we now turn.

It will be helpful to focus most of this discussion on the governing elite which developed in Gwynedd in the thirteenth century.[3] Gwynedd's institutional development in this period was not unique, but it left far more evidence than can be seen in other parts of Wales. What we can see quite clearly is the development of what I have described as a ministerial aristocracy.

From the early years of the century, we pick up references to an increasingly important official of the prince of Gwynedd (*princeps Norwallie*): the *distain* or steward (Latin *senescallus*). In the

Introduction

law-texts the *distain* is usually listed as the third in seniority of the twenty-four officials of the court, and this seems to reflect that officer's early rank; but in a telling reference in the law-book *Llyfr Iorwerth* (produced in Gwynedd, c.1230) it is noted that the men of Gwynedd do not include the *penteulu* (the captain of the household troop) in the twenty-four officials *y adan y dysteyn* (under the *distain*). This suggests very strongly that the *distain* had become the senior officer of the court by that date.

A somewhat similar rise in the power and prestige of the *distain* is revealed in record sources. From early in the thirteenth century Gwyn ab Ednywain is probably to be identified as the steward in the entourage of Llywelyn ab Iorwerth (and perhaps of his kinsman Gruffudd ap Cynan, who was clearly powerful in the 1190s), as he appears to have been particularly prominent in witness-lists (heading the non-royal lay witnesses) and in other duties. He was usually not given any specific designation as *senescallus*. That fact may not indicate that he was not *distain*, but rather that that office was not yet of such eminence that its holder was specially designated as such. The court, in its administrative as opposed to 'domestic' aspects may still have been significantly undifferentiated, with its members appointed to undertake specific duties on an ad hoc basis. It is possible, even likely, that Gwyn ab Ednywain was succeeded initially by the poet/lawyer and administrator Einion ap Gwalchmai.[4]

It is difficult to be precise about the point at which things changed. By the late 1220s/early 1230s a major figure had emerged, whose rise to prominence seems to have coincided with a rise in the importance of the office of *distain*. This was the celebrated official Ednyfed Fychan. Ednyfed is well known as the leading figure in the administration of Llywelyn ab Iorwerth in the decade before Llywelyn's death in 1240 and in that of his son Dafydd in his short principate (1240–6). Ednyfed was an almost legendary figure, famed in folk-memory as a great warrior, so that when he was accorded a coat of arms, almost certainly significantly after his death in 1246, it featured the heads of three Englishmen, said to have been severed by Ednyfed in the course of a battle against forces of the earl of Chester.

But in the record sources (charters of the two princes and letters emanating largely from the English court) we see another side to Ednyfed. He appears frequently in a diplomatic capacity, on one occasion engaged in travel – clearly a pilgrimage – to the Holy Land, in the course of which he stayed in London when Henry III planned to give him a silver cup to the value of five marks. This suggests something of Ednyfed's importance in the court of Llywelyn ab Iorwerth, as well as the esteem in which he was held by the English king. Other records reveal Ednyfed acting in a judicial capacity, as when it was recalled, long after the event, how two lords of Mechain had pleaded in a case regarding disputed lands in that region, before Ednyfed, the prince's justice. All told, the number and variety of records show a minister who was virtually omnicompetent.

Two more aspects of Ednyfed Fychan's importance need to be emphasised. The first is that he left an expectation that his descendants would follow him in the highest levels of administrative and other aspects of service to the princes of Gwynedd. The second is that his marriage to Gwenllian, daughter of the Lord Rhys, raised his descendants by Gwenllian to the status of the offspring of a royal house. In the first of these cases, it is clear that three of his sons followed him in turn as holders of the post of *distain*. The first of these was Gruffudd (served 1247– c.56), the second Goronwy (served c.1257–68) and the third Tudur (1268– c.81). Of these, Goronwy seems to have been particularly active in all spheres of governance – administrative, military and diplomatic. In a period when the court poets seem not to have been very active in producing compositions in praise of the prince,[5] Llywelyn ap Gruffudd, there are several examples of praise poems to the family of Ednyfed Fychan. Ednyfed himself was the subject of a *Marwnad*, while of his sons, Gruffudd is known to have been the subject of one *Marwnad*, Goronwy of two more, and a son of Goronwy of yet another. These figures contrast with the situation in Gwynedd in the twelfth century, when no examples of poems praising lay officials have survived. In this respect it would seem that the leading officials might have been beginning to rival the prince himself.

Introduction

In the case of Ednyfed's marriage to Gwenllian, daughter of the Lord Rhys, it seems clear that the sons to whom Gwenllian gave birth were favoured, as they succeeded to their father's office, and to lands which Gwenllian brought to Ednyfed in south Wales. This meant that the descendants of Goronwy and Gruffudd, who inherited those lands, had the advantage of royal blood.[6]

A further and crucial aspect of the emergence of a ministerial aristocracy, beyond the birth of its members into families with records of administrative and genealogical eminence on both paternal and maternal sides, is the form in which they held their lands. If we look at lands held by descendants of the probable *distain* of the early thirteenth century, Gwyn ab Ednywain, we find that their description in the great surveys of the middle decades of the fourteenth century is what we should expect of territories held by 'ordinary' freemen. The descendants of Gwyn ab Ednywain paid rents to the prince for their lands, paid certain 'circuit dues' to officials of the prince, investiture fees upon inheritance of lands, *amobr* dues with respect to their daughters upon marriage or in cases of fornication, and often paid for their corn to be ground at the lord's mills. The situation was very different in the case of descendants of Einion ap Gwalchmai.[7] It became still more evidently a matter of special privilege in the case of descendants of Ednyfed Fychan (and of his brothers who were also important administrators, even though the tenure by which they possessed their lands was known as 'Wyrion Eden' – the tenure of the descendants of Ednyfed[8]). These men paid no rents, they paid no circuit dues, no investiture fees, no *amobr* dues, and they had their own mills and so did not pay for the grinding of their corn. They did owe suit to the prince's courts, and they did have the duty, or perhaps the right, of performing military service – a privilege rather than a burden – but this was to be at the prince's cost. In other words, the descendants of Ednyfed's father, Cynwrig ab Iorwerth, held their lands by privileged tenure, which gave them immunity from almost all the usual payments and services which the free population owed to the prince or subsequently the king. Here we have the marks of an aristocracy of service and sometimes an aristocracy of the sword.

It is not only the descendants of Ednyfed and his brothers who were thus marked out as superior types of freemen. In the thirteenth century a number of other descent groups within Gwynedd became similarly privileged. They generally represent lineages whose members had served the prince in an administrative context. We have already noted the development of privileges associated with Einion ap Gwalchmai, very prominent in the prince's service in the years c.1209–23, whose descendants possessed significant lands in Gwynedd, some of which were held by privileged tenure. Einion ap Gwalchmai's father and grandfather Gwalchmai and Meilir, were important court poets, as was Einion himself.[9] I have argued that Einion ap Gwalchmai, who is seen in record sources in ceremonial, diplomatic and judicial roles, which to a certain extent reflect those of Ednyfed Fychan himself, was the father of the Einion Fychan who was second only in administrative eminence to Ednyfed Fychan for around a quarter of a century, and was followed by his equally eminent son, Dafydd ab Einion Fychan. I have further argued that Dafydd ab Einion Fychan is to be identified as the *distain* who succeeded Tudur ab Ednyfed (d. c.1281), and who led a large segment of Prince Llywelyn's army in the direction of Brecon lordship in December 1282, after the prince had divided his forces at Llanganten.[10] On that campaign, the *distain* (i.e. Dafydd) met his death. As one who had died 'against the peace' Dafydd left his heirs severely penalised, but their willingness to help the new regime of Edward I appears to have resulted in the lifting of the penalties against them. They thus continued to enjoy the tenurial privileges and immunities which applied to many of their lands, and which appear to have been the result of grants made to Einion ap Gwalchmai by Llywelyn ab Iorwerth. In that context it is important to note that one of the lands which enjoyed tenurial immunities was a Trefddisteiniaid in Malltraeth, Anglesey.[11] The plural 'townland of the *distains*' is important. It fits an analysis that suggests that both Einion ap Gwalchmai and his descendant Dafydd ab Einion Fychan may have held the office of *distain*. It is possible, therefore, that we may have in Einion ap Gwalchmai in the second decade of the thirteenth century an additional chief officer of the prince's court.

Introduction

The identification of Einion ap Gwalchmai as a *distain* is strengthened by two further considerations. Firstly, the work of Ben Guy on the medieval pedigrees, and specifically the group designated as the Llywelyn ab Iorwerth genealogies, has revealed that Einion ap Gwalchmai is very possibly to be regarded as the compiler of the original text of the Llywelyn ab Iorwerth group, and in that context Guy's detailed argument that the text was marked by 'attempts to bolster the position of Einion ap Gwalchmai's family' as 'the dominant land-holding group in the cantref of Aberffraw' is important.[12] It is most interesting to see a genealogical compilation being developed for the ruling prince of Gwynedd, but at the same time putting great emphasis on the pedigree of the likely compiler, as paramount among the ministerial elite of western Gwynedd.

Secondly, doubt must be cast on the validity of the argument that Einion is unlikely to have been *distain* because he is not so described in the original sources, where he is not accorded any title.[13] It is more than likely that the holder of the office of *distain* in the first decade of the thirteenth century was Gwyn ab Ednywain, but it is interesting that though he was referred to as *senescallus* of Llywelyn ab Iorwerth in an English financial record of 1209, and in Llywelyn ab Iorwerth's grant to Cymer abbey in the same year, he appears without any such designation in several Gwynedd charters. This suggests that the early thirteenth century was a period in which the eminence of the office of *distain*, though already developing, was not such that it was felt that it should be emphasised. On the other hand, the notion that Einion ap Gwalchmai may have held the office of *distain* for some years is rendered uncertain by the fact that in one charter, that of Llywelyn ab Iorwerth to Morgan Gam, issued in 1217, Ednyfed Fychan precedes Einion ap Gwalchmai in the witness-list. It may be that this document was issued at a time when the order of precedence at the court was still somewhat unstable.

In spite of inevitable uncertainties, the important aspects of the examination of the families of Einion ap Gwalchmai and Ednyfed Fychan reveal that both were a very important element in the administration of Gwynedd (and beyond) for much of the thirteenth century, and that the same period saw the steady rise in esteem of the post of *distain* with which both families can be connected. From a position of close to parity with other senior offices in the prince's entourage, the post of *distain* rose from a situation in which it was seldom differentiated from other posts by a distinct Latin title in official records, and in which its holder was not marked out by grants of privileged tenure, to one in which it was normal to designate the *distain* first as *senescallus,* and ultimately as *justiciarius,* while members of both families enjoyed important immunities from tenurial obligations which increasingly distinguished them as superior to the bulk of freemen in Gwynedd.

It clear that there were at least two extremely prominent and privileged kin groups in Gwynedd in the thirteenth century, who retained their eminence into the post-conquest era. To these we can add some three other descent groups whose political position in that century was more precarious, but who retained signs of their importance into the same post-conquest years.[14] There are signs that princely patronage, in the form of grants of privileged land holdings, was drying up in the later years of the principate of Llywelyn ap Gruffudd, but the grants made earlier in that century ensured that the descendants of recipients continued to flourish.

The above discussion has examined only Gwynedd, and principally western Gwynedd. But it is important to note that similar trajectories of ministerial kin-groups can be identified in most areas of Wales in the thirteenth century, so that in most regions a potential ministerial elite was present into the middle and later years of Edward I. It was from these groups that a Welsh governing class could be constructed when the need arose. And it is a representative selection from their more prominent members that we shall now discuss.

The thirteenth-century development of ministerial elites beyond Gwynedd

The first general point to be made is that the thirteenth century witnesses the growing importance of Welsh officials in the

Introduction

service of Marcher lords in all sections of the March. Such officials – above the ranks of those in close contact with the Welsh population as reeves or estate stewards – are scarcely visible in the twelfth century, an age of consolidation of lordship in the March. But it is in the thirteenth-century documentation that we see the rise of a Welsh administrative class whose more ambitious, talented or fortunate members begin to be visible at the senior levels of Marcher governance. By the later years of that century, Welsh officials of the highest rank have become visible in most regions of Wales. They will be examined in Chapters 2 and 3 below.

One of the most impressive exemplars of the rising officialdom of the March is Gwilym ap Gwrwared of the Dyfed lordship of Cemais. Gwilym ap Gwrwared was a descendant of famous poets of the eleventh and twelfth centuries: Gwynfardd Dyfed and his son Cuhelyn Fardd. He was also an ancestor of a still more renowned poet, Dafydd ap Gwilym himself, of the middle decades of the fourteenth century, a line of descent which suggests that we should envisage Gwilym ap Gwrwared as a member of a lineage in which poets were prominent over several generations, and in which cultural patronage played a significant part. There was yet another element to his emergence as an important figure in administration in the south-west in the central decades of the century. His father, Gwrwared ap Gwilym, is recorded in the Welsh genealogies as having married Gwenllian, daughter of the most prominent of the Welsh administrative class in the thirteenth century, Ednyfed Fychan of Gwynedd. Gwilym ap Gwrwared therefore had ancestors on the side of his father and of his mother who lent him prestige both within Dyfed and more widely in Wales. To this ancestry he was clearly able to add formidable abilities: a servant of the Fitz Martin lords of Cemais, he rose to high office, as constable of Cemais by 1241, as royal steward of the north Ceredigion lands of Maelgwn Ieuanc in 1252, as a royal envoy conducting negotiations with Llywelyn ap Gruffudd in 1258, and as royal constable of Cardigan castle. His last appointment is particularly significant, as it mirrors a similar appointment of Nicholas Fitz Martin, lord of Cemais as constable of the royal stronghold of Carmarthen. The two appointments were made in almost identical terms, suggesting that in royal eyes there was little difference between Gwilym and Fitz Martin. By September 1267 Gwilym was appointed, together with the English official Guy de Bryan, to carry out all arrangements in south Wales which related to the forthcoming Treaty of Montgomery between Llywelyn ap Gruffudd and Henry III.[15] Gwilym's successors, as we shall see, maintained his progress to eminence in Dyfed and beyond.[16]

Across Wales, close in time to when Gwilym ap Gwrwared was active, another example of an ambitious and highly successful member of the emerging Welsh ministerial elite can be traced. He was Hywel ap Meurig, whose forebears had acted as reeves of the manor of Gladestry, as did Hywel himself and some of his descendants. But Hywel's horizons extended far beyond Gladestry. By the 1260s he had appeared as acting for Henry III in negotiations with Prince Llywelyn ap Gruffudd and also, in 1262, serving Roger Mortimer as castellan of Cefnllys. The 1270s saw Hywel in royal service as a surveyor of Crown castles and lands in Carmarthen and Cardigan, while still acting on Mortimer's behalf in the March. His eminence in the March was evident when he appeared in the war between Edward I and Llywelyn ap Gruffudd as the leader of forces from the Middle March, totalling at least 2,700 men, against Prince Llywelyn. In one royal document he was described as the steward of the lord king, of Roger Mortimer, and of Humphrey de Bohun, earl of Hereford. He was clearly central to the administration of much of the March. After the 1277 war, Hywel was active as a member of the Hopton Commission, a judicial bench established to hear and determine plaints arising from the period before, during and as a consequence of the war. He was also closely involved in the building and management of the new royal castle of Builth. By the time of his death in late 1281, Hywel had assumed a coat of arms, and had been knighted. He had also fathered several sons, some of whom would be of great importance in Wales and the March in the next generation, while one, William, would be the progenitor of a branch of the family who would take the name of Clanvowe, and would become significant not only in

Introduction

south Wales and the March but also in the royal court and even internationally.[17]

Not all of the identifiable members of the administrative class have descendants who can be traced through the decades which marked the era of the Edwardian settlement. The point is, however, that many such officials survived the Edwardian wars to emerge as models of what energetic and ambitious Welshmen might become: prominent members of a Welsh administrative and military elite. Two more figures from the Middle March represent this group of officials who appear to have left no male descendants, but whose influence surely lived on after them.

An early example of a regionally significant magnate who was eventually prepared to work with the English lords and the royal administration rather than with Llywelyn ap Gruffudd is provided by the case of Ifor ap Gruffudd of the Marcher lordship of Elfael. Ifor ap Gruffudd first appears in May 1276, as the bailiff of the lord Llywelyn ap Gruffudd, prince of Wales and lord of Snowdonia, for Elfael is Mynydd. He led a group of ten notable figures from the Middle March, including two of the lords of Elfael uwch Mynydd, the prince's bailiff of Gwerthrynion, a leading figure of the lordship of Builth, and some prominent ecclesiastics, including the dean of Elfael. These men had been brought together to secure the release from the prince's prison of John, son of Hywel ap Meurig. They had pledged sixty marks of silver, to be paid to the prince if John should presume to withdraw from Llywelyn's fealty and unity at any future point. The document in which this arrangement was recorded specified that the sureties were bound in the sum of six marks (four pounds) each. Perhaps more importantly the document was said to have been given at *Brynysceuyll* in Ifor's manor. The mention of Ifor's manor marks him out as a man of magnate status. The place name *Brynysceuyll* has not yet been identified, but a location in Rhos Goch a little to the north of Painscastle and within Elfael is Mynydd, which is marked on William Rees's *Map of South Wales and the March* and is described in Jonathan Williams's 1824 *History of Radnorshire*, which has the name Llys Ifor, or Ifor's Court, and it seems quite likely that this court was named after Ifor ap Gruffudd.[18]

Entries in records of the early 1280s make it likely that Ifor ap Gruffudd had lived a somewhat turbulent life in that period, for an entry in the Patent Roll 1282 records a pardon to him for an offence against Walter de Baskerville, whose family held the lordship of Eardisley, while entries in the Welsh Assize Roll indicate that he had clashed with John de Braose, who is known to have recovered lands in the manor of Glasbury, as a result of an action in the court of Humphrey de Bohun, earl of Hereford and lord of Brecon at around the same period.[19] Both Eardisley and Glasbury lay in the March, close to Elfael is Mynydd, and this suggests that the Ifor ap Gruffudd concerned is to be identified as the prince's bailiff of 1276. But, if so, it seems that Ifor's loyalty to the prince (as opposed to his own self-interest) was somewhat fragile, and had collapsed in the war of 1276–7. The first sign of this comes with a royal letter to Henry de Lacy, earl of Lincoln, empowering him to receive into the king's peace Ifor ap Gruffudd (*Ivorius Agriffy*) with his men and goods. The reference to 'his men' is undoubtedly significant. This letter was remembered in 1281, when Ifor seems to have been in some trouble: the point being to establish that his reception by the earl of Lincoln had legitimised any subsequent actions by him.

Rather more important is the fact that by the late summer of 1277 not only had Ifor seized the opportunity to transfer his allegiance from Prince Llywelyn to king Edward, but he was recorded as a constable of troops from Elfael Is Mynydd, who were part of the central Wales army fighting for Edward I and led by Ifor's near neighbour in the Middle March, Hywel ap Meurig whose territorial interests included Gladestry and Hergest. The army – and we have seen that it was not insubstantial, consisting of at least 2,700 men – was an important element in the forces which drove Llywelyn back into Gwynedd Uwch Conwy, the only territory which remained under his control by the end of the war, as marked by the Treaty of Aberconwy of 9 November 1277. It is clear that Ifor's defection from the ranks of Prince Llywelyn's supporters in the Marchland did not bring his career to a halt. In 1292 he appeared as one of the two chief taxors for the lordship of Elfael is Mynydd acting for Ralph de Tony, the lord of that land.

Introduction

It was de Tony who was the lord, but it was Ifor who knew the people and the terrain, and who remained a crucial figure in the administration of the lordship.[20]

A rather similar role to that adopted by Ifor ap Gruffudd was assumed by Einion ap Madog, a man with association across several parts of the middle and southern March. Early references to Einion ap Madog provide strong hints as to how he began a career which saw him form part of the ministerial elite of the Middle March. The accounts of the lordships of Abergavenny and the Three Castles in the mid-1250s show him as a soldier from those lands, actively involved in operations in Builth lordship, where he may be assumed to be engaged against forces of Llywelyn ap Gruffudd, who was beginning, after his victory over his brothers at Bryn Derwin in 1255, to push into the Middle March. Substantial payments made to Einion covering the second half of 1257 reveal that he was being paid at the rate of one shilling per day, the rate appropriate to a knight or other troop-leader. In a further move which establishes him as a soldier of some repute, it is recorded that he received a gift of £12 6s 8d with which to buy himself a light horse, a robe, a shield, iron greaves, and other pieces of armour and equipment.

But over the next decade Llywelyn ap Gruffudd asserted control over much of the Middle March, in which major lordships were conceded to him in the 1267 Treaty of Montgomery. This presented Welsh soldiers and officials with a dilemma as to their career options. When Einion ap Madog appears in records of 1276, it is as Prince Llywelyn's bailiff of Gwerthrynion. It is undoubtedly significant, however, that he is found acting as one of the sureties for the loyalty to the prince of John, son of Hywel ap Meurig. And in the following year, the fragility of his former loyalty to the prince is revealed when he appears as one of the centenars, or troop-leaders, in the central Wales army led by Hywel ap Meurig against Prince Llywelyn. The centrality of men of this rank and experience in the politics of the March is underscored by a deed in which a prominent man of Builth, Owain ap Meurig, who had in the past acted for Henry III in making and receiving amends with Llywelyn ap Gruffudd for breaches of a truce between the prince and the king, made over to Einion ap Madog lands at Rhosferig near Builth castle. The land of Rhosferig has been identified as the likely territory in which Prince Llywelyn was killed, in December 1282, in a trap set by the Mortimers and, it would seem, their Welsh associates such as Einion ap Madog.[21] It is entirely likely that Einion ap Madog, with his contacts and lands in Builth, is to be identified as the man of that name who was one of the two chief taxors for the lordship of Builth on the occasion of the assessment of the lay subsidy in 1292. His colleague, unsurprisingly, was William ap Hywel, a son of Hywel ap Meurig and also dean of Builth.

Other prominent *uchelwyr* of the Middle March in the thirteenth century might claim descent from old ruling houses, long gone from the political scene. Such was the case of Einion Sais of the lordship of Brecon. Einion and his descendants were supporters of the de Bohun lords of Brecon, and suffered and prospered accordingly. Further north, the great principality, subsequently the lordship, of Powys witnessed the development of a group of leading officials who became central to the politics of the region. A decision made by a group of prominent freemen from the region north of the Dyfi to transfer their allegiance and their lands from Gwynedd to the lordship of Powys south of the Dyfi resulted in the establishment of a hereditary succession to the office of *distain* within that family. One of those who actually made the transfer of people and lands to Powys, Goronwy ab Einion, was not actually designated as *distain*, but he appears at or close to the head of the list of laymen in the witness-lists of charters issued by Gwenwynwyn in the period 1185–1202, so that he can be identified as a prominent courtier and a probable *distain*. His son Gwên ap Goronwy, does appear as *senescallus* (= *distain*), and is followed by his son, Gruffudd ap Gwên, the better-evidenced *distain* of the second half of the thirteenth century who is also designated as *distain* but sometimes appears as *justiciarius*, as does Tudur ab Ednyfed in Gwynedd at roughly the same period.[22]

Still in eastern Wales, the lordship of Gwynllŵg provides another example of hereditary succession to the office of *distain*, this time in the early thirteenth century. The line was begun by

Introduction

Caradog, *distain* to Morgan ab Owain (d. 1158), in whose entourage he appears possibly as early as the 1150s, under the almost archaic title of *dapifer*.[23] He was subsequently *distain* (*senescallus*) to Hywel ab Iorwerth,[24] Caradog was succeeded in that office by his son Iorwerth and then his grandson Adam.[25] Close to Gwynllŵg, the lordships of Gwent saw the rise of Welsh officials in charge of castles in the middle decades of the thirteenth century. Such were Rhys ap Meurig, constable of Bronllys castle in 1251, and Philip ap Goronwy, constable of White Castle in the 1270s.

The above brief and selective survey of some of the more prominent instances of the rise of a ministerial elite in native, royal and Marcher polities in Wales in the thirteenth century serves to demonstrate simply that we are dealing with a widespread phenomenon of the greatest importance, fit to be set alongside the shifts in the basis of Welsh society in the period 1100–1300 which Thomas Jones-Pierce and Glanville Jones believed they could discern,[26] or the impact of changing ecclesiastical features with the development of more vertebrate diocesan structures and with the arrival of reformed monasticism, especially that of the Cistercians.[27]

The native administrative elite would come to play a crucial part in the governance and politics of Wales in the late thirteenth and earlier fourteenth centuries. Before we analyse that development in detail, we need to examine the sequence of events that made the dominance of the Welsh elite appear not only possible but necessary to stable governance in the post-conquest decades.

Beyond the ministerial aristocracy: the development of a more complex and sophisticated society in Wales in the twelfth and thirteenth centuries

Outside the area of state development, it seems that other categories of experts were developing in the later twelfth and thirteenth centuries. The emergence of prominent and influential jurists, who were preserving and reshaping Cyfraith Hywel, is a well-known example, but another particularly interesting case is that of the physicians. I have argued that we can detect a system in which a physician was resident in each commote, or in the March each lordship, or component of a large lordship. This system seems to have originated in the twelfth century, and was almost certainly not the result of an initiative by rulers but by the physicians themselves. But it reflects the advance of expertise as a feature of Welsh life in that period.[28]

The propagandists: the court poets. The development of court poetry was an adjunct of state development in the twelfth century: poets acted to underscore the eminence of rulers like Madog ap Maredudd of Powys (d. 1160), Owain Gwynedd (d. 1170) and the Lord Rhys of Deheubarth (1197). The classic exemplar was Cynddelw Brydydd Mawr, who was pre-eminent as a poet of all three of the rulers noted above. He does, however, represent not only a tradition of the poet as one who celebrated the achievements of a ruler, but one in which the poet judges the ruler and, in some cases, subjects him to criticism. The vogue for critical comment by the court poets developed further in the thirteenth century, although poets such as Prydydd y Moch in the early decades of the century, and Llygad Gŵr in its middle period, continued the tradition of supporting the princes – in these cases Llywelyn ab Iorwerth and Llywelyn ap Gruffudd respectively. But, during the ascendancy of the latter ruler, the emphasis on independence and even of criticism of the ruler on the part of the court poets was accentuated, to an extent that suggests a significant breakdown in this aspect of princely dominance.

Crucial developments took place with respect to ecclesiastical structure and spiritual care. The advance of parochialisation and a stronger structure of diocesan management, with the development of decanal chapters and archdeaconries in the twelfth and thirteenth centuries brought the clergy close to the people and was a source of increased pastoral vigour. The development, under the impact of the arrival and influence of Norman clerics, of a more vertebrate ecclesiastical structure of the Welsh Church, seems to have gone hand in hand with changes in the structure of lay governance in Wales, and there can be little doubt that the former supported and, in some instances, influenced the latter. The foundation and patronage of monastic houses, particularly those of the Cistercian order, offered support and counsel to Welsh secular rulers.

It is fairly clear that, in many areas of life, the twelfth and thirteenth centuries saw considerable advances in the development of a culture of expertise within the native Welsh society at many levels and in many respects: in administrative structure and attainment, in military organisation and equipment of all sorts, in medical care, in the poetic arts, in increasing use of seals and heraldic devices, in ecclesiastical structure, learning and provision, in developing sophistication of the built environment with developments in castle-building, in the structure of courts (*llysoedd*), in advances in law and the recording of law and legal cases, and in many other ways. These developments meant that a conqueror of large parts of Wales – for that is exactly what Edward I was – would be able, well-advised, and in significant measure compelled, to retain a very significant proportion of the procedures and achievements of the people on whom he had imposed his rule. In other words, the momentum of change in Welsh society would work to make conquest a more superficial thing than is often reckoned. A process of accommodation to realities was a sensible reaction to what had happened in the period 1277–95, years which had seen the collapse of Llywelyn ap Gruffudd's regime and his aspirations from both internal resistance and the application of external force, and then the extension of practical dominance to other regions, particularly in the March. It is to a key aspect of that process of accommodation that we must now turn.

Chapter 1

Edward I's Developing Policy in Wales: The 'Charm Offensive'

In the course of establishing first his primacy in Welsh politics, and subsequently his effective dominance in both *pura Wallia* and the March as he challenged the pretensions of Llywelyn ap Gruffudd, Edward I had become aware that he could count on the support of Welsh magnates. They might be lords of regal descent, like Gruffudd ap Gwenwynwyn of the lordship of Powys, and his sons Owain and Llywelyn. They might be members of what we have termed an administrative aristocracy, of whom figures such as Hywel ap Meurig in the March, or Rhys ap Gruffudd and his brother Hywel, active both in the heart of Llywelyn's principality and in the service of the king, are examples. In spite of what his propagandists frequently depicted as a struggle between the rightful supremacy of the English king and the treacherous manoeuvring of the Welsh, Edward had cause and opportunity to reflect that not all Welshmen were his enemies, while many could be led to become his loyal subjects. His victorious wars against Llywelyn in 1277, against the same ruler and his brother and successor Dafydd in 1282–3, and the leaders of risings in 1287 and 1294–5, left Edward financially drained. They also left him facing the challenge of bringing Wales to a peace sufficient to allow him time, money and energy to meet the other great challenges that he faced, both in domestic politics and in foreign policy. It is perhaps in these matters that Edward I's rule is in greatest need of re-evaluation of the sort that will be attempted in the present chapter, which traces the ways in which Edward acknowledged the problems he faced, and developed trends which over many decades had both facilitated and challenged the governance exercised by native elites.

In any assessment of the way in which Edward I dealt with Wales after his military victories in Wales, the words of Rees Davies in his classic analysis of Welsh history from 1063 to 1415 are of fundamental importance:

> Edward I's fault ... as in so many other directions, was that of lack of imagination. His rule was not particularly oppressive; but he had not learnt from his earlier experience that, in the governance of a subject people, restraining the zeal and greed of his officials, taking the leaders of native society into his confidence, and working with the grain of local custom were quite as important as a military occupation and a legal and administrative settlement.[1]

It will be the argument of the present chapter that Davies was, very unusually, simply wrong in this contention. Davies further declared with reference to the revolts of 1294–5 that:

> Edward's immediate response was to institute punitive and security measures to ensure that the settlement was not challenged again.

That comment was buttressed by his reference to the 'spirit of apartheid' which 'pervades ordinances which Edward I issued almost certainly in the wake of the revolt.'[2]

More nuanced verdicts on Edward's attitude and activity after the years of conquest were provided by Davies himself, albeit relatively briefly,[3] and by shorter surveys of medieval Wales which appeared after the publication of Davies's book. David Walker observed that once the revolt (*sic* in the singular) of 1294–5 was over Edward 'showed little animosity towards the Welsh leaders, and he set in motion a thorough investigation into the underlying causes of complaint and unrest ... Where the revolt might have sharpened divisions, it seems rather to have created a sense of common interest between the king and the Welsh elite.'[4] And A. D. Carr, who was responsible for some excellent work on aspects of Wales in the fourteenth century, saw that Edward 'does seem to have realised that it had been caused by real problems and there was a conscious attempt to remedy Welsh grievances'.[5]

More recently, a volume focusing on developments in Wales in the period 1064–1332 by the present author has noted that 'it is depressingly easy to point to the widespread oppression and discrimination suffered by the Welsh population in many regions of Wales, where in matters of administration, law and economic opportunity, there was a rigid distinction, in theory at least, between the privileged English and the "mere Welsh"'. But the same work has emphasised that 'on closer examination, the uniformity and, after some years, the severity of the Edwardian settlement, begin to appear less severe'.[6] Further, 'one of the most striking features of royal governance in the lands of north and west Wales is the sensitivity of the king to complaints from the Welsh communities of those lands, and the resolve to rectify matters.'[7]

We shall embark on an exploration of developments in the upper ranks of Welsh society in the decades that followed the conquest, in an analysis of the sort that has not previously been attempted. But before that can be attempted, we must chart the process by which Edward I showed himself sensitive to Welsh feelings and situations in the years after the outbreaks of 1294.[8]

Edward's attitude to the rebel leaders of 1294–5 is also revealing of a more positive and less than vindictive approach. It has now been established that there were five major risings in Wales in 1294–5. Four of these have long been known: that of Madog ap Llywelyn in north Wales; Maelgwn ap Rhys in Ceredigion; Morgan ap Maredudd in Glamorgan; and Cynan ap Maredudd in Brecon and neighbouring lordships. To these we must add a fifth rebel, Meurig ap Dafydd in Abergavenny.[9] Of these we can now confidently establish that Madog ap Llywelyn and Maelgwn ap Rhys were imprisoned after the revolt, Madog in the Tower of London and Maelgwn in Bamburgh Castle, before the latter moved with two Welsh lords and rebel leaders captured in 1282–3 to Newcastle on Tyne, with the king's stipulation that they should not be put in irons. Maelgwn was clearly accompanied by his own groom, and his wages – as in the case of his two companions

– were relatively generous, as was his robe allowance.[10] His companions were recruited for Edward I's campaign in Flanders in 1297 but there is no mention of Maelgwn ap Rhys. It is likely that he remained in captivity in Newcastle.[11]

Madog ap Llywelyn's imprisonment in the Tower of London was also relatively comfortable.[12] He was also joined by at least one of his sons, Maredudd, who went on to be an esquire of the king's household – a position of some trust. And some at least of Madog's lands on Anglesey were returned to his family: another of his sons was recorded as holding them in 1352.[13]

Even greater leniency was shown to the most successful of the rebels of 1294–5: the rising in the lordship of Glamorgan had been led by Morgan ap Maredudd,[14] who had driven the Gilbert de Clare, earl of Gloucester, from the lordship. The earl had enjoyed only limited success in re-establishing himself in Glamorgan, before Morgan made his peace with the king in early June. Edward's leniency to Morgan is reported to have been extended only against the earl's will while de Clare was forced to accept Edward's seizure of the lordship into his own hands.[15] Glamorgan was restored to the earl only after some four months, shortly before Gilbert's death towards the end of the year. The only rebel leader to be executed was Cynan ap Maredudd, not to be confused with his namesake who was one of the princelings captured in the war of 1282–3 and became one of Maelgwn ap Rhys's fellow prisoners at Bamburgh Castle. The rebel of 1294–5, who appears to have been active in the March region of Builth/Brycheiniog, attempted to escape punishment, when his rising had clearly failed, by passing himself off as a leper. This attempt failed and he was sent to Hereford, where he was brutally executed.[16]

The generally lenient treatment accorded by Edward to the leaders of the risings of 1294–5 suggests that the king was ready to accept that the Welsh might have legitimate grievances against both royal and Marcher governance. This forms the background to what can be classified as a constructive royal policy in such matters, which in the years after the risings touched most parts of Wales.

Edward I's Developing Policy in Wales: The 'Charm Offensive'

Examples of Edward's interventions, actual or threatened, to protect the Welsh are easily traced in the aftermath of the risings of 1294–5. On 4 and 24 August 1295 Edward issued grants to, respectively, the bishop-elect of St Davids and John de Hastings, lord of Abergavenny and of Cilgerran, making donations of the forfeitures of their Welshmen and tenants lately in arms against the king in the late war in Wales and whom the king 'has admitted to his peace and has given up to the said bishop and John, saving to the said Welsh their lives and limbs and lands and tenements, and reserving to the king the power of reasonably mitigating grievous fines, should they impose any'.[17]

In a different matter, but only shortly after the grants to the bishop-elect and John de Hastings, a commission was issued to John de Havering, justice of North Wales and William de Cycon, constable of the castle of Aberconwy, on 1 September 1295, to investigate complaints by the men of the commonalty of North Wales touching 'trespasses, injuries, extortions, oppressions and grievous losses inflicted on them since that land came into the king's hands by the sheriffs, bailiffs and other ministers of the king in those parts'.[18]

A most remarkable letter was issued to the good men and commonalty of Snowdon[ia] on 3 December 1296, informing them that:

> the abbot of Aberconwy, Thomas Danvers, Tudur ap Goronwy, and Hywel ap Cynwrig, sent by them to the king's presence, have related to the king the rumour which disturbed and grieved them, to wit, that the king held them in suspicion; and begging them not to believe such rumours for the future, as no sinister rumour of their state or behaviour has reached the king in these days, and he has no suspicion towards them, but rather, by reason of their late good service, holds them for his faithful and devoted servants.[19]

In fact, Edward had certainly received prior notice of the rumours about his lack of trust in the men of North Wales, for the Close Rolls contain a letter from him to John de Havering, dated 24 November 1296:

> It is shown to the king on behalf of the men and whole community of Snowdon and Anglesey that they have been told that certain things have been suggested to the king concerning them by reason whereof the king ought to hold them suspect, and they are much disturbed and aggrieved thereby. As the king does not wish that their minds shall be further vexed or disturbed by the lying stories of such speakers of evil, he has intimated to them by his letters patent that nothing at all of sinister rumour concerning their estate or behaviour has come to his notice at the present time, and that he has not conceived against them any suspicion, as is more fully contained in his letters. For these reasons the king orders John to so chastise any such liars as shall be found henceforth in his bailiwick that the punishment shall strike terror into others saying the like things.[20]

But quite the most remarkable aspect of the king's protestations of 3 December is the fact that one member of the deputation sent to him, Tudur ap Goronwy, had been the steward (*senescallus*) or *distain* of the rebel leader Madog ap Llywelyn in 1295. This means that Tudur had been deeply implicated in the rising, so that it would hardly have been surprising if Edward had held him in some suspicion.

A further example of Edward's concern for the conditions of the Welsh population and the governance being exercised in his name comes in a commission of Oyer et Terminer dated 10 March 1297, to Peter Malore and Henry de Guildford regarding reported oppressions of the people of West Wales by bailiffs of the king and of barons and magnates of those parts. Such cases as they could not resolve were to be referred to the king to be dealt with in the next parliament.

While West Wales was not neglected, the period after the revolts of 1294–5 saw a significant burst of activity aimed at the Welsh communities of the eastern borders and Marches of Wales. It was recalled in 1309 that after the war of Madog ap Llywelyn Edward I had made a grant of liberties and customs to the Welshmen of Hope and Hopedale (in the newly created county of Flintshire).[21] In 1297, at least three regions of Wales saw the granting of charters confirming the Welsh tenants in rights which had been threatened or ignored by the lords. The first case is that of Maelienydd, a significant region of the lands between Wye and Severn, over which lordship was exercised by Edmund Mortimer of Wigmore, who issued two charters to his Welsh tenantry of the lordship on the same day. The first begins by stating that Edmund's grant had been made in response to complaints by the men of Maelienydd alleging oppressions committed by officers of the lord, both in Edmund's time and in that of his father. The charter thus emphasises the role of the community in challenging the ways in which lordship had been exercised, and suggests that some at least of the complaints were not of recent origin. It sets out a procedure for dealing with grievances relating to lands, tenements and amenities which have been unjustly taken from a complainant, or to other injuries or trespasses suffered at the hands of Edmund, his father or his bailiffs. The plaint was to be brought into the court of Cymaron, to be dealt with by judgment of twelve jurors, according to the laws and customs previously used there. Edmund thus appears to be picking up long-standing grievances which are to be remedied in accordance with time-honoured customs. A proviso is introduced that no one should bring any plaint regarding the demesnes of the castles of Cefnllys or Knucklas, and the lands of Pilleth. In what looks like a partial repetition (which may suggest hasty drafting) it is stated that cases touching fees 'or other matters' should be determined in the court of Cymaron by verdict of twelve jurors. It is then provided that the goods and chattels of the freemen of Maelienydd should not be taken for the lord's use, unless in cases of necessity. If those goods should be saleable, they should be taken at a just price, to be paid within three weeks. It was also provided that if anyone had been taken and imprisoned but was according to the laws of Maelienydd 'repleviable or manucapable' (i.e. fit to be released upon finding suitable pledges), he was to be released should such pledges be found. For every crime whatever, the common law should be granted without money ransom.

A further section of the charter relates to mercantile matters and notes that all pleas touching the lord's tolls (*tolnetum patriae*) in that land should be held in the 'hundred' (court) of Cymaron, as was usual in the time of Edmund's father, though those relating to the markets of Cefnllys and Knucklas should be held in those places. These mercantile provisions were important firstly in that they do, in contrast to others, suggest that problems had intensified in the time of Edmund Mortimer, while they imply that the courts of the urban foundations attached to the castles of Cefnllys and Knucklas were a special source of lordly revenue. The dispositive clauses of the charter conclude with a provision that anyone holding wood or pasture in the land of the abbot and convent of Cwmhir by the monks' grant should enjoy those rights peacefully.

A second charter, with the same date, place of issue and witnesses as the first, granted the men of Maelienydd the right to hunt and take deer in that land, with the exception of the demesne lands of Knucklas and the demesne of the wood of Swydd, as well as in the lands and demesnes of the abbot and convent of Cwmhir, though three granges of Cwm-hir were withdrawn from this prohibition. It provided that, if anyone should hunt beyond the permitted bounds and should kill any kind of game and should be convicted by being taken in the act or by the inquisition of twelve lawful men, a fixed scale of penalties should apply. If the hounds should go beyond the permitted bounds and take deer, the beasts should remain the property of the lord and the hounds should be given back to their owners. In addition, it was provided that the whole of the river Ithon from the bridge of Llanddewi to the ford called Rhyd yr hen bont should be free for hunting.[22]

On first examination it appears that these elaborate charters had been conceived by Edmund Mortimer in response to pressure from the Welsh community of Maelienydd. But initial doubt may be cast on this view by the fact that this region appears to have been quiescent during the risings of 1294–5. More significantly, an alternative and much more convincing explanation is provided by an entry on the Close Roll, in the form of a royal order to Edmund Mortimer, dated 16 May 1297:

> The king has received divers complaints from the community of Welshmen of Maelienydd, Edmund's men and tenants, setting out

that he grievously disquiets and molests them by imprisonment of their bodies and the taking and carrying away of their goods and chattels and by various ransoms, wilfully and without reasonable cause, contrary to justice and contrary to the law and custom of those parts, so that they are now so impoverished that they have little or nothing to live upon, as they assert; and the king, pitying their estate, has given them a day before him in parliament at London in the octaves of Holy Trinity to show their complaints there before him and his council: he therefore orders Edmund to be present in person on that day to answer to the said Welshmen for the aforesaid grievances and other things that they will object against him, and to do and receive what the court shall consider in the premises. He is ordered not to aggrieve or molest them in any way in the meantime in their persons or goods by reason of the complaints aforesaid or for any other reasons.[23]

It is quite evident, therefore, that the moving force behind developments in Maelienydd in 1297 was the king himself. The charters to the Welsh community of the *cantref* were issued on 10th June, almost a week before Edmund Mortimer's scheduled appearance before the king in parliament on 16th June. It is a reasonable conclusion that the issue of the charters was designed to remove the need for that appearance.

The pressure that Edward exerted on Edmund Mortimer to ameliorate the situation in Maelienydd was by no means the only foray that the king made into the March in that year. The situation in the lordship of Brecon was even more drastic. At some point in the summer of that year, in July or August, Edward sent one of his close associates, Morgan ap Maredudd, on a secret mission to that lordship.[24] The nature of Morgan's mission was revealed in a letter from Morgan to the king.[25] He reported that before he had arrived in the region of Brecon, the lord of that land, the earl of Hereford, Humphrey de Bohun, had ordered that his castles should be stocked with food and garrisoned. He had also made it clear that he was against the king's peace. To secure the support of the Welsh community the earl had issued, through his steward, a charter to his tenants, confirming 'all the laws and usages that they had ever had in the days of his predecessors'. It was then that Morgan had made contact with the men of Brecon whom he knew best, and had enquired if there was anyone who would go against the wishes of the earl. It seems evident that Morgan's mission, at a time of considerable tension between the king and the earl, was to probe the resolve of the men of Brecon to stand by the earl, and, if possible, to stir up conflict – presumably to create a pretext for the king to intervene in the affairs of the lordship. But when questioned, the men of Brecon informed Morgan that 'they were all at one with their lord' – that is, with the earl. On this occasion, Morgan's efforts had been frustrated, but there can be no doubt about the king's objective in sending him on the secret mission to Brecon. Just as he had done in Glamorgan in 1295, Edward was preparing to take over the lordship of Brecon, exactly as Earl Humphrey had evidently assumed was his intention.

There was indeed another part of the March which excited Edward's interest and this time it was one in which the king had previous experience of intervention: the great lordship of Glamorgan. Gilbert the Red Earl had died in late 1295, leaving the earldom and lordship in the care of his widow, Joan of Acre – who was a daughter of the king himself. Although Edward had ordered the lordships of Earl Gilbert to be taken into royal custody after his death, Joan succeeded in showing that she and Gilbert had been jointly enfeoffed of the estates, and Edward had had to install her in the inheritance in January 1296. In 1297, the situation took a new turn. In January, Joan had secretly married Ralph de Monthermer, a relatively junior member of the king's household. This cut across Edward's plans to arrange a diplomatically advantageous marriage for Joan; when she told him that she was already married to Monthermer, the king was enraged, and had her husband cast into prison in Bristol Castle. By August of 1297, the king had relented. He released Ralph from his prison, and shortly after that gave him for the term of Joan's life the titles of earl of Gloucester and Hertford.

While she was in sole possession of Glamorgan, it is clear that Joan had issued grants to the Welsh communities of several regions, all former Welsh lordships: Senghenydd, Meisgyn, and Tir Iarll. It is difficult to establish the dates of these grants, but it is possible that Joan made them shortly before, or during the time when, her new husband was in the king's prison, in an attempt to win the support of the Welsh. Whenever the grants were made it is significant that they were confirmed by King Edward, who also ordered remission of sums outstanding which had been promised when the charters were granted. The first such grant by the king was made to the community of Senghenydd in eastern Glamorgan on 2 June 1297. Walter Hakelute, keeper of the land of Glamorgan, was ordered to respite the exaction of 100 marks for which they had submitted to the grace of Joan, countess of Gloucester, the king's daughter, as it is said, and to release any distraint (sc. for non-payment) which he may have made in this matter. In this case the confirmation of Joan's grant, and the reason for it, are both implicit.

The other grants by the king, both made on 3rd July, are clearer and more explicit. That for the community of Tir Iarll in western Glamorgan granted:

> respite during his pleasure for payment of the 100 marks that are still in arrears of the £100 by which they made fine with Joan, countess of Gloucester, the king's daughter, in order to have the laws and ancient customs that their ancestors were wont to use; the king orders the keeper of Glamorgan to cause them to have such respite, and to release to them any distraint made in this behalf.

The king's grant to the men of Meisgyn, to the immediate west of Senghennydd, gave them respite during the king's pleasure, from the 60 marks outstanding from the 500 marks by which they made fine with Joan, countess of Gloucester, the king's daughter, for pardon of their trespasses and for having again their laws and old customs. It appears that the grants made by Joan had all involved significant payments by the community, both in recognition of past offences (probably those committed during the risings of 1294–5), and also, as in the case of Maelienydd, to secure the traditional laws and customs of which they had been deprived. The involvement of the king in making contact with the Welsh communities of much of the eastern March is evident, and comes at a time when he was recruiting heavily in most regions of Wales for his 1297 campaign in Flanders.[26]

Not only was the king ready to foment strife within a Marcher lordship, as in the case of Brecon, to present himself as the defender of Welsh interests. It seems that he was prepared to apply a somewhat selective memory to past events in an effort to present a more favourable image to the Welsh people. The Annals of Worcester contain a relatively full account of the destruction of the abbey of Strata Florida in the summer of 1295:

> When the king crossed into the southern region of Wales the abbot of Strata Florida stupidly promised him that he would bring the population of the county of Cardiganshire to his peace at a specific time and place. But when the king and his army had been waiting for a long time, not one Welshman appeared, so the king, enraged, said 'Burn it, burn it'. And thus, the abbey and its environs were consumed by fire, which never says 'Enough'.[27]

If that is an accurate account of what happened at Strata Florida, it seems possible that the king had developed a selective memory by 1300, when the Patent Roll records a licence for the abbot of Strata Florida to rebuild on its former site the abbey which was burned *against the king's will* [my italics] in the twenty third year of his reign'.[28]

However, the year 1300 was also marked by a development which was arguably of the greatest significance in the relationship between Edward I and the Welsh. As well as attempting to reduce the incidence of oppression by royal officials in Wales and to ensure that Welsh communities in both the principality lands and the March were able to able to enjoy their traditional laws and customs, Edward I went further in hastening the process by which senior administrative positions were filled by Welshmen. The king was in fact already becoming familiar with Welsh abilities in such spheres as administration, law and diplomacy as well as in many aspects of military activity. He had had opportunities

Edward I's Developing Policy in Wales: The 'Charm Offensive'

to become aware of Hywel ap Meurig's skills as a negotiator in the 1260s and as a military leader and administrator in and after the war of 1277.[29] In the years after 1277, Edward employed not only Hywel ap Meurig but also two significant figures from Gwynedd, Goronwy ap Heilyn and Rhys ap Gruffudd,[30] as justices on the Hopton commission and in many other capacities. In the immediate aftermath of Edward's conquests in much of Wales there had been an initial tendency, strong if not without exceptions, to appoint English, and sometimes Savoyard, figures to positions of seniority and oversight in the royal lands in Wales. The exceptions included Gruffudd ap Tudur, appointed as constable of Dolwyddelan in 1283, and Hywel ap Meurig at Builth. It was of course the case that Dolwyddelan was not a castle built by Edward I, while A. D. Carr has noted that 'this castle was not part of Edward's defensive plan for his new lands in north Wales'.[31] It was, however, a place with associations with Llywelyn the Great, the most esteemed prince in the history of Gwynedd, and therefore an evocative symbol of Venedotian greatness. It was a shrewd move to place it in the keeping of a man whose forebears had included significant figures in the courts of the princes of Gwynedd.[32] It is entirely accurate to describe the custodianship of Dolwyddelan as amongst the 'key posts'.[33] Almost inevitably, Hywel ap Meurig's son Philip was also an early example of the promotion by Edward I of a Welshman to a senior position: in 1290 he was appointed constable of Dryslwyn castle, once the chief seat of Rhys ap Maredudd, and custodian of the lands formerly held by Rhys.[34]

Appointing Welshmen to important posts was therefore not entirely a novelty for Edward by the mid-1290s. But in the second half of the decade, Edward was faced increasingly with other challenges, in Flanders, in Scotland, and in the looming political crises at home. He therefore needed both to ensure as far as possible the pacification of Wales, so ensuring that no further costly wars broke out, and to utilise the administrative skills of Welsh magnates and the military abilities of Welsh leaders as well as the rank and file.

It is perhaps little wonder that in the period after the risings of 1294–5 Edward began to move towards appointing more

Welshmen to increasingly important positions in the crown lands in Wales. In the south and west, this was the case with the stewardships of the large regions of Cantref Mawr in Ystrad Tywi, and of Cardiganshire Is Aeron and Uwch Aeron. In the case of Cantref Mawr, consisting of the bulk of Ystrad Tywi, the key development was the appointment to the stewardship of Goronwy Goch in 1299. An examination of Goronwy's background gives us an insight into the qualities that brought him to the notice of the king and his advisers. He was of distinguished ancestry in Ystrad Tywi, and in the Welsh pedigrees he was known as Arglwydd Llangathen – his place of residence. The designation as *Arglwydd* (lord) suggests that he was held in considerable esteem, for *Arglwydd* (Latin *dominus*) had been the title appropriate for rulers. Record sources reveal him as a senior figure at the court of the lord of Dryslwyn, Rhys ap Maredudd, who had given Edward support in the wars of 1277 and 1282–3. Goronwy appears as Rhys's constable of Dryslwyn, his great castle and his principal seat, but when Rhys took to rebellion in 1287, Goronwy Goch did not follow him, but turned to support the king. He appears in crown service as a sergeant, riding a barded (armoured) horse, the mark of a distinctly superior warrior, and receiving wages commensurate with that status – 12d per day.[35] After the rebellion of Rhys ap Maredudd had been suppressed, Goronwy appears as one of the two chief taxors of Dryslwyn lordship in the assessment of liability for the lay subsidy.[36] By 1307 he is recorded as holding a half of Brechfa mill, and rendering for it half a mark per year.[37]

Another Welsh appointment as steward of Cantref Mawr was that of Dafydd Bongam (Dafydd ap Hywel ap Dafydd), who served from 1303 to 1309. An inquest of 1309 recorded that he was regarded as 'the most competent person in the laws and customs of those parts for the preservation of the peace.' The emphasis in Dafydd's appointment, therefore, was his expertise in the law and customs of the region of Ystrad Tywi. The same commissioners who reported on Dafydd Bongam's tenure of the stewardship of Cantref Mawr also reported on the situation in the nearby territory of Emlyn, where Dafydd Fychan was bailiff. Their report included the information that, at the beginning of the last Welsh war (in 1294), the keepers of Newcastle Emlyn had left the castle almost empty, without men or provisions. At that point, Dafydd ap 'Moriz' (almost certainly 'Meurig'), father of Dafydd Fychan, taking with him the said Dafydd Fychan and his other sons, and others of his blood in whom he confided, entered the castle and provisioned it.[38] Together with others, he faithfully held the castle until he died on the eve of Whitsun (1295). Thereupon Dafydd Fychan remained there, with others, until the Thursday after Trinity, in the 23rd year of Edward I, when King Edward, on his progress through Wales, passed by the castle, and commended Dafydd for his faithful service and custody of the castle. The king then conferred on Dafydd Fychan the custody of Emlyn, in which he had faithfully served and which he still held. It may have been as a consequence of the commissioners' report that a plan was formed to move Dafydd Bongam from the stewardship of Cantref Mawr, and Dafydd Fychan from the bailiwick of Emlyn, perhaps because the question of payment to these officials for their services had arisen. For present purposes, however, it is clear that while in Dafydd Bongam's case his expertise in regional law and custom had been central to his appointment, in that of Dafydd Fychan his family's loyalty and military service to Edward I had been the crucial factor in the grant of Emlyn.

Turning to the royal lordship of Builth, where Hywel ap Meurig had been such a guiding figure in the years after 1277, it is perhaps no surprise to find his son Philip ap Hywel being granted custody of Builth castle for a five-year period in 1299.[39] He was to stock and furnish it at his own cost for two years, and then to retain the custody for a further three years. In fact, his possession of Builth castle was to go on until 1311.[40]

In the three counties of north-west Wales, the appointment of sheriffs was not long delayed after the crisis years of the mid-1290s. The first to be recorded was Gruffudd ap Dafydd, who became sheriff of Merionethshire for the year 1300–1[41]. He was widely known as the lord of Hendwr, one of the 'barons of Edeirnion', who held their lordships by a markedly privileged tenure and could trace their ancestry back to the great Powysian king, Madog ap Maredudd (d. 1160) and through him to Bleddyn ap Cynfyn (d. 1075), famous amongst Welsh jurists as a major contributor to the development of Welsh law.[42] Gruffudd ap Dafydd himself had already in 1295 held the office of forester of Penllyn, Ardudwy and Meirionnydd,[43] a substantial part of Merionethshire, and was to go on to be *rhaglaw* of both Penllyn and Ardudwy.[44] In the war of 1294–5 he appears as attached to the royal court, where he was present for fifty-two days. He had thus enjoyed a remarkable series of offices. Gruffudd's prominence in the administration was perhaps reinforced by that of his brother Madog, who also served against the rebel Madog ap Llywelyn in the war of 1294–5, leading troops in Penllyn.[45] There are signs that both Gruffudd and Madog were relatively wealthy.[46] A degree of personal wealth was undoubtedly a significant asset for a man with serious ambitions.

Several other Welsh figures were to be appointed as sheriffs in north-western Gwynedd before Edward I died in 1307, and in some cases they had already attracted attention in the court or administration of the king. But, in 1301, King Edward had created his son, Edward of Caernarfon, 'prince of Wales', and had handed over to him the governance of what became known as the principality lands. That at least was the theory, though it is possible that for much of the time the king continued to be the real force behind decisions. This is particularly the case with the Kennington petitions of 1305, presented by the community and individuals of North Wales to the prince a few months before the serious quarrel between the king and the prince. Hilda Johnstone noticed that the Patent Roll calendar of a passage in which the responses to the petitions were referenced in February 1316 had omitted the important fact that they were *'ordinationes ... de concilio dicti patris nostri et nostro'*.[47] Johnstone's comment that this 'suggests supervision or co-operation' is important. It is noteworthy that, in response to a petition claiming that there were errors in the extents of the new counties of north-west Wales made on Edward I's orders in the aftermath of the conquest of Gwynedd, a commission of five men was set up to investigate the extents and

Edward I's Developing Policy in Wales: The 'Charm Offensive'

to notify the prince of any errors in them. Two members of the commission were prominent Welsh administrators.[48]

It is at least clear that Edward I had initiated, and developed over several years, the granting to Welshmen of important offices in the royal lands in Wales. The king had encouraged Welsh figures of ambition and the required abilities and background, to expect that a well-rewarded career and a significant degree of power were to be had from working within the royal administration or military structure – or in many instances those of the great Marcher lords.

We have already encountered the names of some of those men of ambition who would be prominent and powerful in the later years of the thirteenth century and through many decades of the fourteenth. We must now turn to a more rigorous investigation of these figures who would come to be, in only a few years, the backbone of Welsh societies and governance across most of Wales.

Chapter 2

The New Elite

Introduction

In this discussion we shall distinguish between two groups. On the one hand are the majority of members of this stratum, called here by the contemporary phrase 'the men of position', who dominated Welsh governance and cultural leadership particularly at the level of the commotes and even *cantrefi* or the major subdivisions of the greater Marcher lordships. On the other hand, we shall examine a small group of hugely influential figures, each of whose sphere of activity covered several regions, and whose careers had a decisive impact on the course of events in Wales and the March. It is with this group of primarily administrative and military magnates, here designated as 'the new elite' that we begin our investigation, which will be structured, not in an almost certainly futile attempt to rank them in order of importance, but in the approximate chronological order of their deaths.

We start with two brothers, Philip ap Hywel and Rees ap Hywel. Both were major figures in the March of Wales, and, at times, in the politics and administration of much of Wales.[1] They were sons of the extraordinary Hywel ap Meurig, who rose from relatively modest origins to become one of the most influential Welshmen of his day. Active from the early 1260s until his death in 1281, Hywel was a prominent official of both Henry III and Edward I, and the steward of both Humphrey de Bohun, earl of Hereford and lord of Brecon and Roger Mortimer of Wigmore, two of the most powerful of the Marcher lords. Hywel led an army recruited from the Middle March composed mainly of Welsh troops and commanders against Prince Llywelyn in 1277, and was subsequently in charge of the lordship of Builth, where he was responsible for much of the building of Builth Castle. He was in addition a member of the Hopton commission, set up in 1277 to settle legal cases in Wales arising from the recent war, and was involved in other judicial work. By the time of his death, Hywel had been knighted and had his own coat of arms. Their father's eminence assuredly helped the careers of his sons, at least three of whom were prominent clerics. Both Philip and Rees were of significance in the Church, and a third son, William, became dean of Builth.[2] Philip and William were involved as executors of their father's will, and Philip rendered Hywel's final account as a royal official, but it is Rees whom we shall discuss first.

Master Rees ap Hywel

Apparently a younger brother of Philip and William,[3] Rees was also to become a cleric. He appears as a sub-deacon in Hereford diocese in 1287.[4] Probably born in the later 1260s, most of the documentation of the central decades of his career, however, records his involvement, sometimes with his brother Philip, in very worldly matters. He first achieved administrative prominence in June 1301, when he was associated with Philip and with Walter de Pederton as paymasters to troops being led by William de Camville, William Martyn and Morgan ap Maredudd, already with a record of being deeply involved in the king's Welsh policies,[5] en route to Carlisle for a campaign against the Scots.[6] Master Rees was in the service of Humphrey de Bohun from 1302, and in that of Edward of Caernarfon by 1305, when he was given the task of inspecting and revising the extents of North Wales compiled under Edward I.[7] It is possible that he was emulating the approach of his brother Philip, in building a career which gave him the prospect of advancement in several directions. Rees was also making some of the same contacts, as when he was associated with Walter de Pederton and Master William Hore in an investigation into office-holding in West Wales. It seems that in one respect Master Rees chose a rather different path to power from that of Philip: his connection to royal government was stronger than his links to Marcher lords. Thus in 1312 he became the first Welshman to hold the office of deputy justiciar of South Wales – a signal achievement.

In 1315 Master Rees joined his brother Philip and the senior royal administrator John Walwayn in preparing the defences of Wales against a threatened Scottish invasion of Wales from Ireland.[8] In the following year Master Rees, again with John Walwayn, was responsible for collecting fines from those in Glamorgan implicated in the rebellion of Llywelyn Bren. This, like his activity in 1315, almost certainly brought him once more into contact with Morgan ap Maredudd, in a task of some delicacy.[9] Further work undertaken by Rees in 1316 was the raising of two thousand men for service against the Scots.

Like his brother, Master Rees was notably absent from the records of the royal government after 1316. It is possible that he had more than enough to do to establish his control over the very significant lands that he had been gathering into his hands in the previous years.[10] But it is quite likely that he was alienated by the increasing influence of Hugh Despenser the Younger over the king. A letter sent in January 1321 by Despenser to his sheriff of Glamorgan, John Inge, is instructive.[11] Despenser informed Inge that certain persons had informed the king and him that 'Master Rees ap Hywel makes fresh alliances, and leads a great rout of people with him; if Inge thinks that it would be well for Despenser to have a commission to take Rees, he is to inform Despenser, and also to say how he thinks that Despenser should obtain the commission'.[12]

Amongst Rees's actions at this time was his success in frustrating Edward II's wishes relating to the lordship of Gower. The previous lord, William de Braose, had given Gower to his son-in-law, John de Mowbray, without the king's permission. Despenser had persuaded Edward to size Gower into his hands, and then appoint Despenser as custodian. Rees had organised resistance to this, and was regarded by the king as 'one of the principal abbetors and maintainers of those who had by force of arms prevented a royal official from taking the lordship into the king's hands.'[13]

Rees was pardoned for his offences in August of 1321, when the baronial opposition to Despenser was in effective control of the government, but when the situation was reversed in early 1322 and the king's authority was restored, Rees's extensive lands were confiscated and he was imprisoned in Dover Castle. Here was the danger inherent in becoming a notable figure in the politics of Wales in unstable times. It was small compensation that he was given maintenance for himself and a chamberlain.

Rees was subsequently moved to the Tower of London, where he remained a prisoner until late 1326. The circumstances of his eventual release are fascinating. Roger Mortimer of Wigmore had been imprisoned in the Tower in early 1322, after his surrender to the king, but had escaped and fled to France, subsequently joining forces with Edward II's estranged wife Isabella. Together they planned the downfall of Edward and Despenser, and returned to England with a small invasion force in the late summer of 1326. As Mortimer and Isabella advanced across England, gathering forces, Edward retreated to south Wales. Amongst the beneficiaries of these developments was Master Rees ap Hywel, who was released from the Tower and hastened to join the hunt for the fleeing Edward.

The pursuing force was led by Master Rees, and Henry of Lancaster, earl of Leicester. The chronicle *Vita et Mors Edwardi Secundi* (Life and Death of Edward II) notes that Isabella:

> Misit Henricum comitum Lancastrie et dominum magistrum Rhesum ap Powel clericum, natione Wallum ad comprehendendum regem et sibi adhaerentes. Predictus comes etiam germanus et heres saepe nominati comitis Lancastriae, Thomae; et iste Rhesus secum missus, qui justicia regali in Turri Londoniensi incarceratus erat, sed per reginae potentiam suae libertati restitutus. Tam comes praedictus quam Rhesus habuerunt possessions et ampla dominia iuxta locum in quo rex latitabat. Fuitque Rheso tota regio valde nota.
>
> [(Isabella) sent Earl Henry of Lancaster and (lord) Master Rees ap Hywel, a cleric, to arrest the king and his accomplices. The aforementioned earl was a cousin, and the heir, of the

oft-named Thomas, earl of Lancaster; and Rees, who was sent with him, had been imprisoned in the Tower of London by the king's decree, but was set free by the queen's power. Both the aforementioned earl and Rees had possessions and large lordships near the place where the king was hiding. The whole region was well-known to Rees.]

They found the king and some of his followers near the castle of Llantrisant. He was taken to Kenilworth by Earl Henry, to await his fate. Despenser and others were executed at Hereford. Rees then began the process of recovering his extensive lands. As well as recovering the lordships of Talgarth, Cantref Selyf, with its castle of Bronllys, he was restored to lands in Blaenllyfni, Usk, and Gower in February 1327.

In the last phase of Master Rees's life he was given a number of significant offices: for a brief period he had custody of the castle and lordship of Builth, thus maintaining his family's interest in that land; another short-term appointment, but this time one of greater import, was Master Rees's tenure of the post of justice of south Wales between November 1326 and February 1327 – when he became the first Welsh holder of a justiciarship.[14] He was also called upon to investigate offences committed by royal officials during the regime of Edward II in South and West Wales and in the lordship of Montgomery,[15] and to inspect the condition of the royal castles in South Wales.[16] In terms of his ecclesiastical career, he received several prebends including one at St Davids, shortly before his death in May 1328.

Master Rees was like his brother Philip, enjoying both ecclesiastical and lay careers, but was perhaps more deeply enmeshed in secular politics than Philip was. His achievements in that field, and the dangers to which they exposed him, were considerable. Not least of his successes was to have risen to become in effect a Marcher lord in his own right, having secured possession of Bronllys and Cantref Selyf, as well as a very eminent royal official. He had several children, of whom Philip 'of Bronllys' was his principal heir; he was possibly named after his uncle, Philip ap Hywel, to whom we now turn.

Philip ap Hywel ap Meurig

Philip has already been noticed as having been his father's principal heir in 1281. He emerges as a figure in royal service by 1290, when he was put in charge of the castle of Dryslwyn and the lands which had belonged to the rebel Rhys ap Maredudd. By 1292 he was steward of Humphrey de Bohun, earl of Hereford, in the lordships of Brecon, Huntington and Hay. In 1297 he appears as steward to both de Bohun in Brecon, and to Edmund Mortimer in Maelienydd.[17] In this context it is noteworthy that both of these lords were facing intervention in their lordships by Edward I, which was averted by the issue of charters to their Welsh tenantry, thus, in all probability, depriving the king of a pretext for taking over the lordships. It is notable that common to both episodes of issuing charters was the involvement of Philip ap Hywel, which may suggest that Philip was behind that tactic. Even more remarkable is the fact that while helping the Marcher lords survive the attentions of Edward I, Philip was entrusted by the king with taking charge at Hereford of troops raised in West Wales and the March.[18] He was already emerging as a man whose services were regarded as invaluable, even when they may have involved something of a conflict of interests. In the course of the following year Philip appears to have been furthering his ecclesiastical ambitions as well, when he entertained Bishop Swinfield of Hereford at his house at Hergest.[19]

That Philip was in favour with Edward I was perhaps demonstrated in 1299, when the king granted to him the castle of Builth for five years, at an annual rent of £113 6s 8d, an arrangement that was subsequently extended. In the following years Philip undertook more administrative duties for the king, which included working with the similarly busy Walter de Pederton, a member of Edward II's council while he was prince of Wales, and who had acted as deputy justiciar of South Wales on several occasions. It was not only the king whom Philip (and his brother Master Rees) served. In 1305, as a consequence of one of the Kennington petitions to Edward of Caernarfon, prince of Wales, Philip and Rees were called in to join with Walter de Pederton and other senior officials in order to investigate allegedly oppressive extents in North Wales.[20]

As well as extending the scope of his work from the March into the principality, Philip was making useful and influential contacts. One of those, who was also associated with Walter de Pederton, was the enigmatic figure of Morgan ap Maredudd,[21] who joined Philip and Pederton to raise troops in south and west Wales in 1308. Morgan was another of those few who constituted the new Welsh elite, and any contacts between the various members of that group are of particular interest.

For the years that followed, Philip continued to perform for the royal government a variety of administrative tasks, some of them of only local importance,[22] as well as remaining close to Humphrey de Bohun and Roger Mortimer of Wigmore. In 1315, however, matters of far greater significance had arisen. The defeat of Edward II's forces by those of Robert the Bruce at Bannockburn in 1314 had been a devastating blow to English morale and had raised fears of a Scottish invasion of northern England. Those fears were compounded by events in Ireland, which was invaded in 1315 by Robert Bruce's brother Edward, who was subsequently proclaimed high king. It was feared in Edward II's court that this was the prelude to Scottish intervention in England by way of Wales. There was a suspicion that the Scots might be able to instigate a rising by elements of the Welsh population who were hostile to English lordship. The king's response to the threat was to turn to the small group of Welsh elite figures who had emerged as central to the governance of and stability of Wales, and of whom Philip ap Hywel was a prominent member. Soon it became clear that Edward II was entrusting Philip and Rees with responsibility for arranging the defence of Wales, as the following documents from the Close Roll demonstrate:

> To the chamberlain of Caernarvon. Order to expend such money about the defence and custody of the parts of Wales as shall be directed by Master John Walwayn, escheator on this side of Trent, Philip ap Hywel, and Master Rees ap Hywel, whom the king is sending thither to ordain, together with John de Grey, justice of

North Wales, for the defence of Wales against the threatened invasion of the Scotch rebels who lately attacked Ireland, and to be aiding to the said justice, and John, Philip, and Rees. By the King and Council.

The like to the chamberlain of Carmarthen, substituting William Martyn, justice of South Wales, for John de Grey.

Orders to the bishops, abbots, etc., of North Wales to give credence to John de Grey and the said John and Philip in what they shall inform them on the king's behalf, and to execute what they shall direct.[23]

It seems that Edward had given Philip and Rees, and their colleagues John Walwayn and the justices of north and south Wales, virtual *carte blanche* to spend whatever they thought necessary to ready the royal lands to face an invasion. The orders which set out the powers of those whom Edward was sending to Wales on his behalf were followed by others which paid them their expenses for the journey to the king.

And as it began to appear that the threat of an invasion of Wales had been averted, Philip and his colleague William Martyn, justice of South Wales were able to get back to the matter of a tense situation which had developed in the lordship of Builth. They had begun to work on a resolution in December of 1315,[24] as soon as they had finished their work on the defences of both north and South Wales, work which must have proceeded at a very fast pace. And their efforts in Builth seem to have borne fruit in inducing the contesting parties, the community and the king's ministers, to settle their differences:

> To William Martyn and Philip ap Hywel. Order to permit the men of the king's garrison of Builth and his bailiffs and ministers there, and the men of the counties, town and land of Builth to meet and agree concerning trespasses and injuries committed one upon another, which the king appointed the said William and Philip to hear and determine, the king having been prayed to grant them licence to agree, superseding the execution of their commission unless they be required by either party to proceed further in the matter.[25]

If Philip maintained his work for the king into 1316, this does not imply that he was no longer employed by Roger Mortimer of Wigmore, for in June of that year he was involved in a legal transaction which enabled Mortimer to specify more precisely the descent of his lands after his death.[26] Indeed, after his considerable activity in royal service in 1315 and early 1316 the records are virtually silent about Philip's relationship with the king. He was probably moving away from all involvement with Edward II in the period of the continued rise of Hugh Despenser the Younger. It is very likely that Philip sided with the growing baronial opposition to Despenser, in which his Marcher patrons, the Mortimers and Humphrey de Bohun were prominent. His continued contact with Roger Mortimer of Wigmore has been noted, and in 1322 it was said that Philip had adhered to Humphrey de Bohun, and that he had worn Humphrey's robes for a long time.[27]

By 1321, the discontent with the Despensers had turned into violence. The baronial opposition to Edward and Hugh the Younger, led by Thomas of Lancaster, supported by the Mortimers and Humphrey de Bohun and labelled 'the Contrariants' were at first in the ascendant: Despenser was exiled and the supporters of the Contrariants were pardoned for their actions against the king. But by late 1321, Edward II had regained the initiative. In February 1322, the Mortimers surrendered and were imprisoned in the Tower of London and in March at Boroughbridge de Bohun was killed, while, following the battle, Lancaster was executed. Many of their followers, including Philip ap Hywel, his brother Master Rees, and their nephew Philip Clanvowe, were arrested and imprisoned. In May, however, Philip ap Hywel, along with some others of the de Bohun affinity, was released upon finding sureties for this good behaviour, and in July orders were issued to restore to him his lands and goods.

Following the turbulence of 1322, Philip appears to have kept a low profile. Not surprisingly, he does not appear in the records of Edward II's government. But he is recorded at Pool Castle in 1324, witnessing a charter issued by John Charlton, lord of Powys. Charlton was a former courtier of the king, who had become associated with the Contrariants by 1321. When it became clear that the king's forces were gaining ground late in that year, Charlton had surrendered to the royalists, but after a brief imprisonment was released, and went on to serve Edward II once more. It seems likely, however, that he was still secretly an ally of Roger Mortimer of Wigmore, and after Mortimer's escape from the Tower in 1323 he may have been in clandestine contact with him. When Mortimer returned from France, where he had gone after his escape, accompanied by Edward II's estranged queen, Isabella, Charlton began to hunt down the king's supporters, especially the earl of Arundel, who was captured by Charlton in Shrewsbury and sent by him to Hereford, where he was executed. It seems quite likely that Philip ap Hywel, with his long record as a retainer of Roger Mortimer and his recent record of opposition to King Edward, may have been acting as a Mortimer partisan, perhaps even a contact between Mortimer and Charlton, in 1324. In the witness-list of Charlton's charter of that year Philip was designated as a canon of St Davids, and it is quite possible that he was focused on ecclesiastical matters in this period. Even after Roger Mortimer's return and rise to real power in the government of Edward II's son, the young Edward III, Philip is notable mainly for his advancement in the Church. In 1328 he appears as the archdeacon of Brecon in the diocese of St Davids, and was also a well-known figure in that of Hereford, where the bishop, Adam of Orleton, had appointed him in 1326 to be one of two sequestrators to collect dues for him from the church of Kinnersley, which the bishop had taken into his own hands. It has been argued that a now illegible marginal note in the continuation of *Brut y Tywysogyon* opposite the entry for 1329 records Philip's death and burial in Hereford Cathedral.[28]

In assessing Philip ap Hywel's career and importance, it is evident that he benefited from the reputation of his father. But we should also take into account his ability, and care, to keep all his opportunities open – advancement in the church, eminence in the entourages of both the Mortimers of Wigmore and the de Bohun lords of Brecon, and for many years prominence as a royal official. In a similar vein, he had landed interests in both the March and in Herefordshire. His influence was clearly great – and was buttressed both by his capacity for hard work and his associations with other ambitious and well-connected men, both Welsh and English. He seems to have taken his clerical calling seriously; there is no hint of illegitimate children, in contrast to his brothers Rees and William. Indeed, his heir was the son of William ap Hywel, Sir Philip Clanvowe, who also rose to great eminence in both Wales and Herefordshire.[29] It is a matter for speculation as to when, if ever, Master Rhys and Philip began to lay claim to royal descent which is implicit in later genealogical tracts that show their family as descended from the southern ruler of Ystrad Tywi, Rhys Gryg, and through him from his father, that greatest of twelfth-century Welsh princes, the Lord Rhys. It is quite possible that this pedigree, assuredly based on a fiction, was the product of a later generation. But our next member of the post-1295 elite certainly was of royal descent, on both his maternal and paternal sides.

Sir Morgan ap Maredudd

Sir Morgan remains an enigmatic figure. Many episodes in his career are difficult to interpret, and there is an air of mystery about much of his life. His ancestry is one of royal blood. His grandmother on his father's side, Gwerful ferch Morgan, was descended from the Welsh lords of Caerleon, while his paternal grandfather, Gruffudd ap Maredudd, was a grandson of the Lord Rhys of Deheubarth. His father, Maredudd ap Gruffudd, was the ruler of lordships in Gwynllŵg and Gwent, but these were seized in 1270, the year of Maredudd's death, by Gilbert de Clare, earl of Gloucester and lord of Glamorgan and other lands in south-east Wales. The inheritance of Morgan was thus an attenuated one, consisting mainly of large parts of the commote of Hirfryn. And even that was not to last for long. According to evidence given at an inquisition in 1278, Morgan was called to render homage to Llywelyn ap Gruffudd, Prince of Wales, for the lands of Hirfryn, but when he did so the prince had ejected him. There was no record as to whether this was an arbitrary seizure of lands by Llywelyn or whether Morgan had given cause for his ejection.

Perhaps predictably, Morgan appeared before the Hopton commission set up in the wake of the war of 1277 to deal with the legal issues which had arisen as a result of the war and also those that had been unresolved in the previous years. He can be found involved as a plaintiff in cases against John Giffard and his wife Matilda relating to Hirfryn and associated lands, and also against Gilbert de Clare, earl of Gloucester, regarding lands in Gwynllŵg and Ystrad Tywi. Morgan also claimed against Bartholomew de Mora land in Llanwern (in the commote of Llebenydd). Morgan was unsuccessful in all of these cases, in which he either failed to persist in his case, or else the proceedings were still incomplete when the work of the commission was interrupted by the war of 1282.

Morgan seems to have settled in the few lands that remained to him during 1282: there are no references to any activity on his part in this period. But in early May 1283 he is to be found amongst the die-hard supporters of Dafydd ap Gruffudd, who was now employing his late brother's title of prince of Wales and lord of Snowdon[ia], and holding ever-diminishing lands against the encircling forces of the king. Morgan ap Maredudd witnessed third out of the magnates who were with Dafydd.[30] Of the others who witnessed, some who can be traced were destined to the king's prisons, and one, the steward Goronwy ap Heilin, died 'against the peace'. Dafydd himself was executed in barbaric fashion at Shrewsbury in October of 1283. But of Morgan's fate nothing is heard. He does not appear to have been imprisoned, and clearly survived for decades. Here is the first great mystery of Morgan's career: how did he suddenly appear in Dafydd's entourage in 1283, and why is there no reference to his fate in the aftermath of the desperate events of the middle months of that year?

In fact, Morgan is conspicuous by his absence from the records for more than a decade. He reappears as the leader of the Glamorgan rebels in the risings of 1294–5. He was by far the most successful of the rebel leaders, driving Earl Gilbert out of his lordship of Glamorgan. Though Gilbert was able to return to the lordship he managed to secure a hold only on Cardiff and its environs. The bulk of the lordship remained under Morgan's control. Morgan came to terms with the king in June 1295, when he marched into Edward's camp at Merthyr with seven hundred of his men. He claimed to have been fighting only against the earl of Gloucester and not against the king. This approach was successful: once again Morgan came to no harm for opposing the king: he was allowed to go free, 'against the will of the earl', and handed the lordship of Glamorgan over to Edward, who took it into his own hands.[31] It was returned to Gilbert only some five weeks before the earl's death. He was replaced by his widow, Joan of Acre, who was the king's daughter. Here, then, is a second mystery: how did Morgan escape royal retribution for his rebellion?

It was not long after the events of June that Morgan was once more involved in another episode that might well have had disastrous consequences for him. He appears to have been embroiled in the treasonous plans of Sir Thomas Turberville. Turberville had served Edward I in the Welsh wars of 1277 and 1282–3. He had been engaged in the king's service in Gascony in April of 1295, but had secured his release on giving up his sons as hostages and agreeing to stir up risings against Edward in Scotland and Wales. A letter that Turberville wrote to his contact, the Provost of Paris, contained details of his doings in pursuit of this plan. In the course of this report, he twice mentioned 'Morgan', who can hardly be other than Morgan ap Maredudd. First of all, he described how he had been in the presence of the king, and so had not dared 'to deliver unto Morgan the thing which you well know of'. This appears to refer to a letter of the king of France to Morgan. Later in the report, Turberville notes that 'if those of Scotland rise against the King of England, the Welsh will rise also. And this I have well contrived, and Morgan has fully covenanted with me to that effect.' It is clear that Morgan was deeply involved in the treasonous plan.[32]

Turberville was subsequently betrayed to Edward I and was tried and executed with great brutality. As for 'Morgan', nothing more is heard about him. No investigation, no trial or punishment is recorded. Here is yet another mystery, and another apparently scarcely credible escape for Morgan ap Maredudd.

Events which took place around eighteen months later, in the spring and summer of 1297 may provide a clue to the various mysteries set out above. In May of that year Morgan ap Maredudd was given responsibility by Edward I for raising troops in Glamorgan for service overseas.[33] This in itself suggests that Edward was confident enough in Morgan's loyalty to commission him to recruit troops in a region where he had only recently been, allegedly, in rebellion. An even more illuminating situation developed later in the summer of 1297. Morgan was sent by the king on a highly secret mission to the lordship of Brecon. It is evident from a letter later written by him to the king, that Morgan's mission was to stir up a rising of the leading men of the land against the lord of Brecon, Humphrey de Bohun, earl of Hereford.[34] It seems that the earl, and more particularly his steward, Philip ap Hywel, got wind of Morgan's mission, and countered it by the issue of a charter to the men of the lordship, promising them all the freedoms and rights that they wanted.[35] They therefore told Morgan that they were 'all at one with their lord'.

The point about this incident is that it reveals with some clarity Morgan as a secret agent of the king, and an *agent provocateur*, who was close to King Edward.[36] It may be suggested that here, in his providing covert services to the king, we may have the solution to the mysteries of Morgan's role and repeated avoidance of investigation and punishment in 1283, 1294–5 and again later in 1295.

With one possible partial exception,[37] the events of 1297 seem to end that phase of Morgan's career which involved him in work as a secret agent of the king. Henceforth he rather represents a prominent royal official, much involved in military business. Thus, we see him in 1298 raising one thousand men, again from Glamorgan, for royal service.[38] But it was in 1306 that we have a particularly vivid demonstration of his eminence. The events of late May of that year confirm his value in the eyes of the king. On 22 May there took place the high point of the Feast of the Swans, when in response to a proclamation by Edward I that all esquires eligible for knighthood should come to Westminster, some 266 men gathered there. They were mainly drawn from England, but a few were from Wales, and amongst these latter was Morgan ap Maredudd. First the king knighted his son Edward of Caernarfon, and then the latter knighted the other men who had assembled. This chivalric extravaganza established Morgan as a member of the elite amongst Edward's subjects.[39] Three days later, on 25 May Edward of Caernarfon issued from London a charter to the burgesses of Caernarfon. There was a predictably august witness-list, including Henry de Lacy, earl of Lincoln, and Sir Hugh Despenser. The list was headed by Walter de Langeton, bishop of Coventry and Lichfield. It also included the names of Sir Gruffudd ap Rhys (i.e. Sir Gruffudd Llwyd) and Sir Morgan ap Maredudd. Here was more evidence of social and political eminence.[40]

Finally, on 27 May an order was issued by King Edward, directed at a number of sheriffs, as follows:

> To the sheriff of Salop and Stafford. Order to meet Gruffudd ap Rhys and Morgan ap Maredudd and the Welshmen in their company when they shall enter his bailiwick, and to conduct them in person, throughout his bailiwick safely and securely, not permitting any wrong, annoyance or grievance to be inflicted upon them, and to make proclamation that victuals and other necessaries in places through which they shall pass shall be exposed for sale for their money, as Edward, prince of Wales, is sending Gruffudd and Morgan to conduct certain Welsh footmen from Wales to Scotland to him, there to stay with him for the repression of the rebellion of the king's enemies there. By the king.
>
> The like to the sheriff of Nottingham and Derby, York, Northumberland, Lancaster, Cumberland and Westmoreland.[41]

The great care that the sheriffs through whose bailiwicks the Welsh leaders would pass as soon as they left Wales until they reached Scotland were required to take of Gruffudd, Morgan and their men is striking testimony as to their importance in the eyes of Edward I.

In June of the following year, Sir Gruffudd and Sir Morgan are again seen leading Welsh troops from north Wales and from South and West Wales respectively to attack Robert the Bruce, on what proved to be Edward I's last campaign.[42] It seems that these two eminent men were able to work effectively together.

Advancing years did not mean that Sir Morgan's abilities were ignored. That Edward II continued to have a high opinion of him is suggested by the fact he was called upon to advise the king during a crisis that arose in 1315. In this, the year after Edward II's disastrous defeat at the hands of Robert the Bruce, the fear grew in the court that Bruce might invade England from the north, in conjunction with an attack from the west by his brother Edward. Edward had invaded Ireland with a Scottish army, and had proclaimed himself King of Ireland. The fear was that he would now launch an attack on England through Wales, prompting alarm at the prospect of what may be termed a 'Celtic Alliance'. Edward II's reaction was to call meetings at his retreat at Clipstone tower in Nottinghamshire with very small groups of key figures in Wales, to discuss the issues and to organise defences. Morgan was called to the king together with Einion Sais, bishop of Bangor and Sir Gruffudd Llwyd. They stayed with Edward between 30 November and 2 December. Given that he had acted with Sir Gruffudd in the past, Morgan's association with him in 1315 is not surprising – but it may have had a deep significance for Sir Gruffudd's actions as the crisis developed.[43] These meetings were a crucial determinant of the king's policy in the years after 1315. Along with his knighting in 1306, his role as an influence on Edward's policy in the later period demonstrates his importance to the royal regime in Wales. A further indication of that importance came when he headed a list of Welsh figures called upon after the Llywelyn Bren rebellion in 1316 to advise on the treatment to be meted out to those who were accused of taking part in, or being in some way complicit in, the rising.[44]

Some idea of Morgan's continuing regional importance is given by the fact that he was engaged in raising troops in South and West Wales in 1316, and a thousand infantry in Glamorgan in 1317.[45] Thereafter, references to him relate principally to some of the lands that he held. It is likely that he had gone into retirement from service to Edward II. It may not be entirely fanciful to ascribe that retirement not only to Morgan's age but also to disillusionment with the king's patronage of Hugh Despenser the younger. Morgan died in 1331, when he was recorded as holding significant lands as a crown tenant in chief: Bodfuan in Llŷn valued at 20s per year, and one third of the commote of Peuliniog with Amgoed, together with one third of St Clears in the south-west.[46] He also held other lands, some as life tenancies, in the lordships of Glamorgan and Abergavenny. Morgan had no son, so his heiress was his daughter Angharad. Morgan had hardly had a conventional career, but was involved in episodes of the highest political importance in the reigns of Edward I and Edward II, as well as in service at senior positions in military and administrative matters.

Madog ap Llywelyn (d. 1331)

Madog was particularly involved in the politics and administration of the Marcher lordship of Bromfield and Yale, though his activities took him on significantly wider missions. His father, Llywelyn ap Gruffudd, was a well-to-do freeman in Bromfield/Maelor, but Madog's ancestry through his mother Angharad ferch Maredudd was most distinguished: she was a daughter of Maredudd ap Madog (d. 1256), lord of Iâl, and through him she was grand-daughter of Madog ap Gruffudd (d. 1236) of northern Powys, and descended directly from Madog ap Maredudd (d. 1160), 'king of the Powysians'.[47] Even more than that, Angharad's mother was Catrin, sister of Llywelyn ap Gruffudd, prince of Gwynedd and subsequently prince of Wales. This linked Madog ap Llywelyn's pedigree to the ruling dynasty of Gwynedd. He could thus claim a most illustrious ancestry.[48]

Madog's forebears may well have made it relatively easy for him to emerge as an outstanding figure in Bromfield. In 1308, when he was beginning to achieve some degree of prominence in Bromfield and Yale he acted as a witness to a charter of the lord, Earl Warenne of Surrey, in which he was the only Welshman amongst eleven witnesses.[49] It was perhaps a decade later that Madog's importance in the lordship became even clearer. In that year John de Warenne was forced out of the lordship by the power of Earl Thomas of Lancaster, a grandson of Henry III and the holder of five earldoms. Once Lancaster had secured Bromfield and Yale, one of his first appointments was that of Madog ap Llywelyn, to the crucial post of Receiver in the lordship.[50] This confirmed him as a prime example of the developing Welsh ministerial aristocracy.

By 1321, Lancaster had emerged as the leader of the baronial opposition to Edward II and his favourite Hugh Despenser the Younger. In the course of that year Lancaster and his supporters were able to achieve dominance over the king and his supporters, but by early 1322 the position was reversed, and Edward II was able to regain the initiative against Earl Thomas. In February, Madog ap Llywelyn was commissioned by the king to raise troops in Bromfield and Yale and to take them to the king at Coventry, from where they would go to fight the Scots and the 'Contrariants'.[51] It seems therefore that Madog was had already switched his allegiance to the side of Edward II. In March, the two sides fought a decisive battle at Boroughbridge, in which the king was entirely victorious. Thomas of Lancaster was captured and executed. In the aftermath of Lancaster's death John de Warenne was able to regain his lordship of Bromfield and Yale. Although Madog had served the man who had pushed Warenne from that lordship, this seems not to have caused him to lose his place amongst the key figures in the entourage of the restored earl. In 1323, Madog, his brother Gruffudd and three other Welshmen travelled to Warenne's principal seat at Reigate in Surrey where they witnessed a grant by the earl.[52] In 1330, Madog appears again as a witness to a Warenne grant issued at Holt, his chief seat in Bromfield.[53]

In another sign of a new allegiance, Madog accepted a commission from the government of Edward III, after the execution of Roger Mortimer who had been more than anyone behind the fall of Edward II. The commission of Oyer and Terminer was to Madog and four prominent English officials, to respond to a petition from the community of North Wales complaining about oppressions committed by William de Shaldeford, who had been deputy to Roger Mortimer as justice of North Wales.

Throughout his career, Madog ap Llywelyn seems to have been well regarded in the lordship of Bromfield and Yale. Indeed, the author of the Continuation of the Welsh chronicle *Brut y Tywysogyo*n, composed mainly in that region, recorded Madog's death in 1331. This in itself was unusual – as very few men who were not rulers received such a notice of their death in the *Brut*. More than that, the chronicler accorded Madog what amounted to an obituary notice, noting that he had been buried 'in his own church of Gresford'. Even more telling was the chronicler's comment that Madog was 'the best man that ever was in Maelor'.[54]

The chronicler who wrote the final stages of the Continuation of *Brut y Tywysogyon* may well have been predisposed to praise Madog. It has been suggested by the present author that important stages in Madog's career coincide to a marked extent with changes in the structure of the Continuation.[55] This perhaps indicates that Madog ap Llywelyn may have been an informant of the chronicler. Even more than that, it possibly gives rise to a suspicion that he may have acted as a patron of the chronicler.

Within Madog's church of Gresford is further important evidence of Madog's standing in that region. The church is now a fifteenth-century structure, but it contains some older elements, of which arguably the most important is the tomb of Madog ap Llywelyn, surmounted by his sepulchral effigy. This is a splendid sculpture, presenting him as a military figure, clad in armour with his sword part-drawn.[56] This depiction suggests that there was probably more to Madog's military activities than simply leading men to join the king in early 1322. Madog is also depicted bearing his shield, on which is depicted the lion rampant of the royal house of Powys.[57] These are further indications of the complex foundations of Madog ap Llywelyn's eminence.

Madog seems not to have had the impact throughout much of Wales that characterises the other members of the elite group within which he is numbered in this analysis. But, in spite of that, his regional importance was at times expanded, and was of such intensity, covering so many aspects, that he emerges as a figure worthy of inclusion in the present chapter.

Sir Gruffudd Llwyd ap Rhys

It is difficult to argue with Rees Davies's estimate of Sir Gruffudd as 'the most powerful figure in native Welsh society' – at least as far as Gwynedd was concerned. His pedigree was both very distinguished and of a type likely to interest Edward I: he was Gruffudd ap Rhys ap Gruffudd ab Ednyfed Fychan. His great-grandfather had been *distain* to both Llywelyn ab Iorwerth and Dafydd ap Llywelyn, and was the most celebrated member of the administrative aristocracy that had developed under the thirteenth-century princes of Gwynedd. His grandfather, Gruffudd ab Ednyfed, had been *distain* to Llywelyn ap Gruffudd in the mid-century period. And his father, Rhys ap Gruffudd, had been very prominent amongst those who had gone over from the entourage of Llywelyn in the 1270s to side with Edward I, and had served that monarch until his death in 1284.[58] He had by then had the satisfaction of seeing his son enter Edward's court as a king's esquire. In addition, Sir Gruffudd Llwyd was descended from Ednyfed Fychan's marriage to Gwenllian, daughter of the Lord Rhys, and he could thus claim princely blood. His own mother was Margaret Lestrange, of the prominent baronial family of the Shropshire March, and this probably meant that he was able to make easy contacts amongst the emerging English gentry.

As well as having a favourable genealogical background, Sir Gruffudd was also clearly possessed of the ability to work hard and consistently. As an official of Edward I and Edward II he was frequently engaged on tasks which called for leadership qualities, particularly in the military sphere. He is found leading very large numbers of troops from Wales for the campaigns of those rulers, sometimes taking them north to musters in Carlisle, sometimes to southern English ports for embarkation on continental campaigns.[59] In some instances Sir Gruffudd acted only a leader to musters, but on other occasions he participated in the actual campaigns.

Quite apart from this military activity, Sir Gruffudd had a host of other tasks to fulfil. Most important in this context was his elevation to the office of sheriff, the key official in the county structure of the principality which had been established by Edward I in 1284. He was amongst the very first Welsh holders of this office,[60] and by far the most eminent. In one important respect he was unmatched in terms of his tenure: he was not simply sheriff of a specific county, but in the course of his career was sheriff of all three of the counties of the principality of North Wales.[61]

Put alongside his regular military involvement his record as a sheriff establishes him as an outstanding functionary in positions of wide authority. But his activities on behalf of King Edward II went far beyond this. He undertook many assignments of an *ad hoc* nature, but three politico-military episodes stand out as major contributions

The first of these came in 1315, at a period of considerable tension in Edward II's realm. In the year following the victory of Robert the Bruce over Edward II's forces at Bannockburn, there was considerable nervousness in case Bruce should launch an invasion of northern England. That nervousness was increased when Robert's brother, Edward Bruce, invaded Ireland and took control of Ulster. Edward was proclaimed king of all Ireland, and the government in England waited on his next move. It was feared that he might next invade England, via Wales, where he might hope to get considerable help from the Welsh population.

Faced with that prospect, Edward II called meetings with prominent Welsh figures in order to plan a response. As we have noted,[62] Sir Gruffudd was called in to a meeting in Edward's retreat at Clipstone Tower in Nottinghamshire. He was joined by Sir Morgan ap Maredudd, and by the bishop of Bangor, Anian/Einion Sais. They spent 30 November to 2 December in deep discussions with the king. Perhaps as important as the talks – and meals – with Edward was the opportunity for the participants to talk to each other more privately. Here we should remember that Sir Gruffudd and Sir Morgan were old colleagues. This may be a point of importance, to which we shall return. Along with Philip ap Hywel and his brother Master Rees, and a colleague of theirs, Master John Walwayn, who were also consulted by Edward II, Gruffudd, Morgan and Bishop Anian constitute a very select group of Welsh notables to whom the king turned at this time of crisis.

In the event, there was no invasion of Wales in 1316 by Edward Bruce, though something of that sort had indeed seemed likely. For the moment we can leave the events of 1315–16, only noting that they emphasised the eminence of members of the elite group of Welsh notables. That there may have been another dimension to the scenario is a matter to which we shall return.

A second occasion when Sir Gruffudd showed his importance, and in fact made a decisive contribution to political events, came early in 1322, when Edward II's regime was deep in crisis. We need first to sketch the background. In terms of the 'High Politics' of Edward's realm, especially the relations between the king and the greater aristocrats, bitterness had become acute in the relationship between King Edward and Thomas of Lancaster, significantly as a result of the advancing influence of Edward's favourites, the Despensers – most clearly that of Hugh Despenser the Younger. The rise of Hugh Despenser the Younger was marked by his ruthless acquisition of the whole lordship of Glamorgan, and his elimination in 1318, by what was generally regarded as a judicial murder, of Llywelyn Bren, the Glamorgan rebel leader of 1316. The execution of Llywelyn Bren aroused bitter opposition and revulsion amongst Marcher lords and the Welsh community alike. With baronial unrest mounting, Edward II was forced to exile the Despensers in August 1321, but over the following months the king regained the political initiative. As many of the baronial leaders rallied behind Thomas of Lancaster, it was clear that the struggle for political control of the realm was coming to a head. 'Royalist' and 'baronial' factions gathered troops and manoeuvred for military advantage. In this process, members of the administrative elite played a significant part – though not a united one. On the one hand, the king was able to rely on the support of Sir Gruffudd Llwyd and his cousin Rhys ap Gruffudd.

On the other, Philip ap Hywel ap Meurig and his brother Master Rees stood with the Mortimers of Chirk and of Wigmore, and Humphrey de Bohun, earl of Hereford and lord of Brecon. It was to confront the baronial faction, led by Thomas of Lancaster, a prominent Marcher lord himself, that the king resolved to strike west into the lands of the great Marcher lords.

However, advancing from the Midlands of England, Edward found himself facing what seemed to be an impenetrable barrier of baronial forces along the line of the River Severn. The king was, however, able to call upon forces which Sir Gruffudd Llwyd and his cousin Rhys ap Gruffudd were raising in North and South Wales from November. By January, Sir Gruffudd was able to lead his levies from North Wales against baronial strongholds, including Holt, Welshpool and Chirk, each of which he succeeded in overwhelming. The taking of these castles punched a great hole in the line of baronial 'blocking' fortresses, and that enabled the king to make a crossing of the Severn at Shrewsbury, and to march south towards Hereford, increasing his own strength while denying reinforcements and supplies to the Marchers who opposed him. At the same time Sir Gruffudd (with the support of Giles Beauchamp sheriff of Caernarfonshire), was able to attack, and seize for the king, Thomas of Lancaster's lordship of Denbigh, while also attacking John de Grey's lordship of Dyffryn Clwyd.[63] The contributions to the king's cause made by Sir Gruffudd and by Rhys ap Gruffudd and their allies were of crucial importance in damaging the Marchers and in strengthening the royalist forces.

Thus far, it has been possible to depict Sir Gruffudd Llwyd's career as one marked by a consistent chain of successes. In the last years of Edward II's reign he clearly stood very high in the king's confidence and estimation. From November 1321 to 1327 he was sheriff of Merioneth; he was installed as keeper of the castle and lordship of Builth, and the castle and land of Llandovery.[64] He was called upon to raise troops from north Wales when Roger Mortimer of Wigmore escaped from the Tower of London in August 1323,[65] and again when Mortimer and Queen Isabella invaded the realm in 1326.[66] He was involved in a small number of failures, the principal one being Bannockburn, but this was hardly a fault of his. But at times there was a much darker side to Sir Gruffudd's life. He was, for example faced by accusations of tyrannical and oppressive behaviour. Most seriously, on three occasions he was cast into prison. Rees Davies noted with some understatement that Gruffudd was 'briefly imprisoned'.⁶⁷ This was with specific reference to the second of those periods of captivity, which lasted in fact for some eighteen months, from very late 1316 to mid-1318. As this was the most important, and also the most mysterious of the imprisonments of Sir Gruffudd, we shall consider it last of the three.

Let us examine first Gruffudd's incarceration in the period September 1295 to March/April 1296. This too was a somewhat mysterious affair, coming as it did immediately after Gruffudd had given good service in leading a squadron of cavalry against the rising of Madog ap Llywelyn. The dates of this confinement were suggested in 1915 by J. G. Edwards, who argued that, though 'difficult to explain', it can be fixed as beginning at least six months before Easter 1296.⁶⁸ This date was echoed by Beverley Smith writing in the *Oxford Dictionary of National Biography* in 2004, who suggested that Gruffudd's captivity started 'before the end of 1295'.⁶⁹ Easter in 1296 was in late March. In a petition to the king and his council asking to know the reason for his imprisonment – a petition which is probably to be dated some time before Gruffudd was taken to London from his place of captivity in Conwy castle – Gruffudd noted that he had been a captive for 'half a year and more'. The Chester annals tell us that Gruffudd was taken to London by John de Havering, the justice of North Wales 'after Easter' of 1296.⁷⁰ If we count say, seven months (half a year and more) back from a date around the end of March, we come to a date around the start of September. This is in fact the date of John de Havering's appointment as justice, which was 3 September 1295. This is most instructive, because as well as that appointment, John de Havering and a colleague, William Cycons, were given a commission of Oyer and Terminer on 1 September. The terms were 'on complaint by the men of the commonalty of North Wales' that they should deal with 'trespasses, injuries, extortions, oppressions and grievous losses inflicted upon that land came into the king's hands, by the sheriffs, bailiffs, and other ministers of the king in those parts.' It is difficult to resist the suspicion that Gruffudd Llwyd may have been one of the first targets of the new commissioners. It seems possible that Gruffudd Llwyd had been the subject of accusations, and that Havering had responded too rapidly. Gruffudd himself, in his petition to the king and council, claimed that he had been imprisoned *par encusement et male volence de ses enemis* (by the accusation and ill-will of his enemies). It may be that Gruffudd was right – his position as a Welsh 'man of the court' might well have prompted both the Welsh community and English officials to feel threatened by his presence in North Wales.

An endorsement on the petition is brusque, and suggests strongly that the king was unhappy to hear about his incarceration: 'Let the Justice be heard, or let him be ordered to notify the king of the cause of his capture and his detention in prison.'[71] It would seem that Gruffudd Llwyd was rapidly released. And it is ironic that by the early spring of 1298 John de Havering and Gruffudd Llwyd were working together as commissioners of array for North Wales, gathering troops to serve in a campaign in Scotland.

In somewhat similar fashion, Sir Gruffudd's third period of captivity, in Caernarfon castle in 1327, can be explained fairly simply as a consequence of a change of monarch and of government. Sir Gruffudd had been implicated in a plan in the summer of 1327 to release the captive Edward II, a situation entirely consistent with his record of support for that monarch, and his effective refusal to attend the parliament called in that year to effect Edward II's deposition.[72] Under these circumstances it presumably seemed prudent to Roger Mortimer, the driving force in the new regime, and his advisers to imprison Sir Gruffudd as a danger to peace and stability in the realm. Along with him, twelve of his close associates were also imprisoned, probably in the late summer. But by late October of 1327 orders had been given for the release of all thirteen of the captives – quite probably because their continued detention was seen by Mortimer as an incentive to serious disturbances in north Wales. The comment of Beverley

Smith that the men detained with Sir Gruffudd 'represented a very powerful force in the community of north Wales' is very much to the point.[73]

We must turn now to the second and longest of the imprisonments suffered by Sir Gruffudd. This began at the end of 1316. It was almost certainly no coincidence that it coincided closely with the appointment of Roger Mortimer of Chirk as justice of north Wales in late November 1316, and it may reflect the very poor relations that existed between Mortimer and the leaders of Welsh society of the principality.[74] On the other hand, Mortimer surely needed at least a pretext for any action against Sir Gruffudd. Such a pretext, and possibly more than a pretext, was provided by Sir Gruffudd's apparent involvement in an intrigue with Edward Bruce.

The core evidence of such an intrigue takes the form of letters preserved in a seventeenth-century copy preserved by Robert Vaughan of Hengwrt.[75] In his letter, Bruce raises the prospect of a Scottish invasion of Wales and the removal of that land from English control. In reply, Sir Gruffudd assures Bruce that if the Scots come the Welsh will be ready to rise, and emphasises that 'the intention of the English is to try to delete our name and memory from the land'.[76]

Given that the letters exist only in much later copies, there have to be reservations about how genuine they are, but there is a widespread consensus that they reflect authentic documents of the later part of the second decade of the fourteenth century. It cannot be denied that the tone of Sir Gruffudd's letter is hard to reconcile with his record of loyalty to Edward II and his father, and particularly with his position in late 1315. Beverley Smith noted that 'indications of date within the letters themselves are perfectly consistent with a possible deviation on Llwyd's part in the period immediately preceding his imprisonment', and suggested that:

> treacherous activity on the part of Gruffudd Llwyd might, on the one hand, help to explain the reappointment of the formidable marcher baron to the justiceship so as to provide for the greater

security of a key quarter of the realm in what was still a period of real danger. On the other hand, the letters may be interpreted as an ill-judged response on the part of Gruffydd Llwyd to the return of Mortimer to a position in which he had already aroused the ire of influential persons in the Welsh community.[77]

A more recent view of the situation is that of Adam Chapman, who accepts that the letters represent genuine communications between Bruce and Sir Gruffudd,[78] and notes that:

> letters were exchanged between Sir Gruffydd Llwyd, undisputed leader of the Welsh elite, and Edward Bruce who had been crowned 'king of Ireland' in May 1316. Bruce offered the prospect of invasion. Sir Gruffudd's reply, extraordinary for a man who owed his position and status to the English Crown, but presumably speaking for his community, was that if Bruce were to come to Wales, the nobiles of Wales would join him. Whatever the reality of Bruce's sentiments or the prospects of invasion, that Sir Gruffydd Llwyd, of all people, should make such an offer indicates how low Edward II's stock had sunk. The discovery of these wavering loyalties ... was certainly the reason that Sir Gruffudd was imprisoned in Rhuddlan Castle late in 1316 by the justiciars of North Wales, Roger Mortimer and Roger de Grey of Ruthin. The existence of the letters between Bruce and Sir Gruffudd Llwyd demonstrates the independence of thought of the *uchelwyr* a generation after the conquest. Gruffudd Llwyd and his contemporaries had, in their minds at least, taken on the mantle of the princes and felt able to reconsider the settlement imposed by Edward I with independent action.[79]

The interesting point about these commentaries on the Edward Bruce/Gruffudd Llwyd letters is that they take the correspondence at face value without looking for a rather more complex context for them. This applies particularly to the letter from Sir Gruffudd, which seems so out of character from a man who was such a prop of the regime of Edward II. We shall do well to search for another approach. Fortunately, one possibility seems to me to stand out. This is Sir Gruffudd's relationship with Sir

Morgan ap Maredudd. The point has been made above that the two men had quite frequently shared elements or all of the same military assignments over several years. Most importantly, they had both, together with the bishop of Bangor, met with Edward II at Clipstone Tower in late November and early December 1315 to plan responses to the threat posed by Edward Bruce. It is a matter for speculation whether, in the course of the Clipstone meetings, or in private discussions with Sir Gruffudd alone, Morgan may have talked about his experiences at an earlier stage of his career as a secret agent of Edward I. It seems tolerably certain that some of Morgan's secret work for that king had involved activity as an *agent provocateur*.[80] This in turn raises the possibility that Sir Gruffudd may have learned enough from Morgan about such manoeuvres to employ one when contacted by Edward Bruce.

Perhaps the most interesting aspect of this approach to the Edward Bruce/Gruffudd Llwyd correspondence is that it follows very closely the pattern of the contacts between Thomas Turberville and Morgan (ap Maredudd) in 1295. Turberville had introduced the possibility of linking a rising of the Welsh against English rule to a similar Scottish rising, and Morgan had assured him that in the event of the Scots rising the Welsh could be persuaded to do the same.[81] Morgan's relationship with Turberville thus offers a possible template for Sir Gruffudd's relationship with Edward Bruce in 1316. While hardly constituting proof that Sir Gruffudd was emulating Morgan's actions in 1295, the parallel between the two cases surely makes that a distinct possibility.

Even if Sir Gruffudd's career was marked by occasional sudden downturns in his fortunes, there can be no mistaking the great power and influence that he wielded. There are constant reminders of this, not only in the poetry in which his landed possessions and his martial abilities are celebrated,[82] but in record sources. Thus, in the course of the Scotto-Irish invasion scare of 1315–16, a proposal was drafted for instructions to be sent in the king's name to commissioners in Wales. Amongst those instructions was one that they 'should not forget to consult with Sir Gruffudd Llwyd'. That was a view from the king's government in England. There was also a view of Sir Gruffudd from the men whom he had led, as expressed in a letter from Roger Trumwyn, lieutenant of the justice of North Wales, to the Black Prince and his council, probably written in late May, 1345.[83] In the course of the letter, Trumwyn reports that Welsh troops selected to serve overseas had apparently demanded that they should be led by an Englishman, as they had not been led by a Welshman since the time of Sir Gruffudd Llwyd, 'who was a Welshman and a man of the court'. Trumwyn added that, if Welshmen were chosen as leaders, they should be chosen from 'amongst those who hold by franchise of barony … rather than from among men of lesser estate'. In North Wales, at least, men looked back on the days of Sir Gruffudd as a time when leadership was provided by one who was fully acceptable as a Welshman of excellent stock, and 'a man of the court'. We must now turn southwards to examine the situation there.

Sir Philip de Clanvowe

Philip Clanvowe was a close kinsman of the brothers Philip and Master Rees, sons of Hywel ap Meurig. He was their nephew, the son of William ap Hywel ap Meurig.[84] The background to Philip's abandonment of his patronymic is unclear, but the strongest suggestion is that it relates to a manorial name of Clanvowe in the 1340 extent of Hay lordship.[85] It may have been adopted to facilitate a career in England, or it may have been intended to obscure Philip's parentage, for William was a cleric, and became the dean of Builth.

Early record references to Philip show him to have been involved in the political tensions of the reign of Edward II. It is evident that he was in some way involved in the killing of Piers Gaveston, the king's favourite, after he had been condemned to death by an assembly of barons, led by the earls of Lancaster, Warwick, Arundel and Hereford. The actual killing was the work of two Welshmen, but we do not have their names. In 1313, those who were in some way involved in the killing were pardoned. And Philip de 'Clannon' (i.e. Clanvou) was amongst them. But there are some five hundred names on the list of pardons, and it is impossible to establish what part, if any, Philip Clanvowe had in the deed.

Again, some years later, in 1321–2, Philip appears to have been involved in the opposition to the monopoly of the king's favours enjoyed by the Despensers, Hugh the Elder and Hugh the Younger, which produced a similar hostility amongst the English and Marcher nobility to that which had been aroused by Gaveston. In a period of baronial ascendancy, Philip de Clanvowe was amongst those pardoned 'on the testimony (to be read as "at the insistence") of the earl of Hereford'.[86] It seems clear that the family tradition of support for the de Bohun lords of Brecon and earls of Hereford was being maintained by Philip. Also on the list of those pardoned (again a long list) were the names of Philip ap Hywel and Master Rees ap Hywel. But in February 1322, with the king's fortunes very much improved, new orders were sent out for Philip Clanvowe's arrest.[87] Somewhat oddly, shortly after the king's crushing of the baronial forces at Boroughbridge in March 1322, when Thomas of Lancaster was executed and Humphrey de Bohun killed, Philip Clanvowe's lands, goods and chattels were restored to him.[88] Why this should be so is a matter for speculation, but it is noteworthy that his was not an isolated case: others were similarly treated. It was in the following months that it becomes evident that his focus was more on Herefordshire than on Wales. In November he represented Hereford in a parliament, and he was also involved in acting as a surety for Herefordshire men who had been suspected of opposing the king and the Despensers.[89]

Philip was interestingly quiet in the records of the mid- and later-1320s, but reappears after the tumultuous period which saw the fall of Edward II and the dominance of Roger Mortimer of Wigmore. Thereafter, from the early 1330s, he emerges as a prominent official of Edward III first of all in Wales. As early as 1331, he acted as deputy justiciar leading an enquiry into the administration of justice in the southern principality. In 1332, he arrayed a small force in south Wales for service in Ireland, and two years later he recruited many more troops for a Scottish campaign. He acted in a variety of roles in 1334: enquiring into lands and rents granted by the bishop of St Davids, investigating homicides in Is Cennen and consequent widespread disturbances, and raising forces in south Wales and taking them to the king at Newcastle upon Tyne; and, in the following year, together with Owen of Montgomery, taking on the role of keeper of ports and coasts in south Wales, and organising the arrest of Scottish ships.[90] In the same year, Clanvowe was sent to deal with complaints about the ruinous state of Builth castle – thereby maintaining the family link with that place.[91] In 1536 he would be sent to inspect and report on other castles in southern Wales,[92] and in 1339 he would be sent back to continue work on the problems of Builth.[93] A somewhat delicate task faced him in the latter year when he was tasked with surveying and reporting on the lands of his illustrious contemporary Rhys ap Gruffudd in and around Lampeter.[94] In the same year, he began raising six hundred men for a campaign in Flanders, while in 1341 he was involved in recruiting troops for a Scottish campaign.[95]

Increasingly, however, from the later 1330s Philip Clanvowe was drawn into the governance and politics of Herefordshire once more. He acted as member of parliament for Hereford in 1337, and for Herefordshire in 1339 and 1340.[96] More even than that, Clanvowe was deeply involved, from 1339 onwards, in the administration of Herefordshire. In that year he was arraying men in the county to provide a defence force should the French invade.[97] In 1340–1 he acted as a seller of the proceeds of a tax in kind, and in 1344 he was one of two men acting as the collectors for Herefordshire of a tax of a fifteenth and a tenth of moveables.[98] The two taxors were to 'go in person from place to place, and summon two men and the reeve from every township, and the mayor and bailiffs and four good and discreet men from each city and borough enjoining on them to cause the money to be levied by one or two of each township city and borough and delivered to them'.

He was also appointed as a commissioner of the peace for the county, with wide powers. The commissioners were, for example, charged with the task of enquiring into 'vagabonds, and those who form unlawful assemblies or otherwise disturb the peace, and arrest and imprison them, notifying to chancery the names of those who flee the county, and cannot therefore be brought to justice by them, and of those arrested'.[99]

Philip was also involved in issues in Wales in the 1340s. He was responsible for arraying men for service overseas in 1346, and keeping them in readiness should the Black Prince call for them.[100] He was brought in to deal with the problem of a Flemish ship which had been stolen and taken to the port of Fowey. The Black Prince had ordered its arrest, but the crew had succeeded in sailing it away from Fowey to the port of Haverford. The Flemish authorities suspected that the English government was not serious about recovering the ship and its cargo, and so impounded a consignment of wool which belonged to the Black Prince. The prince therefore sent one of his men to Haverford to recover the ship and return it to Zeeland, but his officer was chased away and threatened by the townsfolk. The prince turned to Philip, who was sent in to recover the ship and avert the crisis in relations with the Flemish authorities.[101]

In the following year Philip, still designated as the deputy of the justice of South Wales, was tasked to find persons to 'farm' the town of Llanbadarn Fawr, and was able to report that the burgesses of the town had agreed to take over the farm (i.e. the rent) for three years.[102]

Philip Clanvowe did therefore maintain a role in matters relating to the southern principality and associated lands, but it seems that in the 1340s those matters were for the most part highly specific issues into which he was brought as a kind of trouble shooter; they contrast with his involvement in Herefordshire, in which he was repeatedly brought into contact with the people of the county, high and low. His contributions to the governance of Herefordshire were in fact laying the foundations for a continuing involvement by his family, which over time would take them away from a meaningful engagement with Welsh matters.[103] As far as can be seen, although Philip was by no means removed from Welsh governance, the majority of his close associates were now English officials.[104]

Sir Rhys ap Gruffudd

Rhys was the last of the great figures who played such a dominant part in Wales in the two generations after 1295. A second cousin to Sir Gruffudd Llwyd, Rhys shared his descent from Gruffudd ab Ednyfed Fychan. This alone gave him a most illustrious pedigree. But his ancestry was given added lustre by the fact that his grandfather, Hywel ap Gruffudd, had fallen fighting for Edward I. He had been one of those who died in the disaster that took place at the attempt to cross Menai by the 'bridge of boats' in November 1282. Hywel's fame was such that the Welsh chronicle made him the leader of the force that tried to make the crossing.[105] On the side of his mother, Nest ferch Gwrwared ap Gwilym, Rhys was descended from Gwilym ap Gwrwared of the lordship of Cemais in Dyfed. Gwilym ap Gwrwared acted as the constable or chief official for Nicholas fitz Martin, lord of Cemais. But Gwilym also acted as an important Crown official, and was so distinguished that the English government treated him as the effective equal of Nicholas fitz Martin.[106] Rhys ap Gruffudd therefore had the sort of immediate ancestry that makes Ralph Griffiths's description of him as being of 'respectable lineage' seem somewhat inadequate.[107]

Probably born in the early 1280s, Rhys went early into the administration of the southern principality, holding the office of steward of Cardiganshire from 1308 to 1312, and again from 1316 to 1327. He was frequently to be found leading troops for Edward II: in 1316 he led forces against the revolt of Llywelyn Bren in Glamorgan, and in 1319 he took 1,200 men from south Wales into Scotland. He acted many times as deputy justiciar of south Wales, in 1321–2, 1322–5, 1326, and then, after the 'Mortimer interlude', 1334–40. There were early signs that his administrative style could be harsh: he had to be removed from office in 1320 pending investigations into complaints against him. It seems, however, that he retained the confidence of the king, who made him chief forester of Snowdon in August of that year.[108]

He was soon back in military action: in what was effectively the civil war of 1321–2 he led attacks on rebels in south Wales and west Wales and in February 1322 he seized the lordship of Gower into the king's hand from John de Mowbray.[109] In the same month, as events moved to a showdown between the king and the 'Contrariants', Rhys arrayed all the men of Cardiganshire between sixteen and sixty, so that they might be ready to answer the king's summons at any stage;[110] he was then commissioned to raise a further 1,850 men from South Wales and another 800 from Haverford and Pembroke. Rhys consolidated the king's increasing mastery over the rebel forces by taking control of the Mortimer castle of Narberth and any other lands in west Wales of Roger Mortimer of Chirk. He was subsequently given control of Narberth for life, with an annual grant of 100 marks. He went on to raise forces for a Scottish expedition, and was given custody of the castle of Llandovery. Ralph Griffiths's verdict that 'Rhys had become the king's principal sentinel in the west' is entirely justified.[111] It was perhaps around this period that Rhys was honoured in a poem by Einion Offeiriad, in which he received lavish praise for his military exploits and was compared to famous Welsh heroes.[112] In contrast to Einion Offeiriad's long poem, Rhys was also the recipient of four short *englynion* by an anonymous poet in which his ferocity in battle is emphasised, and his lordship is said to extend even to Gwynedd.[113]

There was, however, to be no chance that Rhys could rest on his laurels. In August 1323, he was raising troops to search for Roger Mortimer of Wigmore, who had escaped from confinement in the tower of London.[114] In fact, Mortimer had succeeded in crossing the channel to France, where he was eventually to meet and join forces with Queen Isabella, the estranged wife of Edward II.

Orders issued in 1325, which principally concerned Rhys, give some idea of how busy he was at that time:

> Order to Edmund [Fitz Alan], earl of Arundel, justiciar of Wales, and Rhys ap Gruffudd, the justiciar's lieutenant in South Wales, to array in the king's land of South Wales 200 foot-soldiers, both from those men that the earl was previously ordered to array, and from others, and two constables, suitably equipped. Rhys and Roger Pychard, whom the king has assigned with Rhys, are to lead the men, well

arrayed, to Hereford by Tuesday 12 March, receiving their wages from the chamberlain of Carmarthen from the time of their departure from their region until their arrival at Portsmouth. They are to be there by 17 March. The king also orders Rhys to select six men from Cardiganshire and Carmarthenshire, and from the stewardship, to go with him to ensure the safe conduct of the foot soldiers to Portsmouth so that peace is maintained in the king's lands. The chamberlain of Carmarthen has been ordered to go to Hereford on 12 March to pay the customary wages of the men, constables and leaders as far as Portsmouth. The king had previously ordered the earl and Rhys to array 200 Welsh men-at-arms and 1,000 Welsh foot soldiers, the men-at arms to be mounted, armed and equipped according to their status, and the foot soldiers suitably arrayed, to be brought to Portsmouth by 17 March to go with the king, at his wages, to the duchy of Guyenne for its relief and defence. But now, because there is not enough time to array the men, the king has postponed his passage to the duchy until 17 May at the request of the earls and barons of the realm. Nevertheless, he does not want the duchy to be left undefended, and has ordered that some men-at-arms and foot soldiers be sent there on 17 March, some of whom he wishes to be from South Wales.[115]

When Mortimer and Isabella invaded England in September 1326, Rhys ap Gruffudd was prominent among those who assembled men to resist the invaders when they reached Wales – to which Edward had fled. When it became clear that her advance could not be stopped, it was Rhys who headed a group deputed by the king to negotiate with his wife. That mission failed to save Edward, who was captured and imprisoned in Berkeley castle. Rhys was involved in a failed attempt to set the king free, and fled to the Scots. It may have been a sign of his importance that he was pardoned in February of 1328, and had his lands restored to him in April. Alternatively, it may have been that the government of Roger Mortimer decided that Rhys was more dangerous in Scotland than he would be in Wales, where he was more easily accessible and visible. Rhys ap Gruffudd was implicated in the plot of the earl of Kent against Roger Mortimer in 1330 and was forced to escape abroad, while his estates were once again seized. The fall of Mortimer later in that year, however, meant that Rhys was restored to favour, and his lands were returned to him in the course of 1330–3.

For several years, he was much occupied once more in raising troops for the king: 1332 saw him gathering foot soldiers from North Wales for Ireland, while in 1334 he led some four hundred and fifty men from Builth to Scotland. Additional duties intervened between raising and conducting troops: thus, in 1335, for a second time, he was appointed as constable of Carmarthen castle – a post he took over from Philip Clanvowe.[116] He raised more men for Scotland in the same year and in 1337 acted as keeper of the coast and ports of South Wales together with Philip de Clanvowe. Rhys appears to have been the senior of the two.[117] The terms of their appointment are fully set out in the Gascon Rolls:

> Order to Rhys ap Gruffudd and Philip de Clanvowe that they should keep all ports and the coast where ships can land, and all the coastal land in South Wales, and manfully resist those who may presume to invade the realm, and that they ordain for the safe and secure keeping of those parts diligently and without delay. The king assigned them to this because he has been informed that the king of France, is coming to those parts. The king has commanded the sheriffs, and all his other ministers and faithful subjects to be intendant on, consult with and aid Rhys and Clanvowe as often and when they are warned to do so. Rhys and Clanvowe are given full powers of arresting and taking all those who they will find refuse to obey the orders, and committing them to prison where they are to remain until further orders are received.[118]

As well as his responsibilities as a keeper of coasts and ports, Rhys was also ordered in 1337 to conduct troops from south Wales and the March to Canterbury, though this order was subsequently cancelled.[119] In November of 1337, he was apparently acting as lieutenant of the justice of South Wales, Gilbert Talbot.[120]

He was raising troops again in South Wales in 1341 when he recruited both lancers (spearmen) and archers, while in 1342–3 he assembled over eight hundred archers for a campaign in Britanny; and in 1345, interestingly, it was reported by Richard Talbot, deputy justice of South Wales, that the Welsh troops 'will not for various reasons be led to the profit and honour of the king, unless they are led by Rhys ap Gruffudd'. Talbot therefore urged that Rhys should be commissioned to lead them, commenting that 'the choice of Welshmen was never better done for the king's honour, wherefore it is the more important that they be well led'.[121] Rhys was on the royal campaign of 1346 that included the battle of Crecy, and it was on that occasion that he was presented with a courser by the Black Prince. The following year he was recruiting again, this time another thousand men from South Wales.

A particularly significant point about Rhys ap Gruffudd's later years is that his financial situation was becoming fragile. In spite of the fact that his wife, Joan de Sommerville, whom he married as a very young woman, was an heiress, and had brought him significant estates in Staffordshire, his acquisitions of territories had been remarkable, but in some cases had been financially reckless: his lands included estates in Llansadwrn and Abermarlais in Carmarthenshire, Llanrhystud, Llangybi, and Betws Bledrus in Cardiganshire; he was given Lampeter, Trefilan Maenorsilian, Eglwys Cymmin and land in Llanllwch; Lampeter was given free of renders and for life; many more lands and lordships were given to him on a more temporary basis, with Rhys acting as 'farmer', paying to the Crown a rent and making what profit he could – or suffering what losses might occur. Such acquisitions included the forestership of Chirk, in 1333, and the custody of the lordship of Builth in 1334. Some, but by no means all, of such grants were converted into life grants, such as Narberth, first granted to him as custodian in 1321, but in 1322 given to him up to a value of 100 marks per annum for life. The life grant of Lampeter was confirmed by Edward III in 1339.

In spite of his very large land-holdings, as Ralph Griffiths has pointed out, 'his financial commitment to the crown was immense',[122] with the result that his debts mounted. They were increased by penalties for oppressive and extortionate activity: £192 16s 8d (in 1344) imposed by Sir Gilbert Talbot, justiciar 1330–46, and 500 marks imposed by Sir William Shareshull (1349).[123] Rhys may have been honoured for his efforts, by a knighthood,[124] by gifts and by favours, but his conduct of administration was becoming tyrannical. This last development will be more fully examined in a subsequent chapter.

Rhys's financial embarrassment was lessened as a result of pardons granted by the Black Prince, and his negotiating payment by instalments; it was considerably eased by his inheritance of the Llanrhystud and Llansadwrn lands of his kinsman Ieuan ap Gruffudd Llwyd, the late archdeacon of Anglesey in 1355, and his wife's inheritance of lands in five English counties from her father in the same year. However, his access of wealth came a little late: Rhys died in May, 1356.

With the death of Sir Rhys ap Gruffudd we come to the end of our survey of the careers of the individuals who constituted the group which is here designated 'the new elite', those Welsh figures who can be described as having national eminence in the governance of Wales. Few in number but possessed of great power and influence, it is possible to discern a number of common characteristics which distinguish this group, and set its members above the great majority of their Welsh contemporaries.

It is evident that, by the late thirteenth century, Welsh communities, both in many Marcher lordships and in the lands taken into his hands by Edward I, were beginning to articulate complaints about the governance to which they were subjected and to express demands. It also seems that both the king and some Marcher lords were beginning to listen and respond to this trend. The process was facilitated by the emergence of Welsh figures who achieved administrative and military eminence. These were men who were able to take advantage of the favourable conditions created by the willingness of Edward I to extend his protection to the Welsh population of the royal lands, and to advance the careers of his Welsh supporters there. Some benefited from the readiness of increasing numbers of Marcher lords to promote Welsh administrators. These new leaders, often the descendants of leading officials of the old Welsh rulers and contemporary

Marcher lords, and in some cases able to trace their descent from the old ruling families, developed into a powerful and influential stratum in Welsh society. The history and importance of this ministerial class, whose members sometimes included significant elements of spiritual or cultural patronage in their activities in the post-conquest generations, are investigated in the chapters that follow.

Chapter 3

'The Men of Position: Those Who Can Be a Help or a Hindrance'. A Biographical Gazetteer Arranged by Region

At this stage it is important to establish the criteria for inclusion amongst the 'men of position' who will be examined. In any one case it will not be necessary for a 'candidate for inclusion' to meet all of the following criteria; meeting two or three of the conditions should be enough to confirm inclusion, while meeting a single criterion very fully may in some circumstances guarantee addition to the list.

Important criteria for admission to the list of 'men of position' are as follows:

1. Appearance in a chronicle. The few examples include the thirteenth-century figures, Ednyfed Fychan and Goronwy ab Ednyfed. But chronicle material relating to Wales in the period from the Edwardian conquest to the age of the plague (1349–62) is not plentiful. However, Madog ap Llywelyn from the lordship of Bromfield and Yale, and Goronwy ap Tudur from the northern principality are both noticed in the Continuation of *Brut y Tywysogyon*.
2. The leaving of visible remains: hardly any signs of residences except castles survive for the period before the fifteenth century; but other material remains, such as sepulchral effigies or inscribed slabs do exist, particularly for Welsh persons in north-east Wales. The possession of an elaborate seal which emphasises its owner's high status may come into this category.

3. Appearance as a subject of a praise-poem, or as a patron of poets.
4. Appearance in record sources as a significant office-holder. This is a particularly important category. The bulk of governmental records are of English origin; some deeds and similar documents may originate with Welsh figures.
5. Possession of a particularly distinguished genealogy – such as one that includes members of ruling families, or of eminent figures in the 'ministerial aristocracy', such as Ednyfed Fychan.
6. Possession/acquisition of extensive lands or other substantial wealth was an important underpinning of centrality in the Welsh community.

It is necessary to point out at once that the documentary evidence relating to elite figures is to a significant degree skewed in favour of materials derived from sources which have been carefully and successfully preserved, such as English official archives. Those regions which lay within the scope of such archives, such as the principality lands of north-west, south and west Wales or the county of Flintshire are marked by much fuller and detailed evidence of their prominent Welsh figures than is the case in many of the Marcher lordships, where preservation of archive materials is of uneven quantity and quality, and is sometimes almost non-existent, as for example in the case of the lordship of Powys, in contrast to the far more abundant material in, say, the court rolls of the lordship of Ruthin (Dyffryn Clwyd). Again, it is quite clear that the incidence of late-thirteenth and early-fourteenth century sepulchral slabs and effigies relating to important Welsh figures is far greater in north Wales, and especially in north-east Wales, than in many other regions. In our pursuit of the powerful and influential figures in the Welsh communities we have of course to be led by the evidence, but we also have to understand that each category of evidence is often potentially misleading in its emphases.

The following gazetteer is intended to be representative but it is by no means comprehensive, and it is hoped that more names will be added to it over time.

The south-eastern March

Llywelyn Bren

Until his rebellion in 1316, Llywelyn Bren appeared to be a model of a successful Welsh leader, combining distinguished ancestry, closeness to a major Marcher lord, possession of relative wealth and an attractive personality. He was the son of Gruffudd ap Rhys, the last native lord of Senghennydd in eastern Glamorgan, who had been captured by Gilbert the Red, earl of Gloucester, and taken away from Wales to the Clare castle of Kilkenny in 1267, and had apparently died in captivity. In time, and somewhat surprisingly, Gruffudd's son, Llywelyn had become close to the last of the Clare lords, the 8th earl of Gloucester (1307–14), who had been killed at Bannockburn. The well-informed author of the *Vita Edwardi Secundi* reports that Llywelyn had held high office (*magnum officium*) in Earl Gilbert's administration,[1] while it is clear from a record source that he had held several bailiwicks.[2] The *Vita Edwardi Secundi* also notes that Llywelyn Bren was 'a great and powerful man in his own country',[3] and that verdict finds a modern echo in a comment by Rees Davis that such was Llywelyn's power that even the Cistercian abbey of Llantarnam/Caerleon could not deny him lands that he wanted.[4]

Llywelyn was clearly a wealthy man by the standards of the *Blaenau*, the uplands in which his lordship was based: the inventory of his possessions drawn up after his revolt revealed that he had 77 oxen, 250 head of cattle, 36 horses as well as sheep, goats and pigs; he had a chest holding records of his diverse lands and gold and silver items such as clasps and rings. He had been granted by Edward II, before the events which provoked his rising, both money and a site on which to build a fortress at Whitchurch. He was, moreover, a cultivated man, who possessed a missal and three service books, as well as three books in Welsh and a copy of the *Roman de la Rose*. But by late 1315 he had become exasperated by the attitude and actions of Payn de Turberville, the custodian of Glamorgan who had been appointed by Edward II in July of that year. Llywelyn Bren's resulting appeal to the king had been rebuffed, producing only a demand from Edward that he should appear before parliament to face a treason charge which, if proved, would mean a death sentence. Fearing the worst, Llywelyn took to rebellion.

His rising in early 1316 was widespread in Glamorgan and well supported, but when he realised that large royal forces, under the direction of Humphrey de Bohun, earl of Hereford, supported by the Mortimers (Roger of Chirk and Roger of Wigmore), were closing in, he nobly insisted on giving himself up to save his supporters. His bravery and conduct impressed de Bohun, who urged the king to do nothing before he and Edward had talked. But Edward handed Llywelyn, after a period of imprisonment with his family in the Tower of London, over to Hugh Despenser the Younger, the new lord of Glamorgan. Despenser had Llywelyn savagely executed, a deed that provoked revulsion amongst Welsh and English alike.

Amongst the English, Humphrey de Bohun felt particularly aggrieved by Llywelyn's execution, and provided material support for Llywelyn's widow, Lleucu, and their sons. Those sons joined in the hunt for Edward after his fall in 1326, and one of them, Gruffudd, was appointed constable of Senghennydd,[5] while he and his brothers began to reassemble their father's lands. Lleucu was maintained on a pension by the de Bohun lords, until her death in 1349.[6]

The verdict of the author of the *Vita Edwardi Secundi* was surely prompted by his observation of the progress and ultimate fall of Llywelyn Bren. 'The Welsh', he wrote 'keep quiet for ten years and are then suddenly athirst for battle, and their achievements over a long period are brought to destruction.'[7] In the present context, it is not Llywelyn Bren's destruction on which we should focus, but on his 'achievements over a long period'.

Hywel ap Hywel
Clearly an important figure in Glamorgan in 1331 when, in a document relating to William la Zouche as lord of Glamorgan, Hywel appears as *dominus* ['Sir'] Hywel ap Hywel *vicecomes* and is clearly the lord's principal official.[8] Some two years earlier he was one of a group of knights who witnessed a charter to Margam

abbey issued by William la Zouche, lord of Glamorgan.[9] He is possibly the same person as Hywel ap Hywel of Brecon lordship.

Madog Fychan
Best known perhaps as an adherent of Llywelyn Bren, there is much more to be noticed about Madog Fychan of Tir Iarll. He had almost certainly held high office under the earl of Gloucester in the lordship of Tir Iarll in the earlier fourteenth century, for in an elegy for him composed by Casnodyn he is described as *maer*, an archaic designation for a senior commote officer.[10] He was one of those who rose with Llywelyn Bren, and he was one of those consigned with Llywelyn and his family to the Tower of London in the aftermath of the rising.[11]

He was also amongst those leaders who were recommended for perpetual imprisonment by the commission, which included Sir Morgan ap Maredudd and Leisan d'Avene, that was set up to advise on sentences for the leading rebels.[12] The poem by Casnodyn praises Madog for his savage slaughter of the English,[13] and this suggests that he may have played a particularly prominent part in the rising of 1316 – and perhaps that of 1314. It is, however, clear that Madog Fychan did not suffer perpetual captivity: it was arranged that he should be freed in November 1316 – though his release may have been delayed until the next year.[14]

Madog Fychan's rehabilitation after his imprisonment in 1316 did not prevent him from taking part in the attacks on the Despenser regime in Glamorgan in 1321, though on 17th May of that year he obtained an early pardon for adhering to the baronial rebels who had invaded that land.[15] That he once again became a significant political figure is suggested by his receipt in October 1326 of a commission from the king to raise forces in Tir Iarll and *Aveneslonde* (Afan) to oppose the invasion of Roger Mortimer and Queen Isabella, which was to topple Edward II.[16] Once again, Madog Fychan survived this reverse, and must have made his peace with the new regime, for he is still found witnessing a charter in 1329.[17] It seems that he died soon after that, and was buried in Margam abbey – a further clear sign of his eminence.[18]

In the lordship of Tir Iarll, Madog was a consistently important figure, associated with men of the calibre of Llywelyn Bren and members of the d'Avene dynasty (for whom see below). His career suggests that he was too regionally powerful for kings and lords of Glamorgan to risk alienating him and his family.[19] It is a further sign of Madog's eminence that his son Owain was called upon to raise forces for Edward II in 1326.

Leisan d'Avene

Leisan was a member of the family of lords of Afan, who had adopted a 'Frenchified' version of their name (d'Avene) in the thirteenth century.[20] The d'Avene lords could in fact demonstrate descent from Iestyn ap Gwrgant, last of the native Welsh rulers of an entire kingdom of Morgannwg. As the Normans occupied much of Glamorgan, the Welsh lords were driven into diminished polities in the uplands, but those of Afan remained significantly free from Norman control into the thirteenth century, and continued to maintain a significant degree of autonomy into the fourteenth century. Leisan was the seventh lord of Afan, having succeeded his father Morgan Fychan in the 1280s. The most significant passages in the career of Leisan d'Avene came in the period c.1314 to the mid-1320s. Leisan claimed that he had spent forty marks of his own money in defence of Glamorgan from 'the tumults of the Welsh' and in defending the castle of Kenfig from a Welsh rising in Neath and Tir Iarll in 1314.[21] He remained aloof from the rising of Llywelyn Bren in 1316, and was a member of the commission set up to advise on the punishment of those involved in the rising.[22]

The evidence relating to Leisan's stance in the tumultuous months of 1321–2 is somewhat confused. He appears to have been aligned with the baronial faction which rose up against Edward II and the growing power of Hugh Despenser the Younger, triggering the 'Despenser War' in Glamorgan. On 20 February 1322, as the king was developing his assault on his baronial opponents, Leisan d'Avene was amongst a group of prominent figures whose lands, goods and chattels the sheriff of Glamorgan was ordered to take into the king's hands.[23] In December of the same year, arrangements were made by the king for the keeping of the lands 'in Kilvey in Wales late of Leisan d'Avene, recently the king's enemy and rebel, which are in the king's hand by his forfeiture'.[24] On 14 February 1322, however, Leisan had been one of three men appointed by the king to raise 2,000 infantry in Glamorgan for service against the Scots and the Contrariants.[25] It would appear that the king was acting on the assumption that Leisan, the loyal defender of the royal interest in 1314–16, would be ready to afford similar help in 1322. Leisan is not recorded as receiving a pardon for activity against the king and his favourite in 1321, in contrast to many of the Contrariants, and this suggests that he had not been involved in the earlier stages of the baronial opposition to Edward and Despenser. It seems, however, that he had at some point thrown in his lot with the rebels, and that he was subsequently pardoned. His date of death is uncertain, but was probably c.1328/9.[26] He was succeeded by his son **John d'Avene**, lord of Afan, Cilfai (Kilvey) and Sully,[27] who appears prominently in Glamorgan documents in the 1330s and early 1340s.[28] The Inquisition Post Mortem of Hugh Despenser, in 1350, records that John held Afan (Avene) by the service of three knights' fees, and that five corn mills, a fulling mill, a fishery in the water of Glyn Nedd, another in the water of Glyn Tawe and a ferry at Britton had been demised to John de Avene in exchange for the manor of Sully.[29]

Llywelyn ap Cynwrig ap Hywel

Llywelyn ap Cynwrig and his father stood by the king in the rebellion of 1316, and both were included amongst those who gave advice on how the adherents of Llywelyn Bren should be treated.[30] Llywelyn had extensive lands partly acquired through service to Hugh Despenser the Younger. He also appears in royal service.[31] Very interestingly, the last reference shows Llywelyn ap Cynwrig heading a group of seven men – the others all English – raising 1,000 *English* foot-soldiers from Glamorgan for the king in February 1322. J. Beverley Smith suggested that opponents of Edward II like Lleucu the widow of Llywelyn Bren, and Madog Fychan of Tir Iarll were joined in opposition in 1321 'by Leisan de Avene and Llywelyn ap Cyfrig and other former collaborators'.[32]

However, while the references given by Smith in support of this statement do apply to Leisan d'Avene, they contain no indication that Llywelyn ap Cynwrig was an opponent of the king at this time. And yet there is a somewhat mysterious record of Master John Walwayn being ordered to arrest Llywelyn ap Cynwrig and to cause him to be taken to Bristol, and there delivered to the constable of the castle or to him who supplies his place. No reason is given for this order, which came ten days after the battle of Boroughbridge (March 1322) had restored royal authority in the realm. Llywelyn was, however, commissioned by Edward II to raise troops from Meisgyn, Glynrhondda, Tal y Fan, Rhuthin and Glynogwr, to oppose the invasion of Roger Mortimer and Queen Isabella in 1326.[33] He is, however, found occupying a senior position in the administration of Glamorgan in the late 1330s.[34]

A problem case: Dafydd ap Meurig

Dafydd ap Meurig represents something of a mystery. In the crisis period, after the invasion of England by Roger Mortimer of Wigmore accompanied by Queen Isabella in September 1326, and the subsequent appeal by Edward II for military support from within his realm, Dafydd appears in a prominent role across much of Glamorgan, specifically being tasked to raise troops for the beleaguered king in Ruthin and Glynogwr on 27th October and given a more far-reaching commission, covering all of Morgannwg on 29th October.[35] In the second case, Dafydd ap Meurig's name occurs after that of Owain ap Madog, who is to be identified as the son of Madog Fychan. This suggests that he was regarded as less important than Owain, but still of significance. He is almost certainly to be identified as the Dafydd ap Meurig ap Hywel, who was asked to raise troops in Meisgyn and Glynrhondda on 30th October. It will be noted that all of Dafydd ap Meurig's assignments place him in Morgannwg, and this makes his identification as the son of Meurig ap Hywel, who was descended from a former monarch of that region, Iestyn ap Gwrgan, both credible and highly significant.[36] With such a pedigree and with an impressive range of appointments in October 1326, it is tempting to consider Dafydd ap Meurig as one of the 'men of position'. On the other hand, his appearance in the record sources appears to have been brief, and the fact that he appears in an apparently junior role to that of Owain ap Madog in the record of the Morgannwg commission suggests that he may not have been that important. It may be that he was a young man, thus explaining his sudden appearance, and that he may have been killed or injured as the invaders made their way through Glamorgan, thus explaining his apparent disappearance after 1326.

With the exception of a few cases such as that of Llywelyn ap Cynwrig and possibly Dafydd ap Meurig, the most noteworthy characteristic of the Welsh magnates discussed above is their ability to change sides in the often-tortuous politics of Glamorgan. Less evidence is available to chart the activities of important figures in Gwent, but it is clear that men such as **Adam ab Ifor** in Monmouth achieved significant power in the first half of the fourteenth century. He was steward of Monmouth in 1333–4 and 1347–50.[37] His son Philip held the manor of Llanfair (Cilgedyn).[38]

The Middle March

The significance in this region – and indeed beyond it – of Hywel ap Meurig and his sons William, Philip and Master Rees, and indeed in the case of Sir Philip de Clanvowe, one of his grandsons, has already been examined in the previous chapter. We now turn to two of the numerous offspring.

Ieuan ap Rees

A grandson of Hywel ap Meurig, and son of Master Rees ap Hywel, Ieuan (John) was a partisan of Humphrey de Bohun, earl of Hereford and lord of Brecon in the conflict of 1321–2, and was amongst those whose arrest was sought by Edward II in February of the latter year.[39] He is probably to be identified as the Ieuan ap Rees who was recorded as deputy Justiciar of South Wales in May 1337 in an enquiry held at Blaenllyfni into payments made to the steward, constables and other officials at Blaenllyfni and Bwlchydinas.[40] In 1339, Ieuan appears as deputy to Hugh Tyrel, keeper of the manor of Radnor, and in the same year he accompanied Philip de Clanvowe, his kinsman, and Edmund Hakelute to survey the lands of Rhys ap Gruffudd at Lampeter. In 1340, Ieuan acted as the steward of the Mortimer of Wigmore lordships, but thereafter seems to disappear from the records.[41]

Philip ap Rees

Philip was also a descendant of Hywel ap Meurig, and son of Master Rees ap Hywel whose heir he was; he is sometimes described as Philip de Bronllys. He was knighted – but the date of his knighting is uncertain. In 1335, Philip raised 500 men for the king from the de Bohun lordships – including Cantref Selyf/Bronllys.[42] In 1342, Philip took the final accounts of ministers who had held the lands of the earl of March.[43] He was given a commission to raise troops from Pencelli, Blaenllyfni and Cantref Selyf. But this provoked confrontation with Humphrey de Bohun, who objected to a subordinate lord – Philip de Bronllys – acting for the king in lands which were held from de Bohun.[44] By 1343, Philip was constable and keeper of Builth castle and lordship. But he was absent from Builth when commissioners came to take the oath of fealty to the Black Prince: his deputy was also absent – the possible reason for Philip's removal from office.[45] Renewed tension with de Bohuns in 1347 led to a 1349 Quo Warranto in de Bohun's court and the confiscation of his lands by 1351. The case was resolved only when Sir Philip exchanged Talgarth Welshry, and all of the lordship of Bronllys with Earl Humphrey's brother, William de Bohun, earl of Northampton, for Shifnal – and retained Talgarth English down to his death in 1369.[46]

Descendants of Einion Sais

Einion Sais ap Rhys (and his cognomen suggests that he spoke English, or had personal connections with the English) achieved prominence as an opponent of Llywelyn ap Gruffudd when that prince took over the lordship of Brecon in the early 1260s. He was obliged to appear before Llywelyn at the castle of Rhyd y Briw in September 1271 to provide sureties in 200 marks for the release of a hostage held by the prince.[47] Einion Sais appears to have possessed the fortification of Penpont in Brecon, and to have been prominent in the society of the lordship. His most important descendants can be set out in the following lineage: Hywel Fychan ap Hywel ab Einion ap Rhys.

Hywel ab Einion Sais appears in a long list of men pardoned outlawry for non-appearance before the king in 1301 to answer regarding a plea of trespass of Roger Mortimer, on condition that they agreed to surrender to Clifford gaol before Easter to take their trial.[48] It is clear that this represents an episode in which men of Humphrey de Bohun were involved in an encroachment on Mortimer lands. Hywel was still alive in 1313.[49] Hywel ab Einion Sais had a son, Hywel, sometimes known as **Hywel ap Hywel** and sometimes as Hywel Fychan ap Hywel. It is clear that he was a person of considerable importance in the lordship of Brecon and possibly beyond; see the reference to a man of the same name in Glamorgan,[50] Hywel ap Hywel was clearly an important and influential figure in south-eastern Wales in the late1320s and/or the early 1330s but it is far from clear whether how many persons were covered by that name. The crux of the problem is that it was unusual to describe a man whose given name was the same as that of his father as X ap X; it was far more common to find the son described as X Fychan, where Fychan = 'Junior' rather than 'Small (in stature)'. Of course it remains possible that a man might be described on different occasions in both ways. The most securely identifiable figure is Hywel Fychan ap Hywel ab Einion (a grandson of Einion Sais ap Rhys of the lordship of Brecon) raising troops in the lordship of Abergavenny to defend the king in late October 1326.[51] By 1329–31, he or a similarly named man appears in documents relating to William la Zouche as lord of Glamorgan. Hywel appears both in a group of charter witnesses designated as knights (1329) and as dominus ('Sir') Hywel ap Hywel vicecomes (sheriff) in 1331, when he is clearly the lord's principal official.[52]

There must remain some doubt as to whether the Hywel ap Hywel who appears in Glamorgan in 1329–31 is identical with the grandson of Einion Sais of Brecon, noted in 1326, or is an individual from Morgannwg with the same given name and patronymic. But it is worth noting that it was not unknown for a high-ranking official to be part of the structure of governance of two lords – as witness Hywel ap Meurig and Philip ap Hywel who both acted in both the Mortimer and de Bohun interests. A further consideration is that if dominus Hywel ap Hywel the sheriff was simply a Glamorgan official, and a very senior one at that, it seems a little odd that we cannot trace his career for very long before he became sheriff.

The balance of probability seems to be in favour of an assumption that the Hywel ap Hywel descended from Einion Sais was the man of the same name who was in the lord of Glamorgan's entourage in 1329, and was sheriff of Glamorgan in 1331. It is possible that he was too young to be involved in the killing of Piers Gaveston in 1312, as he was apparently still alive and active in 1361; it may be significant that his father was not mentioned in the list of those pardoned for involvement in Gaveston's death. It seems, however, that Hywel Fychan ap Hywel was with Earl Humphrey de Bohun, lord of Brecon, in the rising against Edward II and Hugh Despenser the younger in 1321–2. As the king's position became stronger at the end of 1321, the order went out that Hywel ap Hywel's lands, goods and chattels were to be taken into the king's hand – an order to the sheriff of Gloucester which appears to have related to lands which Hywel held in the Forest of Dean.[53] In the aftermath of the battle of Boroughbridge, in which de Bohun was killed and the baronial forces destroyed by Edward, it was recorded that Hywel ap Hywel had been obliged to find the huge sum of 500 marks, and had found sureties who included Philip ap Hywel (ap Meurig). It should be noticed, however, that the order relating to the fine is marked as cancelled in the Fine Roll.[54] It may be that the fine was never levied, though Hywel's lands and goods in the Forest of Dean were still amongst those for which arrangements for their custody were made on 2 August 1322. Hywel Fychan ap Hywel clearly survived the tumults of 1322, and must have recovered his lands for in October 1326 he was surprisingly appointed by the king to raise troops against Roger Mortimer and Queen Isabella from the lordship of Abergavenny. It is entirely possible that Hywel made no move to fulfil this appointment, which may be an indication of Edward II's desperation.

Under the rule of Edward III, however, Hywel evidently settled to a routine of effective power in the lordship of Brecon, which saw him acting as the sheriff of the lordship from 1332 for some sixteen years, and on occasion adding the office of steward to that of the sheriff. He received signal rewards from Earl Humphrey for his services, such as the gift of a saddle. With one of his kinsmen, he was able to pay 100 marks per year for the lease of valuable lands in the lordship. And more importantly, he was still of sufficient standing in Brecon lordship to be appointed as one of its custodians in 1361.

If, as seems possible, the various references to Hywel ap Hywel, and to Hywel Fychan ap Hywel, are to the same man, then we may be dealing with someone with sufficiently wide interests and prominence – in Brecon lordship, Glamorgan, and the Forest of Dene – and sufficient wealth, to be considered for an entry in Chapter 2, as representative of the new elite. However, it is difficult to be confident of such an identification, so it has seemed better to exercise some caution in the matter and to retain here notes on a Hywel ap Hywel under the South-Eastern March and again under the Middle March, with reference to the present discussion.

Meurig ap Rees

Here we have another possible member of the family of Hywel ap Meurig.[55] A charter of 1313 names him as Meurig ap Rees ap Meurig; he seems to have acquired lands in Cantref Selyf and passed them on to Master Rees ap Hywel.[56] If not a family member, he manifested plentiful signs of closeness to the descendants of Hywel ap Meurig. Like several members of the family, he was pardoned for his hostility to Edward II and the royal favourite Hugh Despenser the Younger in 1321 on the evidence of Humphrey de Bohun,[57] but then commissioned on 14 February 1322 together with Robert de Morby to raise 400 footmen in the land of Brecon,[58] and to have his lands and goods in the lands of the castle of Bronllys and Cantref Selyf restored to him on 15 February, but was ordered to be arrested for his opposition to the king, on 16 February 1322.[59] On 9 March, Meurig's brother William was ordered to be released from prison, and to have his lands and goods restored to him, as William la Zouche, of Ashby, had agreed to act as William's surety to be before the king to answer to any charges whenever required.[60] To complete the complex picture of Meurig's allegiance in 1322, he was pardoned by the king, on 23 September of that year, for his past adherence to Humphrey de Bohun, a rebel.[61]

The probability is that Meurig ap Rees had followed the lead of his putative kinsmen and taken the side of the earl of Hereford and lord of Brecon. In the first place, Meurig had been amongst those who were pardoned for their actions against the Despensers in August and September 1321, when the baronial opponents of the king were in the ascendancy. Meurig, like figures such as Philip de Clanvowe, was pardoned on the testimony of Humphrey de Bohun, earl of Hereford on 20 August. Others, such as Master Rees ap Hywel, were pardoned on the same day – in his case on the testimony of Roger Damory, another of the baronial leaders. Philip ap Hywel, brother of Master Rees, and almost certainly a close kinsman of Meurig, was pardoned, with many others, including William ap Rees, Meurig's brother, on the testimony of the earl of Hereford, on 25 September. So Meurig ap Rees was associated in 1321 with other prominent opponents of Edward II and the Despensers. Further and near-conclusive evidence is provided by another reference in the Patent Roll in 1322:

> 3 June 1322 Commission of Oyer and Terminer to William de Herle, John de Bousser and Adam de Brom on the king's information that Hugh de Audley the younger, Roger Mortimer of Wigmore, Roger de Mortimer of Chirk, Master Rees ap Hywel, Richard do Lymesy, Meurig ap Rees, John Counter, Trahaearn Ddu, Maredudd ab Einion, Meurig de Cemmeys, Hugh de Rath', David Syuuagh, Ieuan ap Gwyn, William ap Rees, Nicholas de la March, William Sart[us], John Curteys, Richard le Barber, William le Rede, Nicholas de Usk, Adam Gybbe, Hywel ap Madog, Iorwerth ap Philip's son and Madog ap Einion with others mowed the king's corn and grass at Newport, Stowe, Diflais, Machen and Rhymni in Gwynllwg, and committed divers trespasses there. The jury is to be of the parts of Gwynllwg, Glamorgan and Morgannwg, and Usk.[62]

The case recorded here began 1 June 1322; by that time some of the accused were in prison – so the actions of which they were accused must have taken place before their imprisonment. The key persons in this respect are the two Roger Mortimers who surrendered to the king and were sent into captivity on 22 January 1322. The symbolic mowing of the king's grass and cutting of the king's corn must thus have happened in the autumn of 1321. In the event, the Patent Roll contains, under 23 September 1322, the following information: 'Pardon to Meurig ap Rees, for his adherence to Humphrey de Bohun, late earl of Hereford, a rebel'.[63]

It seems that Meurig's initial appointment to lead troops in support of the king in February 1322 was a measure of his importance in the lordship of Brecon. Within a few days, however, his involvement with the Mortimers – who had already been consigned to a royal prison – and with Humphrey de Bohun, earl of Hereford, had become known to the king and his advisers, with the result that Meurig ap Rhys had been included with his kinsmen in the list of those who were to be arrested on the orders of the king. But with his baronial allies either in captivity or, with his chief patron Earl Humphrey of Hereford dead at Boroughbridge and the king and the Despensers triumphant, it seems that Meurig had succeeded, by a timely submission, in escaping the consequences of his political actions, and had gained a royal pardon.

Meurig had so far recovered from the chaos of 1322 to be appointed Constable of Brecon at some point before 1327, and for some six years in 1332–8.[64] As late as 1339, Meurig appears with his probable kinsman Philip Clanvowe and Adam Lucas reporting on defects at Builth castle.[65]

The Powysian March

Madog ap Meilir
Though the bulk of Madog's activity pre-dates the precise period under review, it is worth including because it reveals the presence in the lands of the barony of Powys of the sort of very prominent local officials who are visible in other regions of Wales. It is the

more valuable because the evidence for internal developments in the lordship of Powys for the bulk of the fourteenth century is exiguous.[66] Some idea of Madog's age can be deduced from his early appearance in a list of sureties for the fidelity to Prince Llywelyn of a named individual. In this list of December 1276, Madog appears as being 'of Caereinion', and his role as a surety in a list of some twenty persons that included the lords of Mechain, as well as significant members of the court of the currently exiled lord of Powys, including that lord's *distain*, Gruffudd ap Gwên, gives an early indication of Madog's importance.[67] He appears in a position of prominence after the wars of 1277 and 1282–3, when he acted as a leader of troops sent to quash the rebellion of Rhys ap Maredudd of Dryslwyn in 1287. Here he acted as a constable leading foot-soldiers for the lord of Powys, Owain ap Gruffudd together with nine other men, each riding a barded (i.e. armoured) horse and each leading one hundred men.[68]

Madog went on, together with one of his co-centenars in 1287 Madog ab Einion, to lead troops in the campaign against the rebel leader from Gwynedd Madog ap Llywelyn, in 1294–5 and particularly in the eventual and decisive battle of Maes Moydog of 5 March 1295.[69] These two men, both prominent in military matters, had also been involved in the assessment of the lay subsidy of 1292–3: Madog ap Meilir had been one of the chief taxors of Owain de la Pole ap Gruffudd's land of Cyfeiliog, and of William de la Pole's land of Mawddwy, while Madog ab Einion had been one of the sub-taxors (or jurors) of Caereinion, Llannerchudol, Ceri and Cedewain.[70] The upheavals of 1292 to early 1295 were not the end of disturbances in Powys and its associated territories. In August 1295, by which time Edward I had finished traversing Wales to ensure that the last fires of rebellion had been put out, it was reported that there was trouble in Powys, following a 'complaint by Joan, late the wife of Owen de la Pole, that William son of Griffin de la Pole, John and David his brothers, Madog ap Meilir and Owen le Say deforce her of her reasonable dower in the lands of her late husband'.[71] So Madog ap Meilir was of sufficient prominence to be named as one of the principals in a dynastic contest following the death in 1293 of Owain ap Gruffudd, lord of Powys. It is thus a matter for little surprise, apart from the evidence it supplies for Madog's longevity, that Madog ap Meilir was amongst those named in 1313 as receiving a pardon for complicity in the murder of Piers Gaveston, the favourite of Edward II, in 1312.[72]

Dafydd ap Cadwaladr

Descended from the elusive figure of Elystan Glodrydd, from whom the twelfth- and thirteenth-century rulers, and most of the subsequent gentry houses of the land between Wye and Severn derived their genealogies, Dafydd was the subject of a praise-poem by Sypyn Cyfeiliog.[73] The poem is interesting in that it describes with some gusto the character of Dafydd's court, in particular the lavishness of the food and drink, and the nature of the entertainment provided. There is considerable emphasis on the copious supply of alcoholic drinks available, in particular 'three-coloured wine', drunk to the accompaniment of music provided by a harpist and a crowther, and of course singing. Perhaps more significant, however, is his description as 'the mighty son of Cadwaladr', thus emphasising his military and governmental fame.

His principal residence was in Bachelldre, an outlier of the lordship of Caus, in which he was a prominent official. In 1322, he appears as the leader of some three hundred troops raised in the lordship, initially for service in the king's cause against the Contrariants and then against the Scots.[74] That he had distinguished himself in royal service is suggested by a subsequent grant to him of property in the royal borough of Montgomery.[75] A decade after the expedition of 1322 he was involved in the investigation of the raid into the Vale of Montgomery by men of Ceri and Cedewain.[76] In 1336, he appears in a list of men accorded legal protection on account of involvement in a Scottish campaign.[77] In 1338, he witnessed a land transfer at Thornbury, in which he appears as *rhaglaw* (the principal local official) of the Corbet lands.[78]

Gwilym ap Gruffudd de la Pole

Gwilym was a son of Gruffudd ap Gwenwynwyn, lord of Powys c.1241–86, and a brother of Owain, similarly lord of Powys 1286–93.

In the aftermath of the death of Owain in 1293 and the apparent death of Owain's previously active brother Llywelyn, Gwilym, having inherited most of Mawddwy as his share of the lordship of Powys, first appears as a military leader in November 1294 in the war against Madog ap Llywelyn, at the head of forty infantrymen and by May 1295 his command had increased to some four hundred men. Following the defeat of Madog at Maes Moydog on 5 March 1295, and the subsequent 'mopping up' operations, Gwilym next appears in a very different role: on 18 August, Joan, widow of Owain, complained that three of the sons of Gruffudd ap Gwenwynwyn – Gwilym, Ieuan and Dafydd – together with senior freemen from Powys,[79] had deprived her of her proper dower in Mawddwy and Caereinion. A similar complaint was lodged by Joan and her husband Roger Trumwyn, in 1298 and 1299, against Hawise, the widow of Gruffudd ap Gwenwynwyn, and her sons Gwilym, Ieuan and Gruffudd. This suggests that Gruffudd was significantly younger than Gwilym, and that Dafydd may have died.

Apart from these dynastic conflicts, Gwilym, now referred to as a knight (miles) with a *scutifer* (shield-bearer, or esquire) continued to appear in royal service. He was involved in raising troops for the king in 1297–8, first for a campaign in Flanders, and then as leader of some three hundred of the best and strongest men of Powys for a campaign against William Wallace in Scotland. From April 1298, Gwilym, together with Roger Mortimer of Chirk, was to raise six 'strong and powerful' men from Powys who were engaged in the victory at Falkirk, at which Gwilym rode a horse worth 20 marks, while Gruffudd's mount was valued at 12 marks. The final reference to Gwilym as a military leader comes in 1301, when he led fifty-four foot-archers from Staffordshire to Scotland. He appears in May 1303, but was dead by March 1305.

Gwilym's frequent appearance in a military role suggests that he may have been the holder of the post of *penteulu* (the chief of the household guard) in Powys.

Gruffudd Fychan de la Pole

Gruffudd Fychan was in fact a claimant to be in legal terms, and in reality, an heir to a Welsh prince, in that he was a son of

Administrative Eminence and Political Peril

Gruffudd ap Gwenwynwyn, ruler of southern Powys at intervals in the period 1241–86, and himself the heir to his father, Gwenwynwyn, ruler of the same territory 1195–1216 and the last ruler of a Welsh territory beyond Gwynedd to adopt, with some consistency, the title of 'prince'. When the generally acknowledged heir to the lordship of Powys, Gruffudd ab Owain ap Gruffudd ap Gwenwynwyn, died in 1309, the barony passed according to English law, to his sister, Hawise the Younger. She was rapidly married off to the Shropshire gentleman and courtier, John Charlton, who became lord of Powys, *iure uxoris*. But Gruffudd Fychan 'de a Pole' (of Pool or Welshpool, the capital of Powys) put forward a claim based on a reading of Welsh law, which gave precedence to male successors to land, as the surviving son of Gruffudd ap Gwenwynwyn.[80]

Gruffudd Fychan de la Pole had already had experience of controlling the barony of Powys, as he had taken over the role of custodian from his aged mother, Hawise the Elder, in 1308.[81] Gruffudd had already got possession, under complex arrangements established by his brother Owain ap Gruffudd ap Gwenwynwyn in 1291, of part of Mechain is Coed; it was also established that he should take over Hawise the elder's land of Deuddwr on her death, and that he should then relinquish his land of Mechain is Coed. But in fact, Gruffudd Fychan de la Pole seems not to have relinquished his hold on Mechain is Coed, while he had taken over Deuddwr by 1309, a year before Hawise died, for in the former year he had been granted a right by Edward II to hold a market and fairs at Llandrinio, the *caput* of Deuddwr.[82] It was thus perhaps unsurprising that first tensions, and then open hostilities, should arise between the new lord of Powys, John Charlton, and the ambitious lord of part of that land, Gruffudd Fychan de la Pole.

By April 1312, Gruffudd had begun to lay siege to Pool Castle, and to move into support for the principal opponent of Edward II, Thomas of Lancaster, probably a move designed to win himself support for his attempts to gain control of Powys.[83] The situation was made more complex by the fact that Charlton was an increasingly important courtier of Edward II, while Gruffudd was a brother in arms of the king, as both were Swan Knights, whose elevation to knighthood had taken place at the great festival of knighting in 1306.[84] Gruffudd had resisted attempts by forces engaged by the king to break the siege, and eventually both parties to the conflict were pardoned in November 1313, when Gruffudd abandoned the siege and Charlton returned lands which he had occupied in Deuddwr and the lordship of Dinas.[85]

Thereafter the dispute was calmed down for a time, but hostilities resumed in 1316, in a period when the eyes of Edward II's government were very much on Wales, as there was rebellion in Glamorgan, and it was feared that this might spread to other regions of Wales, thus making that land vulnerable to a Scottish attack from Ireland where Edward Bruce, brother of Robert, was active. Once more the dispute was calmed, but not settled. Over a decade later, Gruffudd was able to complain that in November 1327 he had been ejected by Charlton from his lands 'which he had held from our lord the king in chief, of which lands he was seised thirty years and more'.[86] Between late 1327 and 1331 Gruffudd was ejected from, and reinstated in, his lands on three separate occasions. Even in the last year of his life, before his apparent death in 1332, Gruffudd was making attempts to gain the support of the earl of Arundel against Charlton.

It seems that Gruffudd had won significant support from the community of the barony of Powys in his quest to obtain at least a share of that land: in the case of the outbreak of hostilities in 1316 it was reported to the English government that 'the people of Powys have commenced riots ... and besieged and assailed the castle of La Pole and committed arsons, homicides, depredations and other evil deeds'.[87] Gruffudd had also obtained support from some of the leading English families of the borderland, such as the Lestranges of Knockin, the fitz Alans of Oswestry, and the Fitz Waryns of Whittington. His struggle had been a serious one, not without its successes. Essentially, however, he perhaps remains a figure of the thirteenth century past, rather than one representative of the realities of the fourteenth century, though he served to remind English governments of how easily regional conflicts might undermine the 'Edwardian settlement'.

Descendants of Gruffudd ap Gwên

These were descendants of the most important ministerial family in thirteenth-century Powys. The family was effectively founded in Powys by Einion ap Seisyll, who appears to have taken territory with which he and his forebears were associated in the later twelfth century from Meirionnydd into Powys. This was 'the land between Dyfi and Dulas' (i.e. north of the Dyfi) which was still claimed as part of Gwynedd by Llywelyn ap Gruffudd in the later thirteenth century. The descendants of Einion were certainly central to the governance of the lords of Powys, providing at least two, and probably three, holders of the office of *distain*, or steward, the central figure in the administration. The last of the *distainiaid* was Gruffudd ap Gwên, who headed Powys administration from the early 1260s until at least the early 1280s.[88]

The fourteenth-century descendants of Gruffudd ap Gwên clearly had a stellar pedigree and would have been obvious choices as significant officials once the Charlton lords of Powys began to look towards Welsh administrators. This seems to have been a practice which was developing by the 1340s, but there are signs of their prominence within the Welsh of Powys before that period.[89] A prime example of this is provided by events in 1322, a year of upheaval in most parts of Wales, but particularly so in Powys. Although the major part of the lordship was in the hands of John Charlton and his wife Hawise, daughter and heiress of Owain ap Gruffudd ap Gwenwynwyn, the last Welsh lord to bear effective rule in Powys, significant parts of it, in particular the large commotes of Cyfeiliog and Caereinion, were in the hands of Joan, widow of Owain ap Gruffudd, as dower provision after Owain's death in 1293. In the late 1290s, Joan was joined in possession of the dower lands by her second husband, Roger Trumwyn.

In 1322, all of the lordship of Powys had been taken into the king's hand following John Charlton's desertion of Edward and his adoption of the cause of the rebellious baronial faction led by Thomas of Lancaster and Humprey de Bohun, earl of Hereford. The Trumwyns had initially suffered the loss of their lands to the king's officers, but by April of 1322 they had found sureties for their fidelity to Edward. However, Joan and Roger Trumwyn were unable to secure their hold on Cyfeiliog and Caereinion, for the Welsh communities of those commotes refused to admit the Trumwyns, an exclusion which lasted for well over a year.[90] An entry in the Patent Roll for 1322 gives a list of those magnates of Cyfeiliog and Caereinion, twenty-eight in all, who denied Roger and Joan control of their lands.[91] This most unusual list reveals the prominence in the Welsh community of two sons of Gruffudd ap Gwên, **Owain ap Gruffudd** and **Gruffudd ap Gruffudd** listed in second and eleventh positions. Owain had been recorded at the head of the list of jurors for Cyfeiliog in the Inquisition Post Mortem of Owain ap Gruffudd in 1293, thus establishing his prominence in that region at an early date.[92] Owain ap Gruffudd was followed in the 1293 Inquisition by Llywelyn ap Gruffudd, a fact that will shortly be of significance, and then by Tudur ap Gruffudd, who seems to have been another of Owain's brothers. By 1322, Owain and Gruffudd, apparently a younger brother, were evidently amongst the elders of Cyfeiliog.

It therefore comes as no surprise that a probable grandson of Gruffudd ap Gwên, **Llywelyn Fychan ap Llywelyn (ap Gruffudd)**, a son of the Llywelyn ap Gruffudd recorded as a witness for Cyfeiliog in 1293, was included in the predominantly Welsh list of witnesses to a charter of John Charlton to the borough of Machynlleth, the market centre of Cyfeiliog, in 1344.[93] It may be that another of the witnesses of 1344, Hywel ap Gruffudd, may have been a son of the Gruffudd ap Gruffudd ap Gwên of the 1322 list. This last identification is a mere conjecture, but the case of the descendants of Gruffudd ap Gwên, and indeed the descendants of Einion ap Seisyll as far back as the late twelfth century, is particularly important in that it provides evidence of the importance of hereditary eminence amongst the administrative elite in a symbolically important region of a major Welsh lordship, a quality extending over several generations.

The northern March

Gruffudd ap Madog

Gruffudd ap Madog was one of the more celebrated of the 'men of position', since he was the grandfather of Owain Glyn Dŵr. It appears to have been Gruffudd's father, Madog ap Gruffudd, who brought Sycharth (Cynllaith Owen) into his possession to form an inheritance with Glyndyfrdwy, to which his son, perhaps six years old at the time of Madog's death c.1304 or 1305, eventually succeeded. Already Gruffudd's future had exercised the mind of his father, for shortly before Madog's death he had arranged and attended his young son's marriage to Elizabeth, daughter of John Lestrange, lord of Knockin. Gruffudd ap Madog ap Gruffudd, was a grandson of Gruffudd Fychan (d. 1293, erstwhile lord of Iâl, and direct descendant of Madog ap Maredudd (d. 1160), king of the Powysians). The inquisition which confirmed Gruffudd ap Madog's age and his genealogy also establishes that Gruffudd ap Madog's lands amounted to three-quarters of a commote, for Glyndyfrdwy was a quarter of a commote, and Cynllaith Owen was a half of one. Gruffudd held by Welsh barony, known as *pennaeth*, directly from the king. And was obliged – or privileged – to go with his men in the king's army whenever given reasonable warning.

In the few documents which can be used to sketch his life, Gruffudd ap Madog's eminence is discernible. In 1324, Gruffudd appeared as the second witness to a charter issued by Edmund, earl of Arundel, to the tenants of his lordship of Chirkland, a juxtaposition that reminds us that though the two men were vastly different in terms of wealth, they were neighbours and fellow-lords.[94] The year 1328 saw Gruffudd obtaining a royal licence to convey his lands to trustees, who would regrant them to him and his wife Elizabeth in entail, a manoeuvre which would ensure that the lands were protected against forfeiture for felony or treason. It is unlikely that Gruffudd was planning such offences, but in the political atmosphere of the late 1320s it was as well for those who might be caught on the wrong side of a political dispute to guard against the impact of their own misfortune or miscalculation on their heirs. In 1332, Gruffudd's status was further demonstrated when he appeared as the keeper of the large manor of Ellesmere, which had but recently been granted to his brother-in-law Eubolo Lestrange. When the magnates of Wales gathered to perform homage to Edward, the new prince of Wales, Gruffudd ap Madog was listed as one of the tenants in chief who had not yet performed homage; it must be a matter of conjecture whether this was the result of infirmity or illness.

Iorwerth and Cynwrig, sons of Llywarch

Of these two brothers, inhabitants of the lordship of Denbigh, far more evidence has survived regarding Iorwerth than there has for Cynwrig. And yet Cynwrig was memorialised with a large surviving fragment of a splendid sepulchral slab, which lies in the church of St John the Baptist, Ysbyty Ifan, in Denbighshire.[95] The slab fragment is finely carved with an inscription (HIC IACET KYNWRICUS FILIUS LLYVARCH: CVI AIE SIT I PACE: Here lies Cynwrig ap Llywarch, may whose soul be in peace).[96] The inscription runs around the border of a shield on which the charge is a lion rampant, with three circular flowers and two fleurs-de-lis as decoration. Below the shield the head and forelegs of a running hare are lightly incised. Cynwrig was the ancestor of a particularly distinguished family.

The sepulchral slab is an apparent testimony to Cynwrig's wealth and importance, but it is his brother Iorwerth who features in the documentary record. He accompanied Henry de Lacy in Paris in 1286.[97] But it was his service to Thomas of Lancaster which was most notable. He stood with Lancaster in the crisis of the murder of Piers Gaveston in 1311–12,[98] and again in the course of the conflict with the king over the prominence accorded to Hugh Despenser the younger in 1321–2. Both the rewards and the penalties for his closeness to Lancaster can be well illustrated. Thus, an inquisition of 21 April 1322,[99] held in the aftermath of the king's victory at Boroughbridge and the execution of the former lord of Denbigh, Thomas of Lancaster, heard that:

Iorwerth de la Chambre, a rebel, had by gift of Thomas, earl of Lancaster, 240 acres of land in Lleweni, of the yearly value of £8; in Berain and Tal y Bryn a watermill and 749½ acres and half a rood of land, two plots a close with wastes and other appurtenances of the yearly value of £20 4s 4d. He had nothing else by gift of the said earl except a bailiwick of the amobrage of Is Aled of the yearly value of 100s. He had lands in Ereifiad and Hafod yr Haidd not of the gift of the said earl, of the yearly value of 8s.

These lands acquired from Earl Thomas, of a total value of over £33 per year, were confiscated in 1322, and only returned in 1330.[100]

Iorwerth had been allowed to retain his hereditary estates in Llyweni, as was set out in the survey of the lordship in 1334, where it is stated that Iorwerth ap Llywarch (who has a house) and Cynwrig his brother (who has no house) hold half a *gafael* of freemen rendering a range of dues and services.[101] But it is emphasised that 'Iorwerth holds as his share one hundred and eighty-seven acres of land, meadow, pasture and woodland in Lleweni. And nevertheless, Cynwrig ap Llywarch occupies thirty acres in Ereifiad and eight acres in Gwytherin in exchange for the same inheritance in Llyweni, by a charter of the Earl of Lincoln.'[102] Clearly Iorwerth's services to the lords of Denbigh were rewarded in a way that elevated him significantly above his contemporaries. They also appear to have set him above his brother Cynwrig, and it must be a possibility that Cynwrig's sepulchral slab, for which see above, may have been funded by Iorwerth.

Llywelyn and Hywel, sons of Madog

Here were another two brothers, this time from the lordship of Dyffryn Clwyd. Their ancestors in the thirteenth century had been prominent in the region, receiving lands from the princes; Hywel was rhaglaw of Dyffryn Clwyd in 1316,[103] but it is Llywelyn who catches the distant observer's eye. He has been described as 'the foremost Welsh landholder under Reginald de Grey' (lord of Ruthin 1282–1308) and as 'a wealthy local Welshman, and the descendant of a family which had grown rich and privileged in the service of the native Welsh princes'.[104] The result was that 'native Welsh society in the early-fourteenth century was dominated by Hywel and Madog ap Llywelyn ... whose territorial fortunes included over 800 acres of land and two mills'.[105]

Within a very few years Llywelyn ap Madog's importance to de Grey was made manifest by substantial grants of land – of 57 acres in Llanynys and Maesmaencymro and 96 acres in Bodangharad in 1292 at the almost token rent of 4s per year.[106] In 1308, he and two of his brothers were members of the jury at Reginald's Inquisition Post Mortem, while Llywelyn was tasked with testifying to the extent of Reginald's lands.[107] His influence was still felt in the lordship under Reginald's successor, John de Grey, when he and his two brothers appear as witnesses to the lord's charter of 1310 creating and endowing a collegiate chapel for seven priests.[108] He was allowed to fine forty shillings to be excused service in the king's army, though he had been appointed to lead the levies in the king's campaign in 1322 against the Contrariants and the Scots.[109] One estimate of Llywelyn ap Madog's importance is the spread of lands that he held at the time of his death in 1343: the grants of 1292 were augmented by more lands held in Colion commote in Ysgeifioig, Bryncaredig and Derwen and in Corfedwen in Dogfeiling. The total effect was that 'Llywelyn was one of the few Welsh landowners to hold substantial acreage in vills with significant English settlement.'[110]

Madog ap Llywelyn
For the importance of Madog in the lordship of Bromfield and Yale, as well as his impact elsewhere, see the discussion in Chapter 2.

The family of Llywelyn ab Ynyr
This family is perhaps best approached by reference to the 1315 Extent of Bromfield and Yale,[111] where two vills in Yale, Gelligynan and Bodidris, are shown as being held by close kinsmen and subject to very privileged tenure. In Gelligynan, **Gruffudd ap Llywelyn**, **Gruffudd Llwyd**, **Maredudd ap Llywelyn** and **Llywelyn Fychan ap Maredudd ap Llywelyn** hold free of all

rents and services, though their tenants mill at the lord's mill.[112] In Bodidris, **Gruffudd Llwyd** and **Llywelyn ap Llywelyn ap Maredudd** hold the vill for one pair of gloves at Martinmas, while their tenants owe a range of services.[113] Llywelyn ab Ynyr can also be identified as the father of Llywelyn Fychan who, as **Llywelyn de Bromfield**, was bishop of St Asaph 1293–1314.[114] Llywelyn ab Ynyr was prominent in the service of the rulers of northern Powys in the period 1247–69.[115] His son Maredudd ap Llywelyn can be identified as the bailiff (or *rhaglaw*) of Gruffudd Fychan, lord of Iâl in 1278.[116] The privileged tenure enjoyed by the family appears to have originated in the mid-thirteenth century, and they were evidently of importance in the later years of that century and the early years of the fourteenth. Their regional eminence probably accounts for Llywelyn Fychan's elevation to the bishopric of St Asaph, which in turn assuredly boosted the family's prestige.

It is evident that this family had been prominent in Iâl for generations, and were particularly eminent in the early fourteenth century. Interestingly, for the period under review, the family appears to have left at least two memorials in stone which have survived: one is an effigy, tolerably intact, and therefore the subject is identifiable; the other is a partial depiction on a surviving fragment of a slab and thus the subject is somewhat conjectural. The complete effigy is that of Gruffudd ap Llywelyn ab Ynyr.[117] And the second and manifestly incomplete work almost certainly relates to the Gruffudd Llwyd noticed above.[118]

The family belonged amongst the descendants of Sandde Hardd, and it is particularly interesting that the Iorwerth ap Dafydd who was associated with Madog ap Llywelyn[119] in raising 700 troops in support of Edward II in February 1322 was also a descendant of Sandde Hardd and a cousin of the descendants of Llywelyn ab Ynyr.[120]

Flintshire

The following survey of 'men of position' in Flintshire (a county created in 1284 by amalgamating three separate areas, Tegeingl/Englefield, Hope, and Maelor Saesneg) is heavily indebted to the work of A. D. Carr, whose many publications have thrown much light on the county and its institutions and inhabitants. In particular, Carr envisaged the county, and especially Englefield, as a region long dominated by the lineage of Ithel Fychan of Halkyn, a branch of the lineage of Edwyn, and it is with them that we shall start.

The contribution of **Ithel Fychan** to his family's fame, and indeed in some cases infamy, in the fourteenth century was based on his extensive lands; in the 1292 assessments for the lay subsidy his holdings were reckoned at £21 12s 2¼d[121] – a figure that puts him clearly in the top bracket of the wealthy in the county. Ithel Fychan's wealth formed a foundation of the fortunes of his family.[122] His wealth was augmented in the later thirteenth century and the early years of the fourteenth by purchases of lands in Bagillt, Rhyl, Llys-y-coed, Halkyn and Llystynhunydd between 1296 and 1309. It was his sons, of whom there were nine, who further developed the family's prominence in Flintshire, with numerous, often small, acquisitions, sometimes using the device of *tir prid* (the so-called 'Welsh mortgage'), particularly in the decades before the Black Death. The (fairly cautious) enterprise of Ithel Fychan's sons, and their sheer number, helped to cement the family's leadership in the county from the 1320s to the 1360s. Some impressive marriages came their way and performed the same function. Thus, one of the most successfully acquisitive of Ithel Fychan's sons, **Tudur ab Ithel**, with a very large concentration of properties in and around Mostyn and Whitford in Englefield,[123] married Erddylad, daughter of Madog ap Llywelyn ap Gruffudd, himself a dominant figure in the lordship of Bromfield and Yale and beyond.[124]

One of Tudur's brothers, **Ithel Person**, although a cleric, rector of Northop, the richest and most important living in the county, was also a key figure in lay matters. He was very important in the Flintshire land market. He seems to have bought out Owain Sais, the grandson of Cynwrig Sais of Northop, revealed by the 1292–3 lay subsidy assessments to have been by far the richest person in the county, with a movable property assessment of £72 15s 4½d. Ithel Person was for some years, possibly beginning in 1320, the *rhaglaw* of the cantref of Englefield, an office which he farmed. In 1331, Ithel Person was joined as *rhaglaw* by two of his brothers of whom one, Cynwrig Sais, became his sole successor. When Ithel Person died in 1341 his wealth was probably distributed amongst his brothers, even though he had a son, Dafydd, who became coroner of Englefield in 1350.

Cynwrig Sais, whose active career record became a by-word for extortion and oppression, was the most famous of Ithel Fychan's sons. By 1336 he was farming not only the office of *rhaglaw* in the whole of Englefield, but also that of Escheator. The two offices cost him £100 per year. He was very successful in turning a profit on this 'investment', which soon involved him in distinctly criminal activity. Complaints were soon made that the *rhaglaw* was amercing men for non-attendance at hundred and county courts who had already paid fines to be excused attendance. Though he was found not guilty the complaints continued and in 1341 he and the sheriff of Flintshire, William de Praers, who happened to be Cynwrig Sais's son-in-law, were forced to answer ten counts of oppression and corruption. These included taking excessive fines from advowry tenants, something between twenty times and one hundred and twenty times the usual payment of 4d per year, and issuing indictments for fictitious offences. It was alleged that when Cynwrig's daughter married William de Praers's son, the bride's father gave her a wedding portion of 180 marks (£120) which he raised by forced contributions from all the tenants in Englefield. The *rhaglaw* and the sheriff were also accused of taking reliefs (entry-fines from new tenants) from lands of people who had died, while the *rhaglaw* was accused of forcing every tenant in the cantref to fill his (Cynwrig's) cart with corn every year. In the event, Cynwrig Sais and five of his brothers and his son Ithel, who were accused of colluding with him, were fined with varying degrees of severity from the 300 marks which Cynwrig was obliged to pay, down through other sums to the £5 which was paid by Ithel, his son. Though the cases of 1341 brought Cynwrig Sais's official career to an end, they marked only the apprenticeship of Ithel ap Cynwrig. Ithel became in 1349 the literal partner in crime of a member of Wyrion Eden, Rhys ap Roppert. As in the case of Cynwrig Sais and William de Praers, Ithel ap Cynwrig and Rhys ap Roppert were linked by marriage ties. Ithel's brother Dafydd was married to Rhys's sister Angharad, while Ithel's cousin, Hywel ap Tudur ab Ithel Fychan was the husband of Lleucu, the daughter of Rhys ap Roppert. In that plague year, the two partners, who shared the offices of constable of Flint and sheriff of Flintshire, were granted the farm of all advowries in Englefield for the next seven years, along with the post of escheator. The extremes to which the two men, particularly Rhys ap Roppert, took their criminality will be examined in Chapter 5.

There were, of course, other significant figures in Flintshire in the period from 1295 to the plague years of the mid-century. Typical of these are the brothers **Roppert and Iorwerth, sons of Rhirid**. They shared assets in terms of movables in the 1292–3 Lay subsidy assessments of £51 8s 9d, making them among the wealthiest persons in the county.[125] Roppert was *rhaglaw* of Advowries for Englefield in 1301–3, while Iorwerth was *rhaglaw* of Englefield in 1302–3 until 1305–6.[126] Both of the brothers were amongst those who swore fealty and performed homage to the prince of Wales in 1301.[127] It would perhaps have been surprising if there had been no contact between this family and that of Ithel Fychan of Halkyn, and indeed Iorwerth's son, Roppert, married Ithel Fychan's daughter Ales. These two had a son, Ithel, who became archdeacon of Englefield.[128] It was said that Iorwerth ap Rhirid was also father of the Matthew of Englefield who became bishop of Bangor in the years 1328–57.[129] So the family was wealthy, with important ecclesiastics as members, and with some important contacts amongst other lay magnates. But their prominence does not compare with that of the descendants of Ithel Fychan.

The Northern Principality

Einion ab Ieuan

Einion was sheriff of Anglesey from 1316 to 1327. A member of the noble lineage of Cilmin Troed-ddu, he appears to have been a great-grandson of the Master Ystrwyth ('Instructus') who was one of the leading officials of Llywelyn ab Iorwerth in the early decades of the thirteenth century.[130] Einion distinguished himself by holding aloof from support of the rebellious barons against Edward II in 1321 – unlike his English colleagues in the northern principality. Einion was imprisoned on suspicion of disloyalty to Edward II, probably in 1322, in the aftermath of the king's triumph at Boroughbridge, but after an enquiry into his conduct was released because 'the king learned by inquisition taken by the justice that Einion has been faithful to the king at all times, and that he never adhered to the king's contrariants in North Wales or elsewhere'.[131] He had, it seems, been imprisoned 'at the procurement of certain of his enemies', and his goods, to the value of nearly £233, had been seized and sold by the chamberlain of North Wales.[132] The calculation of the worth of his goods seems to place Einion amongst the wealthiest persons in Anglesey, a further factor in his prominence. Einion's descendants continued the tradition of loyalty to royal authority in Wales, including his grandson, Tudur Goch ap Goronwy, who was granted an estate in Baladeulyn by the Black Prince, and his grandson, Hwlcyn Llwyd, who died defending Caernarfon castle against Owain Glyn Dŵr's forces in 1404.[133]

Ieuan ap Sir Gruffudd
A son of Sir Gruffudd Llwyd. He was archdeacon of Anglesey, apparently between 1340 and his death in 1352; he was amongst those recorded as attainted of conspiracy in the murder of Henry Shaldeford, in 1345, though not described as archdeacon.[134] Described as still at large in 1345, there is no record of further proceedings against him.

Tudur Hen ap Goronwy and his descendants
Tudur Hen (d. 1311) was a son of Goronwy ab Ednyfed Fychan, and thus a descendant of two holders of the office of *distain* in the time of the princes.[135] It is possible that he was one of the hostages surrendered by Dafydd ap Llywelyn to Henry III in 1241.[136]

In 1286, the chamberlain of north Wales recorded a fine of 40s, received from Tudur ap Goronwy 'for a certain offence'. In

Heirs to the Princes

the course of the rising of 1294–5 the northern leader, Madog ap Llywelyn, issued a charter at Penmachno relating to land in Merioneth which was witnessed by Tudur ap Goronwy 'our steward',[137] a description difficult to reconcile with his appearance as one of the group of four representatives of the people of north Wales in the aftermath of the revolt, who went to Edward I to complain that he was reputed to hold the men of the north in some suspicion. They received an entirely conciliatory response. Tudur like his bother Goronwy, who was also present amongst the witnesses to Madog ap Llywelyn's Penmachno charter, swore fealty and performed homage to Edward, as prince of Wales in 1301.

Tudur was also amongst those from north Wales who presented petitions to the prince at Kennington in 1305.[138] Here he claimed that the Justice of North Wales had removed him from the office of *rhaglaw* of Dindaethwy – the associated demand being one which the prince neatly sidestepped; that he was being charged a rent of 10s per year for a carucate of land at Aber(gwyngregyn) which had been granted to him to hold freely by Llywelyn ap Gruffudd – a claim that was finally allowed four years after Tudur's death in 1311. Tudur also claimed the right to hold his own courts in his lands, excepting only pleas of life and limb, and complained that the sheriff had forced his bondmen to attend the sheriff's tourn and the hundred courts established in 1284. The obligation of his tenants to attend these last courts was upheld by the prince, but Tudur's right to hold his own courts was confirmed.

An insight into Tudur's spiritual convictions and achievements is provided by his relationship with the Dominicans of Bangor. It is clear that the friars had arrived in Bangor by the mid-thirteenth century, so there can at first sight be no truth in the tradition that Tudur had founded the friary. But, after suffering significant damage in the war of 1282–3, the friary was rebuilt in 1293,[139] so the fact that Tudur was buried there in the south wall of the friary strongly suggests that he was a very prominent patron of the building, and perhaps that he was regarded as a second founder.

Goronwy ap Tudur (d. 1331)

Tudur Hen's son, and successor in 1311, was Goronwy ap Tudur. He too was buried, like his father, in the Dominican friary of Bangor. Evidence for his military activity is rather clearer than in his father's case, as he acted as deputy to his kinsman Sir Gruffudd Llwyd, in the 1322 campaign against the Scots which, however, ended ignominiously. That Goronwy was not lacking in courage was demonstrated in 1331 when, along with Sir Gruffudd Llwyd, he became a surety for Hywel ap Gruffudd in the latter's case against William Shaldeford, Roger Mortimer's former deputy as justice of North Wales. Hywel had accused Shaldeford of suggesting to Mortimer that it would be advisable to ensure that the former Edward II was not alive to be rescued by some of his Welsh partisans, and therefore precipitating Edward's death. The accusation was potentially dangerously embarrassing to the government, and those who supported Hywel ap Gruffudd may have been considered foolhardy.[140] Goronwy's death in the same year was probably coincidental.

Goronwy had been one of three men, including Sir Gruffudd Llwyd, who were to raise a large force (1,500 men) in North Wales to be led by Sir Gruffudd on royal service in Scotland in July 1316,[141] but after reaching Chester the troops from western Gwynedd were allowed to return home to counter any Scottish invasion from Ireland. In October of the same year, Goronwy was once more to accompany Sir Gruffudd, this time to Scotland. On this occasion Goronwy was also accompanied by his father-in-law, Madog of Hendwr and Hywel ap Gruffudd.[142] In 1319, again with Sir Gruffudd Llwyd, Goronwy was one of the leaders of a Welsh force sent to attack the Scottish border town of Berwick, which had been taken by Robert the Bruce the previous year. In the same period, Goronwy held the office of forester of Snowdonia, a post previously held by Sir Gruffudd Llwyd.[143]

It is possible to trace something of the land-holdings of the son and grandsons of Tudur Hen. The justiciar of south Wales had reported in 1320 that Goronwy ap Tudur Hen and his forebears had not paid *amobr* or relief in connection with their lands in Cellan, Cardiganshire,[144] while the Inquisition undertaken after Goronwy's death revealed him holding one third of a *Gwestfa* in Cellan (Mabwynion), Rhydonnen (Perfedd), and Llechweddlwyfan (Creuddyn).[145] In 1344, Goronwy's sons were summoned to answer to a writ of Quo Warranto to establish the basis of their claim to hold courts with cognizance of pleas other than those of the crown, in the above three townships.[146] These and other details point to the family as both wealthy and privileged.[147]

Hywel and Tudur, sons of Goronwy ap Tudur Hen

Goronwy's sons, Hywel and Tudur, are memorable for their involvement in the killing of the Black Prince's attorney, Henry de Shaldeford in February 1345.[148] In common with other traceable conspirators of 1345, the brothers survived for some two decades after the Shaldeford murder. Hywel was eventually apprehended by the authorities after taking refuge in England and placed in captivity in Launceston castle in Cornwall. The elaborate precautions taken to guard him, and the instructions given to the constable of the castle to let no one except those in whom he had complete confidence speak to Hywel, suggest that he was considered a highly dangerous prisoner.[149]

Finally, in 1347, Hywel was released from Launceston upon finding four sureties. Their identities are interesting: Sir Richard Talbot, Sir Rhys ap Gruffudd, and Rhys and Dafydd, sons of Madog of Hendwr in Edeyrnion, Merioneth.[150] Richard Talbot was a son of a justiciar of south Wales and a former deputy justiciar;[151] Rhys ap Gruffudd was perhaps the most powerful Welshman in South Wales, 'the 'effective ruler' of the southern principality, and a kinsman of the brothers.[152] The sons of Madog of Hendwr were barons of Edeyrnion, whose sister, Gwerful ferch Madog, was the brothers' mother.[153] The sureties were a tight-knit group, representing some of the high-born and well-regarded members of society in Wales. Beyond this it is clear that the two had pursued divergent careers: elegies by Iolo Goch and Gruffudd ap Maredudd depict Tudur ap Goronwy as a soldier, a brave man who was at home in armour. He had, in addition, succeeded to the office of *rhaglaw* of Dindaethwy, almost a hereditary position as his father and grandfather had held it, by 1343.[154]

Hywel ap Goronwy, on the other hand, was a cleric, who rose to be archdeacon of Anglesey before his death in 1366, a year before that of Goronwy. Already, by 1352, the detailed extents of Caernarfonshire and Anglesey show that the brothers had suffered only temporary inconvenience for their parts in the Shaldeford killing some seven years earlier. They were recorded as holding jointly in Anglesey the vill of Trecastell, half that of Penmynydd, and with Rhys ap Dafydd, their second cousin, that of Erddreiniog, while in Caernarfonshire they held, with others, one and a half *gafaelion* in the vill of Cororion. They had already, in Quo Warranto proceedings in 1348, claimed that they and their ancestors had held since time immemorial three-weekly courts, and the assize of ale with freedom from relief, heriot and *amobr*.[155] It was a strange but instructive career pattern, by which the prisoner of Launceston and the fount of such violence in North Wales should come into the prince's favour and become an archdeacon,[156] and his brother, the apparent leader of the men who actually killed Henry de Shaldeford, should have held a highly responsible office and should be so mourned by the poets.

Madog Gloddaeth
A prominent figure in Caernarfonshire, his importance buttressed by a good marriage – to Morfydd, daughter of Sir Gruffudd Llwyd.[157] He was confident enough to complain to the king against the sheriff of Anglesey in 1318, when he received an encouraging reply. A request to have the office of *rhaglaw* in the Anglesey commote of Dindaethwy was probably less successful,[158] but Madog farmed the office of *rhaglaw* of Creuddyn in 1319, and petitioned Edward II to retain the office, with the bailiwick of Penmaen-Llysfaen and of Euyas (= Eirias[159]) for as long as he comported himself well and loyally in his service.[160] The king replied that he did not wish to remove those who had served him well. Later Madog was deputy sheriff in 1327 and subsequently acting sheriff of Caernarfonshire.[161] In 1341, he helped to levy

troops in North Wales for Edward III's campaign in Scotland.[162] Madog swore fealty to the Black Prince in 1343 when he was farming the office of *rhaglaw* of Nantconwy,[163] and was still *rhaglaw* of Creuddyn in 1350–1, even though he had been on the list of those attainted of conspiracy in the Shaldeford murder in 1345. Madog had begun a family tradition which lasted through the century. One son, Madog Fychan, followed him as *rhaglaw* of Creuddyn. Another, Gruffudd, also held the office of *rhaglaw* in Creuddyn, but was also sheriff and escheator of Anglesey in the period 1355–8.[164] Other members of the same family can be traced holding significant offices towards the end of the century.

Barons of Edeirnion: Gruffudd ap Dafydd of Hendwr and his family

The commote of Edeirnion contained a veritable swarm of descendants of Owain Brogyntyn ap Madog ap Maredudd (fl. c.1160–1218) who became known as the barons of Edeirnion, but, as A. D. Carr pointed out in his survey of 2001, 'the Hendwr family seems to have been the only one from Edeirnion whose members held office with any regularity'.[165] Some of these were sufficiently important to be included amongst the 'men of position'.

Prominent members of the family had shown clear signs of disenchantment with the rule of Llywelyn ap Gruffudd in the later years of his principate. Dafydd ap Gruffudd ab Owain Brogyntyn's house at Hendwr was destroyed by the prince in the course of the war of 1277, and he was one of the barons whom Edward I compelled Llywelyn to release from prison in the Treaty of Aberconwy of November 1277. Edward went further, by ordering Llywelyn to make the manor of Crogen, just outside Edeirnion, over to Dafydd until the house at Hendwr was rebuilt.[166] It occasions little surprise that Dafydd ap Gruffudd's family were to be associated with Edward I and his successor after the conquest of 1282–3. When the revolt of 1294–5 broke out, **Gruffudd ap Dafydd ap Gruffudd** was an esquire of the king's household, while his local importance was recognised by a grant to him of custody of the royal forests of Merioneth.[167] It is clear that he was actively engaged in putting down the revolt.[168] His

Administrative Eminence and Political Peril

brother **Madog** was leading troops in Penllyn at the turn of the year 1294–5.[169]

Gruffudd ap Dafydd is almost certainly to be identified as the man of that name who appears in 1300–1 as the first of the Welsh sheriffs recorded in the northern principality, and by 1304–5 he had been granted the offices of *rhaglaw* of Penllyn and Ardudwy for life.[170]

Gruffudd ap Dafydd was followed as rhaglaw of Penllyn and Ardudwy by his son, **Madog ap Gruffudd**,[171] who led twenty men from Edeirnion to Newcastle in 1316 to join in a campaign against the Scots.[172] Madog was also one of four commissioners of array raising 1,500 troops from Powys in 1322.[173] In the same year he petitioned the king for the office of *penteulu* in the lands of Powys.[174] It is easy to see this office, which derived from the age of the princes, as a mere sinecure in the post-Conquest years, but it is possible that it did give its holder a right to military command in Powys. In 1335, the cousins of Madog ap Gruffudd, probably Gruffudd and Rhys, were summoned to march to Scotland, as part of a large Welsh force.[175]

Several of the barons of Edeirnion of various branches of the descendants of Owain Brogyntyn were involved in military service for Edward III, as well as episodes such as the Shaldeford murder in 1345, after which two members of the family of Hendwr, Dafydd ap Madog ap Gruffudd and his kinsman Rhys ap Madog ap Dafydd, stood sureties for Hywel ap Goronwy of Penmynydd when he was released from captivity in Launceston castle. It is worth noting that Gwerful ferch Madog, daughter of Madog ap Dafydd, was Hywel ap Goronwy's mother.[176]

Ynyr Fychan and his descendants

A family with a most distinguished ancestry, claiming descent from Bleddyn ap Cynfyn, ruler of Gwynedd and Powys 1064–75, and ancestor of the later rulers of Powys.[177] Some genealogies make Ynyr Fychan a brother of Anian II, the celebrated and combative bishop of St Asaph (1268–93), whose opposition to both Llywelyn ap Gruffudd and Edward I in turn earned him the epitaph in *Brut y Tywysogyon* that he was 'the best man and the strongest in maintaining his diocese that anyone saw'.[178] J. E. Lloyd was, however, of the opinion that 'there is nothing to show' that Anian was a son of Ynyr of Nannau; whereas Gresham shows him as such in a genealogy in his *Medieval Stone Carving in North Wales*.[179] However, it is evident from the entry in the *Brut* that Anian was connected with Nannau, the home of Ynyr and his family, for he was recorded in the *Brut* entry as 'The Black Friar of Nannau'.

Ynyr Fychan was involved in the capture of Madog ap Llywelyn, leader of the northern revolt of 1294–5, a feat for which he was eventually granted the office of *rhaglaw* in the commote of Tal-y-bont,[180] where the family may have held a leading position.[181] He is recorded in the Parliament Roll for 1321–2 as one of those involved in the raid on Dyffryn Clwyd in that year, who acted, with others, at the instigation of Sir Gruffudd ap Rhys (i.e. Sir Gruffudd Llwyd).[182] Nevertheless, Ynyr Fychan appears to have been *rhaglaw* of Tal-y-bont until 1330, when he was succeeded by his son Meurig.[183] Another son of Ynyr, Hywel, served as coroner of Ardudwy and Meirionnydd between 1317 and 1344.[184] It seems fairly clear that Ynyr Fychan and his sons constituted the leading family of Tal-y-bont in Merioneth in the early and mid-fourteenth century.

Meurig ab Ynyr Fychan is commemorated by a fine effigy in St Mary's church, Dolgellau which shows him in armour, and with heraldic detail.[185] The armour suggests a date in the middle of the century, while Gresham reports a note in the handwriting of A. N. Palmer, which records Meurig ab Ynyr as living between 1347 and 1349. It must be a possibility that Meurig was a plague victim.

Hywel ap Gruffudd (Hywel y Pedolau: 'of the Horseshoes')

Hywel ap Gruffudd was a semi-legendary figure of the important lineage of Hwfa ap Cynddelw. The legendary (i.e. without any support in known record or contemporary chronicle sources) aspects of Hywel's are mainly two-fold. The first is the story that Hywel was favoured by 'the king' (whether Edward I or Edward II is uncertain) because his mother had nursed the baby who would become prince of Wales and so her son was subsequently knighted. The second is that, when he grew to maturity, Hywel was so strong that he could bend horseshoes with his bare hands. The second story is perhaps more likely to contain an element of truth for it is certain that Hywel's name was used by fourteenth-century poets to indicate physical strength.[186] Hywel was a former esquire of the king's household who was *rhaglaw* of the *cantref* of Aberffraw in 1316–17, and again in 1328–9.[187] The cantref was the location of the chief court of the Llywelyns, and its name was incorporated indeed into the title of Llywelyn ab Iorwerth. The importance of Hywel's immediate family was demonstrated by the petition of his brother Llywelyn to be confirmed as the *pencenedl* (chief of kindred) of the descendants of Hwfa ap Cynddelw. He was one of two men selected by the government of Roger Mortimer and Queen Isabella to attend the parliament of 1327 called to witness the deposition of Edward II, even though Hywel had been one of those (including his brother Iorwerth) imprisoned with Sir Gruffudd Llwyd for a short time after that king's effective fall.[188] Indeed, former supporters of the late king were particularly called to attend the 1327 parliament, thus showing how Mortimer was now in control of the political process. Hywel had shown signs of military prowess early in his career, when he served at the head of ten men in a campaign against the Scots, in 1316.[189]

Holders of shrievalties of whom little is known[190]
A striking feature of the northern principality lands is the presence of a number of Welsh holders of the office of sheriff. The lists are as follows.

Anglesey:
Gruffudd ap Rhys (1305–6)
Gruffudd ab Owain (1306–9)
Madog Llwyd (1308–12)
Einion ab Ieuan (1316–27)
Cynwrig ap Gruffudd (1332–3).

Caernarfonshire:
Gruffudd ap Rhys (1302–5; 1308–1309/10).

Merionethshire:
Gruffudd ap Rhys (1305–6)
Ieuan ap Hywel (1306–9)
Gruffudd ap Rhys (1314–27)[191]
Cynwrig ap Gruffudd (1332–3).[192]

Perhaps the salient feature of the lists of sheriffs above, apart from the prominence of Gruffudd ap Rhys (Sir Gruffudd Llwyd), unique as the holder at different times of each of the three shrievalties of the northern principality, is the concentration of appointments in the first decade of the fourteenth century – first in the later reign of Edward I, then the principate of Edward of Caernarfon (1301–6), when appointments were quite possibly influenced, and even dictated, by the prince's father, and finally in the early years of the reign of Edward II. A significant majority of the appointments of Welshmen to these shrievalties fall within this period. An additional point to emerge is that, in spite of the meagre nature of the evidence, there seems to be a possibility that an effort was made to appoint sheriffs familiar with the shires over which they presided as officials. Gruffudd ap Dafydd, whose career, unusually, can be traced, was one of the barons of Edeirnion, which lay within Merioneth. His home, Hendwr, was a centre of opposition to Prince Llywelyn, until it was destroyed by the prince, leading Edward I to take Gruffudd under his protection. Again, in Anglesey there is a possibility that Einion ab Ieuan was a member of the same kin-group as Master Ystrwyth, the chancellor of Llywelyn the Great of Gwynedd in the early thirteenth century, with strong connections with Anglesey.[193]

The Southern Principality

The story of Welsh governance in the southern principality is of course dominated by those of **Sir Rhys ap Gruffudd** and **Sir**

Philip Clanvowe. But there were several other persons of note, however, whose careers are explored below. Some such men have already been noticed in Chapter 1: these include **Goronwy Goch**, steward of Cantref Mawr (Ystrad Tywi), **Dafydd Bongam** (Dafydd ap Hywel ap Dafydd), also an early steward of Cantref Mawr, and **Dafydd Fychan ap Dafydd ap 'Moriz' (?Meurig)** in Emlyn,[194] a lordship closely tied to the Principality. It is notable that it is in this region that we find clear intimations about the quality of governance with which Welsh magnates were associated, and also about other aspects of magnate activity, such as cultural and spiritual leadership.

Llywelyn ap Philip and his sons Dafydd and Gruffudd

Llywelyn ap Philip appears as a juror for Caeo in the lay subsidy assessments of 1292, was beadle (*rhingyll*) and reeve for Maenordeilo 1301–2 and 1303–4, and was constable of that commote 1301–2 and 1305–6. It is possible that he was the man of this name who was one of a large number of patrons of the church of Llanybydder in 1319–22.[195]

Dafydd ap Llywelyn swore fealty to the Black Prince in 1343 as one of a select group of those who held by barony.[196] The claim to baronial status may have come through his grandmother Catrin, (wife of Philip ap Trahaearn) who was a daughter of Gruffudd ab Ednyfed Fychan. The only other Welsh holder by barony noticed was the future Sir Rhys ap Gruffudd.[197] In 1332–3 Dafydd had been beadle (*rhingyll*) of Caeo commote (Cardiganshire) and in 1335 owed £9 arising from the office, but this was excused as a result of his good service in Scotland. In 1342–3 he led 819 archers on the Breton campaign.[198] He thus appears as an administrator and a soldier, a combination perhaps reminiscent of figures such as Sir Gruffudd Llwyd and Sir Morgan ap Maredudd. Those comparisons are apposite, as Dafydd was a kinsman of Sir Gruffudd through his grandmother Catrin, while his wife was Angharad, the daughter and heiress of Sir Morgan. And the mother of Dafydd and Gruffudd was Elin ferch Llywelyn, who could trace her ancestry back to the Lord Rhys.[199] In genealogical terms alone, this was a distinguished family.

Gruffudd ap Llywelyn appears to have had more spiritual leanings, as he is noted by its scribe, the anchorite of Llanddewibrefi, as the sponsor of the important compendium of Welsh-language translations of Latin religious texts, known as Llyfr yr Agkyr.[200] But Gruffudd too was an administrator: like his father in the early years of the century he was constable of Maenordeilo in 1331–3; he served as beadle of Cantrefmawr in 1337–9, and in 1339 he was acting as bailiff of Ystrad Tywi.[201]

Ieuan ap Moelwyn

One key to Ieuan's successful rise was his parentage. His father, designated in a document of 1271 as Melwyn de Bueld was one of six magnates from the Middle March who organised some twenty-five others to pledge to Prince Llywelyn forty pounds for the deliverance of one Iorwerth ap Llywelyn from the prince's prison.[202] The six men involved in gathering the twenty-five included three lords of Elfael, and two men designated as *ballivi* of Buellt and Gwerthrynion, Only Moelwyn's title remains obscure – but it is clear that he was an influential person within the lordship of Builth. Just over two decades later it was Moelwyn's son who appeared as a directing force in the same lordship. Ieuan ap Moelwyn was given as the bailiff (*rhaglaw*?) of Builth lordship at the time of the assessment of persons for the lay subsidy of one fifteenth of moveables for the tax to be collected in 1293–4.[203] By this time, of course Builth lordship was in Crown hands, as it had been since 1277, following the Treaty of Aberconwy. It is possible that Ieuan had seen, and it is certain that he had been told about, those years when Hywel ap Meurig had been entrusted with the building of the castle of Builth and the administration of the lordship, before his death in late 1281.[204] Ieuan had thus had a clear indication of the rewards which could be won by good service to the king.

By 1303 Ieuan had left Builth for another office, in the service of Edward, prince of Wales, this time further west. In October of that year, he was appointed steward of Cardiganshire, with an annual fee and the profits of four constableships, of Perfedd, Mabwynion, Creuddyn and Caerwedros. He was able to appoint a controller, Walter de Malley, Constable of Cardigan castle, to help with the administration. His tenure of this office was markedly successful: he increased the judicial revenue of the region, without unduly burdening the Welsh tenants. As a consequence, Ieuan received a reward of £10 in 1304–5.[205] He was also able to lease Maenorsilian and Maenor Lampeter in 1307–8. It is possible that he died in the last year, as he was replaced by Rhys ap Gruffudd in October 1308.

Possible local magnates

There is a significant number of men, usually in the records of the principality of South/West Wales who, though noticed only briefly, may be of significance. A sample of those is given below.

Gruffudd Crach was one of the taxors for Mabudryd in 1292, and led infantry from Cantrefmawr to the war in Scotland in late summer 1298; he may also have been a troop-leader of men from South Wales in Scotland in late 1310, and was certainly so involved in July–August 1319, when he led one hundred men from Cantrefmawr to Newcastle upon Tyne. Apart from military leadership, Gruffudd was beadle of Mabelfyw in 1302–4 and in 1310–15. He also acted as beadle of Mabudryd, in 1287–8 and 1301–5, and possibly in 1306–7. He certainly served as beadle of Mabudryd at the same time as acting in Mabelfyw in 1310–15.[206]

John ap Llywelyn acted as an official interpreter in Cardiganshire sessions in August 1348 and deputy justiciar for Sir Thomas de Bradeston, a little later in that year; he also acted as sheriff of Carmarthen in 1349–50. In 1350, he was a member of a commission charged with bringing before the king's council all those who were prosecuting appeals in derogation of a decision by the Bench that the king should have the right to present to the archdeaconry of St Davids (even though the Black Prince's council had claimed that right for the prince). John was the most prominent of the Welsh members of the commission.[207]

Ieuan ap Madog Fychan represents a somewhat puzzling case, which suggests some similarities with the situation in Flintshire. It is not so much the importance of the office that he held which establishes his importance: he was for most of the period between

1307 and 1324 the reeve of Mefenydd. Rather, it is his survival after being fined frequently for misdeeds committed. Ieuan apparently lived dangerously, being fined for misconduct several times – for failing to render account for his office of reeve in 1313, for stealing a cow in 1315, and for harbouring a criminal in 1317.[208] He was then arrested at the Llanbadarn Sessions in 1329, for wrongly appropriating extensive lands in five commotes, including Mefenydd, to the disinheritance of the king, as a result of which he could have expected the most severe penalty, but in 1331 the justice granted him 'life and limb' and commuted his sentence to one of perpetual imprisonment and a fine of £400.[209] He still owed some £80 from his time as reeve of Mefenydd, and he entered into an obligation to pay this off in instalments in 1331. It appears that some of his inherited lands and goods were sold off to help him find the £400. It is probable that once more he failed to pay off the sum he owed, for which failure his lands were forfeited in 1346. He probably died in the Black Death plague in 1349.

The south-western March

Einion Fawr and his descendants in Emlyn and Cemais, a classic case of dynastic transmission of eminence, descended from Gwilym ap Gwrwared of Cemais (fl. 1241–67).[210]

Einion Fawr ap Gwilym, a son of Gwilym ap Gwrwared, probably acquired land in Emlyn after the 1287 rising of Rhys ap Maredudd. A constable of Newcastle Emlyn about that time, and chief taxor in Newport, Cemais, in 1292, Einion held land from the king in Emlyn and Is Aeron in the period 1298–1301. He probably died in or about 1301.[211] Gwilym and Gruffudd, sons and heirs of Einion, held the same lands in 1301–12.

Gwilym ab Einion was given custody of Cardigan castle by Edward II on 17 April 1326, but was ordered to hand it over to Geoffrey Beaufou on 22 October 1327;[212] his sureties on taking office included Rhys ap Gruffudd, and his own son, Einion ap Gwilym, who must have been of some standing at that date. Gwilym ab Einion leased Llansanffraid mill for much of the

Administrative Eminence and Political Peril

period 1307–18.[213] He was the father of three sons: Einion Fychan, Gruffudd and Llywelyn.

Einion Fychan ap Gwilym held lands near Cardigan 1327–42. In 1335, he was 'provost' of Gwinionydd, the land to the north of Newcastle Emlyn. In the same year, he received land called Le Treferet at rent, for his service in Scotland.[214] An undated letter, but probably written in April 1346, shows him as responsible, with Owain ab Owain and Rhys Fychan, for raising troops in south Wales and leading them into England to join the Black Prince's army.[215]

Gruffudd ap Gwilym is little known, beyond a record of his oath of fealty to the Black Prince, 1343.[216] He may be the Gruffudd ap William/Gwilym Goch who was reeve of Anhuniog, 1335–6.

Llywelyn ap Gwilym was the best-known of the sons of Gwilym ab Einion. He, too, swore fealty to the Black Prince in 1343, in his capacity of lieutenant-constable of Newcastle, mayor of the town, and tax collector of the lordship (of Emlyn).[217] Llywelyn's eminence in the region was underscored by the fact that Dafydd ap Gwilym addressed two poems to him as his (Dafydd's) uncle; one of these was a praise poem, and the other his elegy. The former describes his chief residence as being in Emlyn, close to the river Teifi, while the elegy tells us that he had two courts, Dôl Goch and Llystyn, the latter being in Cemais.[218] In the work of his nephew Dafydd ap Gwilym (Poems 12 and 13),[219] Llywelyn appears as a learned man. Most importantly, the *marwnad* contains several veiled references to the fact that Llywelyn died by violence, most notably in its use of the proverb '*A laddo a lleddir*'.[220] Thomas Parry mounted a serious investigation of Llywelyn's demise, in which he made good use of a paper by Gruffydd Evans, which may bring us very close to the context and culprit. Parry notes that during the time when Llywelyn was acting constable the castle had been much neglected and an unfavourable report on it was made in 1340. In 1346, the lordship was handed over to Richard de la Bere on the condition that he would restore the castle and stock it with arms and provisions, all at his own cost, a task achieved by 1349. It is possible that Llywelyn had been removed from office at Newcastle by 1346 or soon afterwards. Gruffudd Evans had suggested that 'the helpless tone of the lines which speak of judgement may suggest that Llywelyn had met his death at the hands of a powerful nobleman and his followers and that the nobleman (sc. Richard de la Bere) was too well befriended to be reached except by the judgement of God'.[221] It seems likely that, while in life Llywelyn ap Gwilym was fully representative of 'the men of position', his death reflected the trend to violence and lawlessness which seems to have overtaken so much of Wales in the middle of the fourteenth century.[222]

Chapter 4

Reflections on the Survey of the New Elite and the 'Men of Position'

It is quite possible that it is only inadequacies in the evidence that have deprived some of those who appear in Chapter 3 of a place in the select group identified in Chapter 2 as the new elite of Welsh magnates in the period after 1295, and that further research will lead to some adjustment of the balance between the two chapters.[1] Nevertheless, the distinction between those whose activities had national impact or implications and those who were important at a more restricted area remains valid.

Chapter 3, surveying 'the men of position', is organised in terms of regional blocs, partly for convenience, but also because this reflects in significant measure the 'on the ground' realities of the period. Rees Davies, writing about the March, noted that the Welsh magnates were 'not only the recipients of seignorial [to which we might add "princely" or "royal"] bounty and office; they were also in their turn the focus of more local loyalties, services and rewards'.[2] This statement applies equally well to the situation in the lands of the Principality and territories like Flintshire and the lordship of Builth. It should be emphasised that the population of Wales in the period 1295–c.1349 was relatively small, at c.250,000–300,00, of whom a small proportion were English burgesses brought in after the conquest and in some cases earlier agrarian settlers,[3] who lived in significant measure beyond the control of Welsh local officials. If we guess at a quarter of a million as the figure for the Welsh population of Wales we shall not be far wrong – before the arrival of Black Death when a significant fall took place.[4] Now this perspective helps us to better understand something of the impact of the activities of the new elite and the men of position, in particular with regard to their role in arraying, paying and leading recruits for the royal armies of the post-1295 campaigns as well as in their positions of political, social and sometimes cultural prominence. They were brought into contact with, and were recognisable to, a significant element of the people of each region of Wales particularly when arraying, organising and leading many hundreds or even thousands of troops. If we make a very rough guess at a figure of around 50,000 adult males at any one time,[5] it is easy to see that the admittedly exceptional 10,900 Welsh infantry calculated by Adam Chapman, or some 42 per cent of the total army assembled by Edward I for the Falkirk campaign of 1297, will have represented a very significant proportion of the active Welsh male population.[6] It must be borne in mind that the estimate of the number of adult males makes no allowance for those who were sick or suffering from injuries or were otherwise physically or for other reasons, such as serious psychological disturbance, unsuitable for military action, or who managed to absent themselves from the process of array and subsequent service. Those members of the Welsh elite who were prominent in military leadership will therefore have been known as leaders to a large element in the adult male population of Wales.

It may be objected that in one crucial respect the men whose careers are examined in this book were markedly unlike the 'princes' of the twelfth and thirteenth centuries: they appear most frequently in a context of service to English kings and great Marcher lords, whereas the 'princes' are usually pictured as enjoying considerable autonomy. This is a reasonable objection to the title of the book, which is perhaps one that requires examination. The use of the term 'princes' to describe Welsh rulers of the central Middle Ages is a form of shorthand which obscures the distinction between those few who actually employed the designation *princeps* in their titles,[7] and the much larger number who were not of sufficient power to be regarded as princes, and who used, if they employed any designation other than their name, the term *dominus* or lord. These lords often appear as high-level envoys or agents of the princes. And even the princes themselves often appear in the role of servants of English kings whom they accept as their overlords. Two of the clearest examples of this relate to Rhys ap Gruffudd (the Lord Rhys), ruler of Deheubarth for most of the second half of the twelfth century, and Llywelyn ab Iorwerth, ruler of north Wales in most of the four decades before his death in 1240. In 1171, following a period of tense relations between the Lord Rhys and Henry II of England, the Welsh chronicle *Brut y Tywysogyon* records that the two rulers were reconciled, and Rhys 'found grace and favour before the king', so that in the next year, when Henry was about to set out for France, 'the king left Rhys ap Gruffudd as justice on his behalf in all Deheubarth'.[8] Rhys's activity in fulfilment of his role as royal justice can be glimpsed in his gathering of Welsh rulers from the southern parts of Wales who had in some way displeased Henry, for a conference at Gloucester in 1175.[9] In the case of Llywelyn ab Iorwerth, perhaps the greatest of the dynasty of princes who ruled Gwynedd and dominated much of Wales in the thirteenth century, the most striking case in which he was pictured as a servant of the English king occurs in 1218. In March of that year, Llywelyn, designated as prince of North Wales, had met with the young king Henry III, his regent William Marshal, and members of the king's council at Worcester. Here agreements were made on a number of topics, including the prince's custody of the castles of Carmarthen and Cardigan, and their appurtenant territories, during Henry's minority. In the record of the agreement, Llywelyn undertook to hold the king's courts in those lands, 'as the king's bailiff'.[10]

These are merely outstanding and explicit examples of the way in which even Welsh princes might be employed as royal officers. Other Welsh rulers were also frequently used by English governments to further royal policy. Thus, in 1254 Gruffudd ap Gwenwynwyn, lord of southern Powys, was included in a group of English magnates appointed by Henry III to hear and determine disputes between Llywelyn ap Gruffudd and his younger brother Dafydd.

In many respects, therefore, Welsh rulers of the twelfth and thirteenth centuries, though sometimes assuming the dignity and powers of princes, had been accustomed to the control frequently exercised by English kings. In the March, those kings might also be able to make their will prevail and to assert mastery. The fate after 1208 of William de Braose, his wife and eldest son provides a simple illustration of the fate that might befall even an apparently mighty Marcher lord who came into collision with the king.[11] But in some ways, the great Marcher lords, no longer needing royal support against the ambitions of the greater Welsh princes, entered into the fullness of their powers in the fourteenth century. With English kings often preoccupied against opposition from within England, and facing wars, notably in Scotland and France, the Marcher lords may have seemed able to consolidate their supremacy in much of Wales. The extent of that supremacy was brilliantly explored by Rees Davies.[12]

Some of the greatest of the Welsh elite figures examined in this study were the agents or servants of the English kings or, in the period 1301–7, and from 1343 onwards, the English princes of Wales. But others operated under at least the nominal lordship of the powerful English Marcher lords, such as the de Bohuns, the Clares or the Mortimers, the FitzAlans or the Warennes. In one crucial respect Rees Davies over-estimated the degree of power wielded by the great Marcher lords. It was indeed very impressive, but it did have its limits, as Edward I had demonstrated in dealing with Earl Gilbert de Clare, lord of Glamorgan and Earl Humphrey de Bohun, lord of Brecon in the 1290s, and even his son had shown in 1322. But more significant, and perhaps more misleading than that, Davies claimed that in the March 'the Marcher lord provided the only major focus of service and reward: there was no alternative ladder of royal service and patronage'.[13] The important point here is that the Welsh magnates of the March were often able to move into royal service, and to balance their obligations to lords with those to kings and princes. At times, a conflict of interest between the monarch and Marcher lords effectively gave to the Welsh magnates the obligation and the privilege of making a choice. This was the case with figures such as Philip ap Hywel, or his brother Master Rees ap Hywel; it was also evident in the career of Madog ap Llywelyn of Maelor,

Reflections on the Survey of the New Elite and the 'Men of Position'

and applied to several of the figures whose careers were examined in Chapter 3. It is important to remember that members of the Welsh magnate class in the March often moved in the same circles as those in royal or Principality lands, while both groups can be identified as undertaking identical missions, such as leading troops in the royal interest or serving as members of the same commissions.

It may seem odd to include in this biographic survey several men who are usually pictured primarily or entirely as rebels or malcontents. But figures such as Gruffudd Fychan de la Pole and Llywelyn Bren were of course not desperate nonentities, but were in contrast established regional leaders who rebelled because they were being denied the respect or position that was their due.[14] It is, however, to be borne in mind that men not thought of primarily as rebels might be caught on the 'wrong' side in political crises: men such as Sir Gruffudd Llwyd, or Master Rees ap Hywel were imprisoned for significant periods, while Sir Rhys ap Gruffudd was obliged to flee for his life on two occasions, and Philip ap Hywel had narrowly escaped a long imprisonment.[15] It had indeed been a frequent occurrence in the 'Age of the Princes' for senior members of ruling houses to suffer incarceration or dispossession. Such were the cases of Cadwaladr ap Gruffudd and even the Lord Rhys, of Gruffudd ap Rhys, of Gruffudd ap Llywelyn and Owain ap Gruffudd and many more. In reality, there may be little to distinguish the story of a successful career from that of the story of a doomed rebel. The marks of honour and worldly advancement might lead to one recipient's loyalty to, or integration into, the dominant structures of the state, while similar or equivalent accolades might prompt another to a greater sense of self-worth and increased sensitivity to real or imagined slights. For some, that is, success might lead to satisfaction with their lot, while for others it might lead to intransigence or rejection of those who did not give them the respect due to them. It had been so for the princes and would-be princes, and so it was for their successors amongst the powerful men who were, as Rees Davies noted, referred to by the poets as the *uchelwyr*, the *barwniaid*,[16] whose residences were *llysoedd*,[17] men who on occasion moved easily amongst the greatest of the realm yet whose exploits, however exaggerated, as slaughterers of the English were as vividly depicted by the poets as those of the princes had been.

It must finally be stressed that this survey makes no claim to be comprehensive. The biographic cases set out in this book are indicative of the presence in the fourteenth century of a native class which provided cultural, administrative and military leadership within Welsh society, at the regional, and sometimes at something approaching the national, level. Sometimes the evidence as it stands is insufficient to allow any more than an educated guess that given individuals were of sufficient status and achievement to be included in a survey of the men of position. In some cases, those individuals' names and the few scraps of career-data currently available are included, in the hope that future research may add more information about some of the more poorly evidenced figures noticed in this volume.

Let us turn now to the principal characteristics of the Welsh magnate class of the two generations after 1295. An important aspect of the new elite and indeed several of the men of position is the possession, in some degree, of royal Welsh blood. The members of the new elite could all boast real or contrived 'royal' blood: thus, Sir Gruffudd Llwyd and Sir Rhys ap Gruffudd were descended from the Lord Rhys, for their common ancestor, Gruffudd ab Ednyfed Fychan was descended from Rhys by way of his mother, Gwenllian, who was a daughter of the great southern ruler.[18] Sir Morgan ap Maredudd was also descended from the Lord Rhys, through the latter's son Maredudd (d. 1201) who was Sir Morgan's great-grandfather. In addition, through his father's mother Gwerfyl, Morgan was descended from the lords of Gwynllŵg.[19] Madog ap Llywelyn of Maelor could trace his ancestry through his mother Angharad, whose father was Maredudd ap Madog, lord of Iâl, whose father in turn was Madog ap Gruffudd, ruler of northern Powys and descendant of Madog ap Maredudd, king of the Powysians.[20]

If we turn to descendants of Hywel ap Meurig of the Middle March, his sons Philip ap Hywel and Master Rees ap Hywel, and his grandson Sir Philip Clanvowe represent a somewhat different case of princely or 'royal' descent. A genealogical tradition shows them as descended from one of Lord Rhys's most eminent sons, Rhys Gryg, lord of Ystrad Tywi. Though the genealogy is demonstrably a fiction, the important point is that the family found it necessary to have it made. It is difficult to estimate when the genealogy was concocted, but it was probably when it was helpful in dealing with the people of South Wales, and at a period sufficiently remote from Rhys Gryg (d. 1234) and his son Rhys Mechyll (d. 1244) for the falsity of the links not to be noticed. A point in the 1330s when the family was developing serious ambitions in Wales might be a possible point at which an initial version of the genealogy may have been constructed. The important element in this scenario is that all of the figures discussed in this chapter had, or could be presented as having had, dynastic links with major Welsh rulers of the twelfth and thirteenth centuries. In that sense they could well be considered heirs to the princes.

Similar royal descent characterises many in the category of 'men of position'. This applies, for example, to Tudur Hen and his descendants, for their ancestor Goronwy ab Ednyfed could claim descent from the Lord Rhys; Llywelyn Bren was a son of the last Welsh lord of Senghennydd, captured by Gilbert the Red Earl in 1267, and subsequently imprisoned in the earl's castle in Kilkenny. Gruffudd ap Dafydd of Hendwr in Edeirnion, and his kin among the barons of Edeirnion were descended from Madog ap Maredudd, king of the Powysians 1132–60 of the lineage of Bleddyn ap Cynfyn. It was from Bleddyn ap Cynfyn, too, that Ynyr Fychan of Nannau and his descendants traced their pedigree.

A further respect in which broad similarities between many of the men examined in this study can be detected is their involvement, in various ways, in the assembling, paying or leading of large numbers of Welsh fighting men in the very late thirteenth and early fourteenth centuries, most often in the service of the English kings in their widespread wars, in Wales itself, but also in England, Scotland, France and Flanders. Into this category come all of the seven men designated in Chapter 2 as 'the new elite', and several of those in Chapter 3. The total number of men discussed in Chapters 2 and 3 comes to around eighty, of whom almost exactly half can be identified as officials raising, acting as paymasters to or leading troops, and sometimes a combination of these roles, for the most part in support of royal military ventures. This high proportion – and it is quite possible that future discoveries will increase this proportion – reflects both the emphasis on military involvement amongst the leaders of Welsh society in the post-1295 decades and the significant militarisation of the Welsh people in the first half of the century.

A notable feature of the new elite and the men of position is the extent to which they tended to be members of clearly defined compact family groups, whether those which had been famously prominent for several decades, a category in which the descendants of Ednyfed Fychan in North Wales as well as lands in the southern principality fell, and they cover men such as Tudur Hen ap Goronwy and his son and grandsons, the son of Sir Gruffudd Llwyd, and possibly the son of Sir Rhys ap Gruffudd, somewhat confusingly known as Sir Rhys ap Gruffudd the Younger, as well as Rhys ap Roppert of Flintshire. Somewhat similar in terms of fame and importance – however different their career trajectory as a family – were the descendants of Hywel ap Meurig in the Middle March and in South Wales. Sons of Hywel included William, who seems to disappear from the records before 1295,[21] but whose son Philip founded the line of Clanvowes, Philip ap Hywel, who apparently died without heirs of his body, but whose heir was Philip Clanvowe, and Master Rees, who certainly did produce children, of whom his principal heir, Philip ap Rees or Philip de Bronllys, was a significant figure, as was his brother Ieuan ap Rees. The Clanvowe branch of the family continued into the fifteenth century, though it became ever more anglicised. But we can also add descendants of Gwilym ap Gwrwared in the south-western March, who ran through several generations of prominent figures in Cemais and Emlyn, in a somewhat similar way to the members of the Hendwr branch of the barons of Edeirnion, while even the sons of Llywelyn Bren of Senghennydd survived imprisonment in the Tower, the execution of their father in 1318 and the danger of death in the royalist reaction of 1322, to emerge as prominent in the pursuit and capture of Edward II in 1327, and to enjoy their restoration to their hereditary lands, while one of them, Gruffudd, became constable and forester of Senghennydd.[22]

It must be acknowledged that there are distinct limits to the uniformity of the backgrounds and the activities of those Welsh notables examined in the present book. It is first and foremost in its coverage a work on men. Women are in some cases clearly important, but not in ways that provide evident, and still less consistent, keys to the careers of the men involved. Some of the women in the families of the men examined in the previous chapters were of English Marcher birth and connections. That may have been the case with Matilda, the wife of Hywel ap Meurig, and probable (though not certain) mother of Hywel's sons. Sir Gruffudd Llwyd's mother was a Lestrange, and Sir Rhys ap Gruffudd's wife was a Somerville. Amongst the 'men of position', English family members followed a similar course. Not surprisingly, members of the ruling house of Afan found wives from the Marcher community, who no doubt helped to reinforce the dynasty's practice of moving from the Welsh patronymic system to the adoption of the name 'de Avene'. Leisan de Avene, and possibly his father Morgan, married members of the de Sully family.

As may perhaps be expected, many of the New Elite and some of the 'men of position' are recorded as having made 'good' marriages or as having impressive dynastic links through a wife or mother – that is those which linked them to potentially helpful local or regional magnates amongst the Welsh community.[23] But in the majority of cases, though we may have suspicions, we are unable to be confident about the influence of a mother's or a wife's family on the career of a 'man of position'.

A potential technique for estimating the significance of the New Elite and the Men of Position identified above

Beyond the common characteristics of the members of the New Elite, outstandingly influential and powerful by almost any criteria, and the Men of Position whose role may on occasion be more difficult to assess, there arises the question of how we may measure the importance of members of these groups, relative to other members of Welsh society. One important way of assessing the importance of the men whose careers have been outlined in the foregoing chapters is to examine them, principally from the standpoint of their perceived military or administrative competence, in the context of major political/military crises. A particularly significant example of this approach is the situation in the initial months of 1322 – particularly in February of that year. The background to this investigation is the revival in Edward II's fortunes after a period in 1321 when the opposition to Edward's governance, which had crystallised around Thomas of Lancaster, Humphrey de Bohun, and the Mortimers of Chirk and Wigmore and other baronial leaders, had seized the political initiative, and had secured the exile of the Despensers, father and son, the king's favourites. But the king had refused to give way to his opponents and had managed to rebuild his position. In late 1321, he began to gather forces to restore his full regal powers, a process which culminated in the return of the Despensers and Edward's preparation for a military showdown with his baronial opponents. Those preparations were well under way in January and February 1322 and involved both very active recruiting of forces from the royal counties and the Marcher lordships of Wales, as well as the sending out of orders for the arrest and detention of the leaders of resistance in the lordships.

By combining the figures relating to the orders for the array of troops to be sent to the king, and those, however incomplete, for the arrest of his opponents, we may obtain a picture of some of the more prominent leaders on both sides in Wales of what had become a widespread civil war. We need to be aware that the orders were issued in some haste, and are therefore subject to anomalies, but nevertheless they are illuminating. The figures are set out below, based particularly on entries in the Patent Roll,[24] with most personal names and place-names modernised and standardised.

Reflections on the Survey of the New Elite and the 'Men of Position'

Table 1 Orders to assemble troops in the king's service[1] 14 February 1322 and to detain those identified as against the king

Source of troops	Number of troops required	Leader(s) of troops specified[2]
Anglesey	800	**Gruffudd ap Rhys****
Caernarfon	800	Giles de Beauchamp
Merioneth	600	
Cardiganshire	600	Walter de Beauchamp
Carmarthenshire	600	**Rhys ap Gruffudd****
Cantref Bychan	300	
Cantref Mawr	350	
Ewyas Lacy	300	John Wroth
Ewyas Harold		John Wynston
Morgannwg	2,000	William Fleming
		John Norris
		Leisan d'Avene*
Gower	400	Robert de Penrees
		Hugh de Lamplugh
Brecon	400	Robert de Morby
		Meurig ap Rees*
Cedewain	400	William de la Beche
Ceri		Madog Foel
Hay & Huntington	500	John de Sexton
		Adam de Walwayn
Pencelli, Blaenllyfni	650	Robert de Morby and Bronllys
		John de Dene
		Richard le Mareschall
Powys	1,500	Robert de Sapy
		Madog de Hendwr*
		Gruffudd ab Owain
		Madog Llwyd
Glamorgan (English)	1,000	**Llywelyn ap Cynwrig***
		William de Oversham
		William de Grey

115

Source of troops	Number of troops required	Leader(s) of troops specified[2]
		William le Walsh
		Philip del Herber
		John Lovel
		Reginald de Somerton
Dyffryn Clwyd	400	**Llywelyn ap Madog***
Radnor	200	Walter le Gras
		Cardigan [? Cadwgan] ap Hywel
Knockin	50	Madog de Hinderston
Ellesmere	100	Llywelyn Foel
Bromfield & Yale	700	**Madog ap Llywelyn****
		Iorwerth ap Dafydd
Land of the lady Audley	50	Madog de Hinderston
Cydweli & Carnwyllion	400	William le Blound
		Robert de Huntley
Monmouth and Three Castles	300	" "
Glasbury & Clifford	60 and all men at arms	Thomas de Thorn, bailiff of Thomas of Lancaster
Pembroke and Haverford	800	Walter de Beauchamp **Rhys ap Gruffudd****

Notes:
1. Men identified as members of the group described in Chapter 2 as the New Elite are marked with two asterisks, while those in the more local or regional category, designated in Chapter 3 as 'men of position' are marked with a single asterisk. All those featured in Chapters 2 and 3 are given in bold.
2. It seems possible that there is real significance in the order in which the leaders of troops are noticed when more than one person is specified. It may indicate superiority of the person placed first.

Reflections on the Survey of the New Elite and the 'Men of Position'

On 15 February 1322, orders to pay troop leaders were as follows:

> Chamberlain of North Wales to pay **Gruffudd ap Rhys** and Giles de Beauchamp
> Chamberlain of South Wales to pay Walter de Beauchamp and **Rhys ap Gruffudd**
> Chamberlain of Chester to pay **Cynwrig Sais** and **Bleddyn ab Ithel**.

To these appointments to gather and pay troops, we can also add the orders to arrest and detain those who were clearly against the king. One such mandate is a writ of aid for Robert de Morby, issued on 16 February 1322,[25] charged with the arrest of the following in the middle March:

> **Master Rees ap Hywel**** and **Philip**** his brother
> **Meurig ap Rees***[26] and **William ap Roys*** (sic) his brother
> John le Receivour of Brecon
> **Philip de Clanvowe**** and Hywel ap Dafydd of the land of Kington
> Walter ap Dafydd
> **Ieuan ap Rees fil Master Rees***[27]
> John Havard and Philip Havard, his brother
> John Parpoynt, Philip Parpoynt and Hywel ap Dafydd of the land of Brecon
> John Ragoan and William, his son
> William ap Gruffudd and Gruffudd ap Hywel of the land of Ewyas
> Richard de Baskerville and his son.

Several days later, however, a further, but in parts similar, list was issued by the king. Once again, the recipient was Robert de Morby, now described as the keeper of the land of Brecon.[28] He was to arrest the following and deliver them to Bristol castle:

> Lleucu, late the wife of **Llywelyn Bren***[29]

Heirs to the Princes

Griffith ap Llywelyn*, Jack ap Llywelyn, Henry ap Llywelyn, Meurig ap Llywelyn, William ap Llywelyn, Roger ap Llywelyn and Llywelyn le Yong, sons of the said Llywelyn Bren
Philip Parpount and his brothers
John Havard and his brothers
Hywel ap Dafydd of the Forest
Philip de Clanvowe
Meurig ap Rees
Hywel ap Dafydd and his sons
Huel Pal (*sic*)
Miles Pychard.

Note also the following order of 22 April 1322 for the arrest of persons in Glamorgan: Writ of aid for John Inge, sheriff of the land of Glamorgan, appointed to arrest Meurig Cammoys, William de Derneford, John Beneyt, John de la More, and Seisyll ab Iorwerth, and to take them to the said land and keep them in prison there until further order.[30] See also a writ to the keeper of the land of Usk, to arrest William de Stretton and Meurig de Cam[m]oys.[31]

A list of somewhat similar mandates issued by Edward II, in even more serious circumstances, is provided, for mainly south-eastern parts of Wales (with the significant exceptions of the principality-wide mandates to Gruffudd ap Rhys (Sir Gruffudd Llwyd) and Rhys ap Gruffudd), in the autumn of 1326, following the landing on 24 September of Queen Isabella and Roger Mortimer of Wigmore, bent on replacing Edward II with his young son, the future Edward III.[32] The mandates were sent out without demands for specific numbers of troops to be raised, but simply directed to the addressees to raise the people of a specified territory against the invaders (or some similar formula) as set out in Table 2.

Apart from some discussion of specific details – mostly dealt with in the notes to the lists above – there are observations about individuals and secondly there are some more fundamental and perhaps far-reaching points to consider.

Reflections on the Survey of the New Elite and the 'Men of Position'

Table 2 Mandates to raise men against the invaders in 1326

Date	Leaders	Specified territory
28 September 1326[1]	**Rhys ap Gruffudd****	South Wales
	Gruffudd ap Rhys**	North Wales
10 October 1326[2]	John Daniel	Keeper of Radnor, *Luggerness* and Pembridge
	Cadwgan ap Hywel	Keepers of Maelienydd
	Dafydd Fychan	
	William ap Rees	Keeper of Elfael
12 October 1326[3]	Robert Clement	Brecknock
	Maredudd ab Einion	
	Walter de Pedwardine	
	Maredudd ab Einion	Talgarth
	William ap Rees	Elfael
	Llywelyn ap Meurig	
	Robert Clement	Hay
27 October 1326	Hywel ab Iorwerth ap Gruffudd	Machen & Gwynllwg
	Hywel ap Dafydd	
	Ieuan ap Meurig	Neath & Kilvey
	Ieuan ap Morgan	
	Rhun ap Goronwy	Senghennydd[4]
	Llywelyn ap Madog ap Hywel	
	Hywel ab Iorwerth ab Llywarch	
	John Beneyt	Usk, Tregrug, Edelygon
	Ieuan ap Philip	
	Hywel Fychan ap Hywel ab Einion*[5]	Abergavenny
	Hywel ab Iorwerth Fychan	
	Llywelyn ap Cynwrig*	Meisgyn, Glynrhondda, Talyfan
	Dafydd ap Meurig	Ruthin, Glynogwr
	Madog Fychan*	Tir Iarll, Avenesland
29 October 1326	**Rhys ap Gruffudd****	County of Pembroke
	Robert de Penrees	Land of Gower
	Robert de Pembridge	

119

Heirs to the Princes

Date	Leaders	Specified territory
	Robert de Penrees	Haverford town and parts adjacent
	Owain ap Madog*	Morgannwg
	Dafydd ap Meurig	
30 October 1326	Philip Fychan	Caerleon & Edelygon
	Hywel ap *Madanewe*	
	John Boneyt	Usk
	Hywel ab Iorwerth ap Gruffudd	Machen and Gwynllwg
	Hywel ap Dafydd ab Adam	
	Hywel ab Iorwerth ab Llywarch	Senghennydd[6] and Cibwr
	Ieuan ab Rhun	
	Llywelyn ap Madog ap Hywel	
	Dafydd ap Meurig ap Hywel[7]	Meisgyn and Glynrhondda
	Thomas ap Cynwrig	Talyfan, Ruthin, Glynogwr
	William ap Philip	
	Madog Fychan*	Wigmore, Tawe Coety[8]
	Einion ap Meurig Fychan	

Notes:
1. *Calendar of Patent Rolls, 1324–27*, p. 331.
2. *Calendar of Patent Rolls, 1324–27*, p. 326.
3. *Calendar of Patent Rolls, 1324–27*, p. 326.
4. Seint Genyth in the text, but we can confidently ignore this odd-looking name and replace it by comparison with the place-name to which note 6 evidently refers.
5. Given in the text as Hywel ap Fychan ap Hywel ab Einion, an obvious error. This is a grandson of that Einion Sais who was active in the lordship of Brecon as an opponent of Prince Llywelyn in the 1270s. He reputedly held the castle of Penpont.
6. Comparison of the names of the addressees of this mandate with those of the addresses of those raising troops from 'Seint Genyth' on 27 October and given above makes it clear that Seint Genyth is a corruption of Senghennydd. The Ieuan ap Rhun given here looks like a son of the Rhun ap Goronwy of p. 119 above, perhaps suggesting that this latter figure had died or been wounded and replaced by a son.
7. Probably to be identified as the Dafydd ap Meurig to whom instructions were issued on 27 and 29 October.
8. This is almost certainly the place hidden by the designation as Cottisland, found in the text.

Reflections on the Survey of the New Elite and the 'Men of Position'

Broad conclusions from the lists of Welsh supporters and opponents of Edward II in 1322 and 1326

As a preliminary to consideration of the significance of the records of developments in 1322 and 1326 set out above, it must be emphasised that in the circumstances of the hasty gathering of royal forces in the former year, and of the desperate situation in 1326, some hasty decisions about the selection of troop leaders may have been made and a number of unfamiliar names may be encountered.

The appointments include several little-known or otherwise unknown figures from peripheral areas – small areas outside Wales and hardly to be counted as lying in the March, yet containing a significant proportion of Welsh inhabitants. Of little more than marginal importance were lordships like Knockin, Ellesmere; in what seem to have been lands from which few troops were expected to serve the king, leaders such as Madog de Hinderston may not have been of great significance and can fairly safely be ignored. The significance of English leaders of Welsh troops has been little discussed in the present study: the reasons for selecting English leaders rather than Welsh ones may be very various, and are not normally made explicit. But some of the English leaders of troops can be identified as men who had significant interests in Wales and who were thus likely to occur to the king's advisers as 'natural' choices to be given important leadership responsibilities. This applies to Robert de Penrees, who was prominent in the areas – Gower and Haverford – where he was appointed to raise troops in 1326. A man of sufficient prominence to hold the position of deputy justiciar of South Wales, he had considerable lands in Gower, and had been granted the castle, town and lordship of Haverford in January 1326.[33] Another English leader of 1326 was Robert Clement, brother of the Geoffrey Clement who was another deputy justiciar of South Wales, but an official whose career had been cut short by his murder in the rising of 1294. Robert Clement's career was also an illustrious one, and he represents the category of English officials to whom the beleaguered Edward II would turn in the final period of his reign. There are, of course, other figures who appear with some regularity in the above lists relating to developments in 1322 and 1326 – again they were probably in the minds of advisers of the king, and so it was natural to call on them. They include Robert de Morby, tasked with heading a small group entrusted with raising 650 troops from Pencelli, Blaenllyfni and Bronllys in 1322. In the same year he was apparently senior partner with Meurig ap Rees as the recruiter of 400 men from the lordship of Brecon, and was also in charge of making high-profile arrests in the same lordship, in one mandate being described as the keeper thereof, as it was in royal hands because of the rebellion of the lord, Humphrey de Bohun.

Particularly in 1322, but also of significance in 1326, the prominence in the lists of royal recruiters of troops, or indeed as those whose arrest was ordered by the king, of men who have been listed as members of the new elite in Chapter 2 or as 'men of position' in Chapter 3, is significant, in that it provides a guideline, however limited, to their importance in the eyes of the royal government. Most importantly, the status of the representatives of the men examined in Chapters 2 and 3 may be gauged by the size of the tasks assigned to them, principally in 1322, but also to a more limited extent in the desperate times of autumn 1326.

Looking first at the king's call for troops in the early weeks of 1322, we can tally up those numbers which were to be brought to Edward by English and Welsh leaders who are not included amongst the elite figures and the men of position named in Chapters 2 and 3. These amount to some 3,410 men. In the total of troops brought by men named as members of the new elite and the men of position, we have to add a figure of 800 men, led by Cynwrig Sais and Bleddyn ab Ithel for whom the chamberlain of Chester was ordered to prepare payments.[34] The combined total is then 11,650, or over 77 per cent of the total force recruited from Wales and the March.[35] This certainly underlines the prominence, at least in the eyes of Edward II's government, of the elite group and the 'men of position' in the large areas from which troops were raised by the king in early 1322. In those limited regions where such dignitaries did not apparently exercise leadership it is clear that the men who headed the raising and moving of troops

Reflections on the Survey of the New Elite and the 'Men of Position'

were mainly English; some 2,600 men were raised and led by Englishmen, without, it seems, some degree of leadership being exercised by Welsh notables.[36] The Welsh involved as leaders of recruitment and command in those regions seem to be of little account, often operating in peripheral or relatively unimportant territories.

Of course, the recruitment for the king does not tell the whole story of the significance of the elite and men of position in military leadership. In 1322, many such men would emerge as the winners in the civil war that was being fought in Edward II's realm. But even though we do not have the sort of details of recruitment and leadership of cohorts of troops on the side of the rebel barons, we do have the evidence of orders for the arrest of those considered important figures on the rebel side.[37] For some parts of the Middle March and associated areas, the details of those who were to be arrested by royal officials are detailed and seem fairly full. The outstanding feature of these lists is the prominence in them of members of the elite and the men of position. Here we have intimations of the importance of these men on the rebel baronial side. Such men come at or near the top of the lists of those to be arrested and held. It is also assuredly significant that in the admittedly peripheral territory of Ewyas, the names of officers raising and leading troops for the king are clearly English: John Wroth and John Wynston. In contrast, the names of those to be arrested from the two lordships of Ewyas are both Welsh: William ap Gruffudd and Gruffudd ap Hywel of the land of Ewyas. This perhaps suggests an ethnic basis for the division in that region. It must be counted a possibility that these figures were of some importance in the English and Welsh communities, respectively, of Ewyas.

A rather more complex picture emerges from examination of the lists of men who were given responsibility for recruiting troops for the king to oppose the invading forces of Roger Mortimer of Wigmore, Queen Isabella and her son Edward, in autumn of 1326. The circumstances were even more fraught than they had been in 1322, with the king in the final desperate months of his reign. It is no surprise that the king called on Rhys ap Gruffudd and Sir

Gruffudd Llwyd to raise all the troops possible from South Wales and North Wales, respectively. This had been their task in 1322, and they were as stalwart in their support for Edward II in 1326. But matters are more opaque in other cases. In the evidently chaotic month from mid-September 1326, there is considerable repetition in orders issued in the name of the king – the products, perhaps, of panic, or of information that orders were not being acted upon, or an indication that the allegiance of addressees was suspect. Orders to raise troops were sent out on 10 October to the keepers of lordships in the Middle March: Radnor and adjacent lands, Maelienydd and Elfael. Those keepers seem not to have been established figures – as was perhaps to be expected in lordships which were normally in the hands of Marcher lords rather than the king. The exception was William ap Rees, almost certainly the brother of Meurig ap Rees.[38] William appears as the royal keeper of Elfael, but the order to him is repeated on 12 October, where he has been joined as a recruiter from Elfael by one Llywelyn ap Meurig, who cannot be identified with any certainty. Thereafter, William disappears from the records for several years. It is interesting, and probably ominous, that his bother Meurig ap Rees does not appear in the king's service in 1326. The two brothers had been closely associated with the baronial opposition to King Edward in 1321: on the testimony of Earl Humphrey, one of the leaders of that opposition, both had been pardoned by the king. It appears that both had at some point subsequently entered the royal service, William in Elfael and Meurig in Brecon. But it also seems that their loyalty was fragile, and it may be that first Meurig and then William stood back from support for the king in 1326. They were still alive, as they both appear in the late 1330s. But in the period of upheaval marked by the fall of Edward II and then the triumph and subsequent fall and execution of Roger Mortimer of Wigmore, they may have kept a low profile.

By late October 1326, the royal entourage, still managing to present the formal appearance of government, issuing orders and pardons, was moving across Gwent and then Glamorgan,[39] with pursuers, including the sons of Llywelyn Bren and Master Rees ap Hywel, who had been released from his imprisonment in the

Reflections on the Survey of the New Elite and the 'Men of Position'

Tower of London, out searching for Edward and Hugh Despenser the Younger. It is little wonder that some of those to whom orders to gather troops to oppose the invaders do not appear elsewhere, while in some cases there is reason to doubt whether they ever acted to fulfil those orders. The issue and rapid reissue in 1326 of orders to raise troops to oppose the invaders suggests that the royal administration had become chaotic, and the fact that many new names were included amongst those selected as recruiters hints at a guesswork born of desperation. Nevertheless, the fact that men who had appeared as responsible for selecting troops for the king in early 1322 do reappear as significant officers of Edward II in the autumn of 1326 reveals a continuing loyalty or at least an expectation of loyalty of some surviving members of the New Elite, and of the Men of Position.

In spite of the ambiguities in the evidence of the 1320s, it seems that material from that decade is especially valuable in shedding light on the significance and the prominence of the men whose careers are noted in Chapters 2 and 3. Those careers underscore the comment of Adam Chapman that 'the post-conquest *uchelwyr*, led by the descendants of Ednyfed Fychan, were inclined to rule large parts of the principality as *de facto* lords rather than servants'.[40] We can, however, go further, and recognise that that phenomenon mutatis mutandis applies not just to the principality but to virtually the whole of Wales, including the March.

Chapter 5

Things Fall Apart

For over a generation after 1295 the ascendancy of the core members of a Welsh elite, supported by a remarkable array of Welsh officials and magnates of considerable seniority throughout much of Wales, designated here as 'the men of position', had been developing steadily. Something approaching a new order at the upper levels of government and society had developed in which Welsh magnates were central. But the 1330s and the two following decades saw that new social and governmental order first eroded and subsequently grievously damaged. When we seek the causes and the course of that change, it rapidly becomes clear that a toxic mixture of forces and situations was involved, both within the upper ranks of Welsh society and in terms of the forces acting upon them. It is the purpose of the present chapter to probe those forces and situations that brought the era commemorated in this book to a close.

The passing of an elite

In the course of the late 1320s and early 30s there were a number of deaths or effective retirements of important figures who had been central to the resurgence of prominent Welshmen after 1295. These include Master Rees ap Hywel, whose death came in 1328, soon after his release from the Tower of London and his part in the fall of Edward II. The following year saw the death of his brother Philip ap Hywel, who seems to have become less prominent in political life after the events of 1326. The tyranny of Roger Mortimer was followed soon after his execution by the deaths in 1331 of Sir Morgan ap Maredudd, after what looks like a long retirement, and that of Madog ap Llywelyn, 'the best man that ever was in Maelor'. Finally, 1335 saw the death of Sir Gruffudd Llwyd, after a period of apparent inactivity. The elimination from national life of so many leading members of the Welsh elite, mostly within a period of some seven years, assuredly marks an important caesura in Welsh political life.

Of the remaining members of the Welsh elite, Sir Philip Clanvowe was significantly involved in political and administrative activity beyond Wales in the period from the later 1330s. Although he was involved in Welsh matters in the 1340s, these were few and highly specific episodes, which did not compare with his regular, high-level and county-wide involvement in Herefordshire. He appears to have died in 1349, perhaps a victim of the Black Death. The final member of the elite group outlined in Chapter 2, Sir Rhys ap Gruffudd, survived until 1356, but his later years were clouded by signs of financial exhaustion and accusations of oppressive behaviour.

It was also the case that several members of the group of 'men of position' across Wales died at the same period as the majority of the elite. Within the period from the late 1320s to the mid-30s, we can include figures like Madog Fychan and Leisan d'Avene of Glamorgan, Gruffudd Fychan de la Pole of Powys, Goronwy ap Tudur and Llywelyn ab Adda in Gwynedd. A further list of deaths in the early 1340s can be assembled, including men such as Meurig ap Rees, Dafydd ap Cadwaladr of Bachelldre, and Llywelyn ap Madog of Dyffryn Clwyd. On occasion, the reason for the absence of one of the 'men of position' was not death but significant exclusion from Welsh territories. This was the case with Sir Philip, son of Master Rees ap Hywel, who had inherited Bronllys castle and the lordship of Cantref Selyf on Master Rees's death in 1328. Twenty years later after deteriorating relations with Earl Humphrey de Bohun, lord of Brecon, of which Cantref Selyf was a subdivision, Sir Philip was faced with Quo Warranto proceedings in the Earl's court. The result was a foregone conclusion – for Earl Humphrey was effectively both plaintiff and judge. By 1351, Sir Philip's lands of Bronllys and Cantref Selyf had been confiscated. They were then acquired by the Earl's brother, William, earl of Northampton, but Sir Philip was compensated by an exchange with Earl William, which meant his acquisition of the large and rich Shropshire manor of Shifnall (Idsall). Although Sir Philip retained some lands in the March, and although he lived until 1369, his link with Wales was in significant degree broken by 1352.[1] He had, albeit in an involuntary fashion, joined his namesake and cousin, Sir Philip Clanvowe, in moving his focus into England.

The declining need for Welsh soldiers

In the closing years of the thirteenth century and the early decades of the fourteenth, one of the defining characteristics of the Welsh people was that they were soldiers. A far higher proportion of the adult male population was involved in military campaigns led by the English kings than was the case with their counterparts in England. The Welsh levies for campaigns in Flanders, in Scotland and in France were central to the military plans of Edward I and Edward II. But in the new age of full-scale war in France under Edward III and his son Edward, the Black Prince, things were changing. A very crude measurement of the change can be had from the figures for Welsh participation in the royal armies in those two periods. Seven campaigns under Edward I and his son between 1297 and 1322 saw just short of 33,000 Welsh troops involved. In the same number of campaigns between 1334 and 1346, the number of Welsh troops employed was under 11,500.[2] These figures are rough ones; for some campaigns not included here, no reliable figures, like payrolls, exist. The totals given here must therefore be regarded as only approximations. Sometimes we must suspect that there was a considerable difference between the numbers demanded by the king and his agents and the numbers who actually served. But they tell an unmistakeable story, which amply supports the conclusion of Dr Chapman that 'by 1346, the "golden age" of the Welsh soldier had passed'.[3]

An increasingly violent society

The number of 'men of position' who survived beyond the early 1340s was small, and replacements were slow to come forward, particularly in the aftermath of the Black Death, which struck Wales c.1349. Before we consider the impact of the plague, however, we must take note of another and crucially dangerous trend in the 1340s: this was the prevalence of politically motivated violence before the Black Death. The most notorious cases took place in the northern Principality, but the incidence of violence was by no means confined to that region. Thus, Llywelyn ap Gwilym,[4] a member of the family of Dafydd ap Gwilym, no less, was apparently killed in an essentially political contest with the new lord of Emlyn, Richard de la Bere, at some point after 1346.[5]

It was, however, in the north that the more notorious events took place. It did not help regional stability when Gruffudd de la Pole, lord of Mawddwy, was removed from the shrievalty in 1331, to be replaced by Walter de Mauny (d. 1372), from Hainault. Mauny, a highly successful soldier fighting for Edward III, and to whom the king was heavily indebted, was given first the office of sheriff, and then in 1341 was granted for life, 'virtually all the revenue raised in Merioneth for which he would normally have accounted at the exchequer of Caernarfon'.[6] The power exercised by Mauny in Merioneth was frequently challenged but never successfully dismantled, so that, late in his life (in November 1370), Mauny could be described as 'lord of the county of Merioneth'.[7] It is probable that Welsh apprehensions about being forced out of offices or the prospect of offices lay behind the murder of John of Huntingdon, Mauny's deputy as sheriff in the early 1340s. This was described in 1345 in terms of Huntingdon's being killed while holding his court in the king's name when 'he was, by the assent and compassing of the leading Welshmen of the country feloniously slain, and robbed of the rolls of the king, and of all his goods and chattels'.[8] This, according to the account given by the burgesses of Caernarfon in early 1345, was just one incident, however atrocious, in a general pattern: 'many other English bailiffs and burgesses have been feloniously slain, and no remedy has

Things Fall Apart

been given; whereby the Welsh have become so proud and cruel and malicious towards the English in the said land that they dare not go anywhere for fear of death'.⁹

The fears of the English inhabitants increased by the events of 1 May 1344, as recalled by the burgesses of Rhuddlan as background to another event, which we shall investigate below. The burgesses noted that:

> on the feast of St. Philip and St. James last, when the men of Rhuddlan were at the fair of St. Asaph (Lanhelewey = Llanelwy) to do their business peacefully, all the Welshmen at the fair rose in arms and wounded several and pursued them to the town of Rhuddlan; there they made an assault on the castle and the town, and slew several men and women, and did not cease from the assault from noon until the hour of vespers [the sunset hour, quite late on 1 May – possibly about 6.00 p.m.], notwithstanding that the arms of the king and the prince were displayed, and they would not cease because of them, but attacked as strongly as before; and at eventide, when the cattle of the town came from their pasture homewards, the Welsh took them and feloniously drove them to their lands, where they still detain them.¹⁰

The murders of John de Huntingdon and those of the citizens of Rhuddlan were, however, overshadowed by that of Henry de Shaldeford and his companions in 1345. Shaldeford was the recently appointed attorney of the Black Prince in the northern Principality, who was on his way towards Denbigh with a guard of six mounted soldiers, on 14th February, when he was attacked by a large group of Welshmen. Some of his guards were killed, and the rest escaped to Denbigh; Shaldeford himself was killed. A letter written by one of the Black Prince's officials contains an early, but informed, explanation for the attack on Shaldeford:

> Henry de Shaldeford was made attorney for the prince, and on account of that office was much hated by the Welsh. When the said Henry was going towards Caernarfon, he was spied by one Tudur, the brother of Hywel ap Goronwy, who had eighty armed

Welshmen with him, and they have slain the said Henry, and one of his *vallets* is dead also, and his brothers are badly wounded.[11] The said Henry had with him only six companions on horseback, and of these two or three have come to Denbigh, and no-one knows what has become of the rest, or whether they are alive or dead.[12]

The letter quoted above was almost certainly enclosed by its initial recipient, Richard de Stafford, the Prince's steward, in a report sent on to the prince's council.[13] Stafford's report contains some additional details, with the dire comment that 'if redress is not made by the prince and his council, the Welsh will be such that it will be impossible for any Englishman or English official to dwell in these parts – and all this through the maintenance of Hywel ap Goronwy.' The specific references to Hywel ap Goronwy are notable, and will be examined further below. Richard de Stafford adds details regarding the motives for the killing: 'the reason why Henry de Shaldeford was slain was that he was my lord's attorney, and had in his possession the evidences of his father, according to which my lord has a very great loss, and so they robbed him of his commission and of all his other goods which he had with him'.

The English inhabitants of several nearby towns flew into a panic, a point that can be demonstrated by examining a few of their utterances following the killing of Henry de Shaldeford. The burgesses of Denbigh expressed their feelings in a letter to the Black Prince's council in response to Shaldeford's death. They refer to warnings from certain loyal Welshmen, that 'the Welsh have never since the conquest been so disposed as they are now to rise against their liege lord to conquer the land from him, if they can attain their purpose'. They go on to urge that 'a speedy remedy' should be found:

> for the Prince's English tenants in these parts hardly dare to go out of the towns of the franchises to plough and sow and trade; and his English bailiffs hardly dare to do their work, for fear of being slain and plundered, so numerous are the evildoers and rebels who are

outlaws in the woods, and are maintained by the greatest men of the land.[14]

At a similar time, the burgesses of Caernarfon, the seat of government in the principality, wrote to the prince and his council to lament 'the great damages and destruction' that they have suffered in the past, and still suffer daily from the malevolence and enmity of the Welsh, who seek to destroy the prince's English ministers and burgesses. In particular, and quite naturally in the aftermath of the Shaldeford murder, they single out for special mention Hywel ap Goronwy and his brother Tudur, 'who have become so powerful that no Welshman dare indict them of the death of the said Henry or of other trespasses which they commit daily against the peace'.[15]

The burgesses of Rhuddlan wrote in a similar vein, though additionally drawing special attention to the events of 1 May of the previous year as well as to the Shaldeford murder.[16] There are signs that the boroughs were either coordinating their lamentations or were following official 'guidance' in preparing them. They each, for example, make specific reference to the need for the prince to 'ordain a speedy remedy' to the current situation. The young but already accomplished Richard de Stafford, a steward to the Black Prince, wrote to the latter's council in March of 1345 to inform them that some arrests had been made, but that up to the time of writing only small fines had been imposed. He continues by writing that action is needed because of the activities of Master Hywel ap Goronwy and his brother Tudur, otherwise in a short time the council 'will have their hands full to check the malice of the country'.[17]

It is possible to detect the repercussions of the Shaldeford murder over the following months. Roger Trumwyn, the lieutenant to the justice of North Wales, reported on the new mood of some of the men being recruited for what would turn out to be the campaigns that culminated at the battle of Crecy in 1346. In May of 1345 he wrote, explaining that, having been ordered to select 250 spearmen and archers to be led to Southampton, he had encountered some problems. The men of Caernarfonshire and of Anglesey had responded obediently; they were inspected, arrayed and ready to march. With those from Merioneth, however, it was a different story: they came as far as the Conwy ferry, but they 'would not cross the ferry or enter the town of Conwy to take their wages, but disobediently remained at the said ferry, so that by their default the march was delayed, nor would they in any way be intendant to the mandates of the prince or of his justice.'[18] As if this recalcitrance on the part of the men of Merioneth were not enough, the rest of Trumwyn's report is decidedly ambivalent.

> As to the men of the other lordships of North Wales, they will be ready whenever the mandate comes to them, except the lord of the land of Powys, who will not obey the mandates of the prince or of his justice of North Wales. And the other lords of the land make great noise, alleging that their men should not go out of their lordships before they have been paid their wages within the lordships.

Trumwyn went on with a dire warning that, if the men recruited from Anglesey and Caernarfonshire should go out of the land, great mischief might come, for four ships had come along the coast of Caernarfon, and, when Trumwyn's garrisons had turned out to try to arrest the crews, the latter had shot at them, with 'unrecognized arrows, not like the arrows of England'. To make matters even more serious, the next development was the appearance of nine ships, which Trumwyn understood to be from foreign lands spying out the land to make attacks.

It looks as though foreign intervention, taking advantage of widespread banditry and a distinctly truculent atmosphere in North Wales and the northern March, appeared imminent in the early summer of 1345. The situation seems to have been even more tense, in the light of the closing section of Trumwyn's report.

> If the prince decides to have another levy from the said land (i.e. from the northern Principality), it would be well to send an Englishman to be their leader by commission of the court, for the Welsh now

chosen say that they were never led by a Welshman since the death of a certain Sir Gruffudd Llwyd, who was a Welshman and a man of the court: and the Welshmen make the request. If the court considers that they should be led by a Welshman, it would be well to order that such leaders be chosen from amongst those who hold by franchise of barony in the said land, and not from among men of lesser estate.

The above final comments in Trumwyn's report seem more than a little Delphic. In the light of widespread ethnic tensions before and after the Shaldeford murder, it appears very odd to see a suggestion that Welsh levies would welcome English leadership. But it is possible that the Welsh troops were reckoning that an English gentry or noble leader would prove more effective in dealing with problems in English regions through which they had to pass to get to the ports, or even in French communities once they had crossed the Channel. The Welsh view may also reflect a belief that the most obvious Welsh leaders of troops may well have been mixed up in the recent murders and therefore were ineligible for leadership appointments.[19] There is also more than a hint that the Welsh troops believed that the quality of Welsh leadership had been significantly reduced since the death of Sir Gruffudd Llwyd.[20]

Perhaps an apt verdict on the events of 1345 is provided by the prince's chamberlain, John de Pirye, writing to the prince's council, perhaps on the very day on which the Shaldeford murder took place:

> there has now happened one of the greatest mischiefs that has ever happened in north Wales by the death of a man, and that is that Henry de Shaldeford, your lieutenant, has been traitorously slain near the house of Master Hywel ap Goronwy, this Monday after dinner, by Tudur ap Goronwy and the men of Master Hywel, who have long been lying in wait for him … The cause of his death was no other than that he was my lord's attorney in North Wales … and all the great men of North Wales, clerks and others were parties to the scheme, as will certainly be found since they feared him because

he had more knowledge than any other man of those who have disinherited my lord.[21]

Pirye's report is a very hurried but seemingly accurate and perceptive one. In particular, his reference to all the great men of North Wales being party to it, can be in part at least confirmed by looking at the list of those attainted of conspiracy or of felony. Well over seventy names are included, and they do indeed include those of several of the 'great men' of North Wales in that number. Senior members of the clergy are included, amongst them the dean of St Asaph, the abbot of Conwy, the archdeacon of Bangor, his brother the dean of Llên, as well as two future archdeacons of Anglesey, Ieuan ap Sir Gruffudd Llwyd and Master Hywel ap Goronwy himself. Several past and future senior governmental officials are there, including Hywel ap Henri, a former deputy sheriff of Caernarfonshire, and several members of Wyrion Eden.

The consequence of developments such as the Shaldeford murder and the other events in the north was, it seems, a sharpening of tensions between the Welsh population and the officials set over them. In 1348, the prince's council ordered arrests to be made:

> on complaint by the prince's tenants and bondmen in the parts of North Wales that the bailiffs and ministers in those parts have taken collections and *commorth* from them, and inflicted divers other hardships on them, in spite of the fact that this was forbidden by the prince's justices lately in eyre in those parts.[22]

It was not only in the north of Wales that a marked increase in lawlessness was noticeable. In August 1347 it was noted in the price's register that:

> Sir Thomas de Bradestan, justice of South Wales, is staying in the prince's service abroad, so that he cannot this time be present in person at the sessions in those parts, and the prince has heard that many extortions, damages, injuries, felonies, misprisions and

other trespasses have been done in the principality of South Wales through failure to hold the sessions which ought to have been held there.[23]

Suspicions of the Welsh at the level of the prince's council are revealed by the order to the steward of Cardiganshire and keeper of Cardigan castle to remove from office 'at once' Adam ap Llywelyn, a Welshman, whom he had made his lieutenant in the office of steward 'in contravention of the ordinance made by Edward I on his conquest of Wales that no Welshman should have the keeping of a castle or other office of charge in those parts'.[24]

The impact of the Black Death

It can hardly be denied that the atmosphere of government was becoming more than a little toxic in the 1340s. The situation was of course made radically worse by the onset of the Black Death in 1349. We have to recognise that, as Matthew Stevens has pointed out:

> it is a great shame that no modern, systematic study of the Black Death in Wales has yet been undertaken. Estimates of plague mortality are notoriously difficult, principally because historians must make estimates from the proxy data such as clerical mortality, fallen rents, and inheritance taxes, but a death-rate of at least a third of the population is generally accepted for the first outbreak of plague, and suits the limited Welsh data.[25]

Those data tend to show that the aftermath of plague was a sharp rise in labourers' wages, even if that rise was not as pronounced as it was in England – where wages tended to double as opposed to what appears to have been a 50 per cent rise in Wales. Such a rise gives us a picture of a lordly class, in Stevens's memorable phrase, 'sourly inconvenienced by that increase'.[26] On the other hand, the same writer emphasises that, for most people, wage labour formed only a small proportion of their income. Given the dearth of suitable evidence, it is difficult to detect clear indications, such as exist for England, of a fall in grain prices in the second half of the fourteenth century. There is thus little sign of a pronounced improvement in peasants' standards of living in the second half of the century. Lords were forced by the fall in population and falling rents to seek other means of maintaining their income, including use of 'the powerful role of judicial lordship and arbitrary taxation in Wales [which] would expose peasants to offsetting exploitation'.[27] A device employed by landlords with increasing frequency, beginning before the onset of plague but intensified thereafter, was the 'farming' of offices, whereby the 'farmer' purchased, often by auction, the right to carry out the functions of a specific official for a given sum – often the winning auction bid – and to raise as much money as possible from the office by way of such methods as exacting payments for breaches of rules enforced by the 'farmer'. It is fairly clear that, as Dr Stevens has noted:

> farming [of offices] became widespread in the first decades of the fourteenth century and intensified after the Black Death, increasing tenants' financial burdens while, in the long term, lords' net incomes nevertheless continued to fall largely owing to their own officials' neglect and fraud, leading cyclically to yet further attempts at decreasingly effective revenue-raising exploitation.[28]

Such are elements of the background to any attempt to gauge the socio-political impact of the Black Death on the upper echelons of Welsh society. There can be little doubt that the plague brought with it consequences which marked significant new developments or accentuated existing ones in the dynamics of the Welsh economy. Most significantly, perhaps, the plague and its consequences changed attitudes in Wales. Office-holders tended to become more exploitive of those whom they were set to govern, and ethnic rifts were deepened, which had the effect of denying opportunities for advancement to Welshmen of talent and good family. The narrowing of opportunities for advancement to ambitious Welshmen was perhaps the most significant impact of the Black Death within Wales. We can take as illustrative of this process the developments at one town in the north-east. We have seen that, at some point after the revolt of 1294–5, Edward I had confirmed their liberties and customs to the Welshmen of Hope and Hopedale in Flintshire. In the case of Hope borough, after rather more than half a century later, some two years after the onset of plague, it was the turn of the town's English burgesses to be privileged. In 1351, the latter were granted by Edward III a new borough charter specifically excluding Welsh burgesses, whose property was apparently confiscated. Hope was not alone in experiencing such attempts at exclusion of Welsh burgesses. Similar developments took place in Cricieth, Harlech and Flint, amongst other boroughs.[29]

The impact of the rule of Edward III and the Black Prince

The situation outlined above was often worsened by the coincidence between socio-economic tensions and changes in governance. The main lines of development here were sketched in the 1930s by W. H. Waters in surveying the administration of the northern principality. Referring to the arrival on the throne of Edward III in 1327, he noted that:

> the change in the kingship ushered in a period distinctly new in atmosphere and in many of its characteristics. The patience and confidence exercised by Edward I in the working of the system which he set up have vanished; so too has the personal concern exhibited by Edward II. Under Edward III deterioration has clearly begun.

The impact of the succession of Edward III had become something of a mantra amongst Welsh medievalists. We may take as examples two senior figures of Bangor University (formerly the University College of North Wales, Bangor). Thus, for Glyn Roberts, writing in a paper published in 1951, and employing terms akin to, and derived from, those used by Waters, the situation was clear, when he noted:

the steady degeneration which had set in under Edward III in the character and efficiency of administration in the Principality. He had never been prince of Wales and he tended to regard the Principality as a mere source of revenue and manpower, or as a means of rewarding his followers. Central authority was capricious, local officers were extortionate and tyrannical. Under Edward I, the policy had been firm; even under Edward II it had been well-meaning; under Edward III it was neither.[30]

A. D. Carr, writing over half a century later, adopted a similar approach:

> The deposition and subsequent death of Edward II seems to mark the end of the political honeymoon which the English Crown and the Welsh political nation in the two principalities had enjoyed since the conquest. Edward and his father had understood the Welsh political leaders and had realised their dependence on them.

But neither under the tyranny of Roger Mortimer, 1327–30, nor under Edward III – nor under his son, the Black Prince – did the basic malaise improve. Carr concluded that 'The understanding and collaboration shown under Edward I and Edward II had gone and would not return'.

A start in understanding the significance of the mid-century decades has thus been made. What has not been emphasised as yet is the extent of the understanding and collaboration noted by Carr, though a significant advance may have been made in the present book, nor the complexity of the forces which brought it to an end. In the light of evidence already assembled in Chapters 2 and 3, it is clear that a crucial factor was the period from the late 1320s to the early 1340s – almost precisely the period from the fall of Edward II to the installation of Edward III's son as prince of Wales – that saw the death of five of the seven men identified as the new administrative and military elite in Wales and the effective withdrawal into English concerns of one of the remaining two. Of the fifty or so 'men of position' scattered across most of Wales, the same period saw the death of nearly a half. Changes in the identity and attitudes of kings and princes, and of the major Marcher lords, were paralleled by changes in the size and composition of the corps of powerful and influential Welshmen. In that context, further shifts in the ethnic balance of the ruling class in Wales became possible, and indeed almost inevitable. This is perhaps nowhere more evident than in the changing composition of senior figures in the Church.

Changes in the Welsh church

There is, it seems, little reason to quarrel with the statement of Glanmor Williams, that 'The Welsh church was fortunate in its bishops during the first fifty years or so after the Conquest'. Compared to an English episcopate of relatively modest attainments, the Welsh bishops deserved Williams's verdict that '[t]he Welsh bishops of this period had no unworthy prelate among them', while most were of Welsh origin or were drawn from families long settled in Wales, and thus found it easier to understand the needs and attitudes of their clergy and their congregations, a feature strengthened by the fact that they all had prior connections with the dioceses to which they were elected. Some of them, most particularly John of Monmouth (bishop of Llandaff 1297–1323) and Henry Gower (St Davids 1328–47) were scholars of great distinction. In the two northern dioceses, the bishops were usually Welshmen, as Edward I and his son both allowed the cathedral chapters to choose the bishops. Thus, in St Asaph, the fiery Welsh figure of Anian II (1268–93) was followed by Llywelyn ab Ynyr (of Bromfield) as his successor; Llywelyn presided over St Asaph for just over twenty years, until his death in 1314. He was followed by a canon of St Asaph, Dafydd ap Bleddyn, who was bishop until 1345.

In Bangor, Bishop Anian (1267–1307), died after a long episcopate and was followed by Gruffudd ab Iorwerth (1306–9), who was succeeded by Anian Sais, another canon of Bangor, whose episcopate ended in 1327. Anian had been archdeacon of Anglesey and dean of Bangor, and the same pattern applied to his successor, Matthew of Englefield, bishop 1328–57.

The Welsh church in this period until the onset of plague and the era of the early stages of the Hundred Years War and the secular dominance of Edward III and the Black Prince was not devoid of tensions, but once more the verdict of Glanmor Williams is pertinent:

> All in all, the half-century or so which followed the Edwardian conquest was one of the few relatively stable and prosperous periods in the troubled history of the church in medieval Wales. It was not without its conflicts or its difficulties. There were ominous portents of future decay. But to many Welsh clerics who lived on into the trials and tribulations of the latter half of the century, its earlier decades may have appeared in retrospect as something of a golden age.[31]

That half-century had been a period in which the cathedral chapters were generally left to elect bishops, whereas in the period from the 1340s the choice of Welsh bishops became very largely a matter for wrangling between the king – and after 1343 the prince of Wales – and the pope.[32] With the death of Henry Gower in 1347, the question of who was to make the choice of bishops of St Davids arose in an acute form. War with France was in full swing, and money and resources were a key factor. The succession to the relatively (in Welsh terms) rich see of St Davids was likely to generate both. The prince's council accordingly acted on the assumption that his grant from his father had included full control of the voidance and succession to St Davids. They even went so far as to raise troops from the episcopal tenants, and to institute the prince's clerks to vacancies in the diocese. At this point the canons of St Davids did have a part to play, in that they advised that the diocese was not included in the king's grant, and sought the king's permission to elect Gower's successor. The end result, in the short term, was that it was decided that the king's council and that of the prince should jointly give the permission to elect.[33] The situation was not clarified for a further decade, when it was decided that the see of St Davids fell outside the grant of the principality to the prince.

Things Fall Apart

When we come to consider the role of the papacy in episcopal elections in Wales, we encounter further complications, and some almost farcical situations. One such arose at St Davids at the time of Gower's replacement as bishop. At first the king appears to have allowed the canons freedom to elect – and they accordingly elected William de Carew, one of the canons and apparently, to judge by his name, a local man. On 30 June 1347, the king signified his agreement to the recent election of Master William de Carew.[34] But that election was then set aside because the pope, Clement VI, had already provided John Thoresby to St Davids on 23 May. In fact, as a senior royal servant, the keeper of the Privy Seal, Thoresby was almost certainly far more likely to have been in King Edward's favour. It is perhaps worth noting that William de Carew would have been something of an exception in the new order which was unfolding at St Davids: in the whole period 1347 to the late fifteenth century, only two out of some eighteen bishops of St Davids had any connection with the diocese before their election.[35]

The other dioceses of Wales had a somewhat similar history in the second half of the fourteenth century. Diocesan chapters were largely discounted in elections to senior positions in which papal and royal – or princely – influence was paramount. Glanmor Williams gave a telling example of this in 1357. The chapter of Bangor in that year elected a canon of that cathedral, Ithel ap Robert – described by Williams as 'a man of exalted lineage, a munificent patron of literature, and one of the outstanding clerics of his generation'. In place of Ithel, the pope, Innocent VI, had provided to the see a Dominican, Thomas Ringstead, who was only the second non-Welsh incumbent at Bangor, the first being the unfortunate Hervé nearly a quarter of a millennium previously. Williams went on to suggest that the funeral of Ithel ap Robert, described in Ithel's *marwnad* by Iolo Goch, reflects a huge demonstration of support and sympathy for a man who had not been treated with the respect that he deserved.[36]

Controversial though Thomas Ringstead's preferment had been, he was a distinguished scholar who 'showed a real concern for his diocese', and in general papal interventions in appointments in the senior positions of the Welsh church were by no means unhelpful. On occasion papal influence and intransigence frustrated the desires of, for example, the Black Prince and his council to impose English candidates largely ignorant of Wales on the Welsh dioceses. Thus, in 1357, the chapter of St Asaph elected their dean, Llywelyn ap Madog in succession to John Trefor as bishop; the Black Prince's candidate was his servant, William de Spridlington, but any collision between the chapter and the prince was averted when Innocent V first annulled Llywelyn ap Madog's election, but then reappointed him by exercising his right of papal provision. Stories such as this one strongly suggest that in the third quarter of the fourteenth century the papacy was able to preserve something of the idea that the bishops of Welsh dioceses should be Welsh.[37] The situation changed with the Great Schism from 1378 onwards for a generation when a much-weakened papacy was less able to enforce its will.

The influence of the lay power (i.e. that of the prince and his council) on church appointments other than episcopal ones is clearer, and in many cases it was a process by which Welsh clerics suffered. This cannot always be seen clearly because of shortage of evidence, but in the period covered by the surviving register of the prince's council for 1347 there are numerous instances of the appointment of the prince's clerks to important Welsh benefices. Thus, February 1347 gives an example:

> Presentation of the prince's clerk, William de Tydolveshyde, to Matthew, bishop of Bangor, for admission to the church of Launvays (Llanfaes), in the diocese of Bangor.[38]

Problems in the Welsh dioceses caused by pressure from the lay power, both in terms of ecclesiastical appointments and with regard to Edward III's and subsequently his son's constant and increasing demands for war-related taxation, could be multiplied many times over. Cumulatively, they made the spiritual life of the Welsh people increasingly restricted in the age of plague. It has to be noted that in some areas of Wales this situation was exacerbated by serious problems of corruption and oppression in the exercise of lay governance. A society increasingly deprived of adequate religious leadership appeared to be losing its moral bearings. This was perhaps nowhere more marked than in the county of Flintshire.

The case of Flintshire: corruption and oppression amongst Welsh officials

It is possible that the situation in that county, and particularly in Englefield,[39] is exaggerated by the survival of its legal records on an unparalleled scale, and particularly by the glimpses of life in that region provided by the existence of registers, however incomplete, of the Black Prince. We must be alert to the possibility that what was happening in Flintshire as we move into the post-Black Death period may have characterised other Welsh communities.

Flintshire governance in the post-Black Death years was characterised firstly by the emergence of a new figure of unprecedented rapacity: Rhys ap Roppert ap Gruffudd, a member of Wyrion Eden, the descendants of Ednyfed Fychan and his brothers. In Rhys ap Roppert's case, his descent was via Ednyfed's son, Gruffudd, the ancestor of Sir Gruffudd Llwyd and Sir Rhys ap Gruffudd, the latter being Rhys ap Roppert's uncle. Rhys thus had an impeccable administrative lineage – though his conduct in office in Flintshire was by no means impeccable. A second figure to emerge in the administrative structure of the county from the later 1340s onwards was Ithel, a son of Cynwrig Sais, the disgraced county official of 1341. The sins of the father were amply shared by his son.

Already by early 1347, Rhys ap Roppert was leading one hundred men of North Wales to aid the prince at Calais,[40] and in April the prince's ministers, lieges and subjects of North Wales and others were warned not to do any harm to him as he had surrendered to the prince to answer to the things which the prince and his council had to say against him. Meanwhile, he was taken into the price's special protection until midsummer.[41] The complaints were already appearing, and the prince's leniency towards Rhys was already apparent. Clearly, whatever the verdict relating to Rees's conduct, it did not damage his standing with the prince, who agreed in October to grant to him and his father, Robert ap Gruffudd, the marriage of a ward of the prince for £20.[42] And, by the close of the year, Rhys had been granted the office of escheator in Merioneth and Caernarfonshire.[43] Ithel ap Cynwrig already had a (somewhat dubious) family history in the prince's lands, but Rhys had an even longer, broken one, and had already undertaken enough tasks for the prince to make himself valued.

Ithel ap Cynwrig Sais and Rhys ap Roppert were to establish a complex relationship, part competitive and confrontational and part collaborative, which is well illustrated in a surviving part of the Black Prince's Register dealing with the earldom of Chester, of which land Flintshire was an administrative subsidiary. Their collaboration began in 1349 when the Chester Recognisance Rolls record that, acting together, they were granted seven-year leases of the farm of the advowries of Englefield for an annual payment of thirty shillings, and of the escheat lands of the cantref for a payment of forty pounds per year.[44] The objective of Rhys and Ithel was, of course, to maximise the return on their investment by exacting as much money as possible from the advowry tenants and from escheated lands.

A further part of their partnership in 1349 was the farm of the constableship of Flint castle and the shrievalty of the county. By 1351, however, the two men were branching out into individual ventures: Ithel took a five-year lease of the constableship and shrievalty, whilst in October of that year orders were issued by the prince's council which reveal an extraordinary bargain that had been struck by Rhys. The lieutenant to the Justice of Chester, and the chamberlain of Cheaster were ordered:

> inasmuch as Rhys ap Roppert has shown before the prince and his council that if he had sufficient warrant, he could profit the prince in several things and in divers ways, (as in escheated lands in Hopedale, Vaynol within franchises and other places which are

not comprised in his commission) – to cause the said Rhys to have a commission enabling him to do the said things for the next two years, to wit, to assess the said lands and make all the profit he can thereof, taking for his trouble a sixth part of all such profits as were never heretofore made for the prince or levied for his use.

There was more. As an afterthought, Rhys was able to wring a further concession from the prince's council:

> inasmuch as the said Rhys has shown before the prince and his council that he could profit the prince in many ways if he could have a grant that none of his under-bailiffs shall be imprisoned for any indictment before a constable or sheriff if he can find good and sufficient security to appear before a justice in the sessions and there make fine or be at common law as shall seem right to the justice, – not to suffer such imprisonment if security can be found as above.[45]

The point here is that not only did Rhys ap Roppert join with the prince to impose additional exactions upon the people of Flintshire, reserving 3s 4d per pound of profit to himself, and thereby making him the prince's partner in oppression, but he negotiated something approaching significant immunity from judicial recrimination for his minions.

By July 1354, however, it must have seemed that Rhys had gone too far when he was seen to have made the prince, his partner, the target of some ruthless action. It came to the notice of the prince's council, which wrote to the senior officials of Chester to launch a full investigation. The council's letter recalled that Rhys ap Roppert had promised to make very great profits for the prince, but noted:

> he has not at all kept his promise, but on the contrary, when certain lands in the township of Backeleye (Bagillt, Holywell) ought to have fallen into the prince's hand by default of heirs, after the death of Dafydd and Ieuan, who held them by charter and were bastards and died without issue of their bodies, he took £4 for his own use from one Dafydd ap Madog ap Bleddyn, who was next in blood

to the said Dafydd and Ieuan for giving him out of the keeping of Llywelyn Goch the charter whereby Dafydd and Ieuan held the lands, which charter pronounces for the prince's right to the said lands, so that the lands are withdrawn from the prince and his right thereto concealed, and moreover he took 20s for his own use from the town of Westbury of Inyoug (Gwesbyr in Llanasa) for handing over the lands of one Dafydd Llwyd of the same town which were in the prince's hands by way of escheat, as well as many other profits to the prejudice of the prince and the concealment of his rights.[46]

What is surprising, if not shocking, about this list of revelations is that they originated 'at the suit of Ithel ap Cynwrig Sais'.[47] The partnership of 1349 appears to have been disintegrating for some time.

Even more interesting is the way in which the accusations against Rhys ap Roppert progressed. The outcome of the enquiries made by the prince's council is encapsulated in an order issued on 17 November 1354:[48]

on information that Rhys ap Roppert has made fine with the prince before them [the justice of Chester's lieutenant and the chamberlain] in 100 marks on account of his misdeeds in Backeleye and Westbury of Inyoug to take from the said Rhys security for payment of 40 marks of the said sum during the next two years by equal portions at Easter and Michaelmas, and to put the remaining £40 [60 marks] in respite on his good behaviour; as the prince has compassion on his estate and wishes to do him a favour in this matter.

So, Rhys was to be able to pay only 40 per cent of his fine, and that by four easy stages over two years. It would seem that the 'compassionate' prince was well aware that even a cheating official such as Rhys was still an asset to be nurtured in the pursuit of effective exaction from the people of Flintshire.

In spite of the Black Prince's toleration of Rhys, the volume of protests from his victims continued to grow, reaching a crescendo in 1358 and 1359. In September of the former year, the prince was petitioned by the men of Englefield,[49] who brought to his attention many complaints about his officials. Amongst their grievances was the claim that 'the *rhaglaw* of Englefield and sheriff of Flintshire [the same person: Rhys ap Roppert] impoverishes and sorely afflicts them by amercing them too heavily for petty trespasses'.[50] A further, and even more serious, claim was that the same official:

> has and maintains divers men who are notoriously in a confederacy of false presenters, swearers and accusers, and by their confederacy and covin with the *rhaglaw* falsely indict the prince's lieges daily of felonies and trespasses, whereupon the *rhaglaw* and sheriff imposes great fines and ransoms on those indicted, and his confederates and false swearers aforesaid, and their wives, by colour of their wicked office, and by the mastership and maintenance of the *rhaglaw* and sheriff demand and collect money, corn, wool and other things from the prince's lieges, well knowing that no one will dare to aid them.[51]

Further complaints directed against Rhys ap Roppert included a claim by the men of Englefield that he oppressed them:

> against right and reason for the sake of gain, receiving complaints from false, malicious and suspected persons no fit to be believed, who make their complaints on the following terms, to wit, that if the plaintiff is convicted in his complaint, he shall only be amerced 6d, but that if he wins his action against the defendant, [the *rhaglaw* and sheriff] shall have a third part or a half of his winnings; on account of which sharing of the winnings the defendants cannot obtain right or law in the county courts and hundred courts.[52]

Again, it was complained of Rhys ap Roppert, and of the former sheriff (Ithel ap Cynwrig Sais), that:

> in his tourns and other courts he takes inquisitions on the matters arising before him and other matters at his pleasure by the oath of his many kinsmen, allies and special friends in the county, and by the oath of those who are his pledges for payment for his farms of

the said offices, so that the prince's lieges, although guilty of nothing, are from day to day maliciously indicted, defamed, slandered, damaged and imprisoned, and endure other grievances against law and reason, because of the aforesaid persons who are thus of the covin of the said Rhys and Ithel.[53]

It is noteworthy that many of the complaints of the men of Englefield were directed at the actions not only of Rhys ap Roppert but also those of Ithel ap Cynwrig. Indeed, the evidence suggests that there was little difference, in terms of abuse of office and criminality in general, between the two men, who came close to controlling between them the apparatus of governance and justice in Flintshire. Nor does it seem that the prince's council was under many illusions about the propensity of Ithel ap Cynwrig Sais to act in highly oppressive ways, for an order from the council in February 1355 had commanded him as sheriff to 'take good care to bear himself well in his office and carry out the promises which he made before the prince's council when he undertook it'. It is difficult to avoid the suspicion that those promises were to ensure the maximisation of profit for the prince, and not to divert the prince's profits into the sheriff's own hands.

Rhys ap Roppert was still, however, in office in Flintshire a year after the complaints noticed above, when a new petition 'touching certain outrages and extortions alleged to have been committed by the sheriff of Flint' reached the prince in August 1359. This one was even more pointed than that of 1358, giving detailed accounts of the sheriff's misdeeds, and the names of his victims. The complaints give a vivid picture of Rhys's methods of enriching himself:

> A complaint by William Colynessone of Babbeley, co. Flint, that he was indicted before Rhys ap Roppert, sheriff of Flint, in the sheriff's tourn in the commote of Colshull, of having feloniously stolen two sheep, worth 2s, of the goods of Ralph, abbot of Basingwerk, for which thing he was taken and brought to the castle of Flint, where he was detained until he had made a fine of 8 marks with the sheriff

for mitigation of prison until the next session of Flint, although he has no lands or goods worth a mark. On being arraigned before the justice touching the said indictment, he was acquitted.

Complaint by John le Saltere of Flint and Wenthlean [Gwenllian], his wife that Gwenllian was maliciously indicted before Rhys ap Roppert, sheriff of Flint, in the sheriff's tourn in the commote of Colshull, of having stolen a mantle, worth 2s of the goods of Bleddyn ap Ithel Llwyd, for which she was taken to prison in the castle of Flint until her husband made a fine of 40s with the said sheriff for mitigation of prison until the following session, although he has no lands or goods worth half a mark [6s 8d], nor anything wherewith to support himself and his wife and children but carries salt upon his back for sale. On being arraigned before the justice the said Gwenllian was acquitted.

Also, the said Rhys has taken for mitigation of prison in the same manner: 20 marks from Iorwerth Goch ap Gwilym; 10 marks from Einion ap Madog ap Saer; 10 marks from Madog his brother; 20s from Einion Fychan ab Einion; 40s from Bellyn de Colshull; £4 from Iorwerth ap Cynwrig of Hendresgair and £4 from Ieuan ap Madog ap Thomas.

Complaint to the prince and his council by Iorwerth ap Gruffudd that he was maliciously indicted of felony by an inquisition procured by Rhys ap Roppert, mayor and constable of Flint, on account of a bushel of wheat and a sack, worth 2s 6d of the goods of William de Praers of Flint, for which thing he was taken and imprisoned in the castle of Flint until the next session of the justice, before whom he was arraigned and acquitted, and that in the meantime the sherif tortured him and hung him up by his feet until he made a fine of £4 in order to secure relief and mitigation of prison although his goods were not worth 10s except for a messuage and two acres of land which are held of the prince in chief, by the service of 2s 6d and which the sheriff wants to take on account of the said fine. He therefore prays that a warrant be granted him to be quit of all amercements of hundreds and counties while he is with the prince for the furtherance of his affairs. Otherwise, he does not dare to return to his country on account of the power of the said Rhys.[54]

There is one further aspect of Rhys ap Roppert's career which demands attention. It appears that he was the father of a Ieuan Wyn, known as *le Pursuivant d'Amour*, who was prominent as a leading figure in a Welsh free company in France in the 1360s and 70s. This was the company led by Owain Lawgoch, the claimant to the principality of Wales and as such the supporter of the French against Edward III and Edward, prince of Wales. Indeed, after the assassination of Owain by an English agent in 1378, Ieuan Wyn became the leader of his company. It was claimed that Rhys ap Roppert had secretly funded the activity of both Owain and Ieuan against the English in France.[55]

Into an uncertain future

In a multitude of ways, therefore, it is evident that the political climate in Wales was changing in the mid-century decades. The ascendancy of a Welsh class of administrators in both Crown and Marcher lands had been a marked feature of the politics of Wales for a generation after the wars of conquest ended in 1295. But in the 1330s that ascendancy was first checked, and then in the 1340s began to unravel. Many of the prominent figures in the Welsh ascendancy that had developed in the period after 1295 had died in the later 1320s and the 1330s; others began to lose contacts with Wales as they moved eastwards. Of course, there were survivors and links with what had been a distinguished era in the history of Wales. One of the elite figures of that era, Sir Rhys ap Gruffudd, effectively a sort of viceroy over the principality of South and West Wales, and much else besides, lived on until 1356. He was succeeded by a son, strangely called Rhys ap Gruffudd,[56] who was also knighted and went on to enjoy a successful career as an administrator and soldier before his death in 1380. But he lived in a period in which ethnic tensions in Wales were becoming more pronounced and more pervasive, and a reaction was increasingly likely. Already in the lifetime of Sir Rhys ap Gruffudd II, the claims of a descendant of the princes of Gwynedd, Owain Lawgoch, to be the true prince of Wales were being advanced and supported by the French government, until his assassination by an English agent in 1378. And already a young man of most august Welsh princely pedigree, whose family were 'men of position', was pursuing a successful career, which involved a spell at the Inns of Court in London, a period of garrison duty at Berwick with the renowned Welsh soldier Sir Gregory Sais, a campaign against the Scots under John of Gaunt, duke of Lancaster, and service with the earl of Arundel at a naval victory over a combined fleet of French, Spanish and Flemish ships off the Kentish coast. He broke off from soldiering to take charge of the family estates in north Wales, where he would be the recipient of several praise poems. These poetic tributes may indeed have encouraged other ambitions. The man's name was Owain ap Gruffudd, but he was known as Owain Glyn Dŵr. He, too, would be an heir to the princes, but of a different type, with different results.

Notes

Preface
1 R. R. Davies, 'Race Relations in Post-Conquest Wales: Confrontation and Compromise', *Transactions of the Honourable Society of Cymmrodorion* (1974–5), 32–56, at 32–3.
2 Davies, 'Race Relations in Post-Conquest Wales', p. 56.
3 A. D. Carr, 'Lineage, Power and Land in Medieval Flintshire: the descendants of Ithel Fychan', *Flintshire Historical Society Journal*, 36 (2003), 59–81, at 81.
4 *Aspects of Welsh History* (Cardiff, 1969) pp. 383–4.
5 'Edward II and the Allegiance of Wales', *Welsh History Review*, 8 (1976–7), 139–40.

Introduction
1 A note on nomenclature: up to the mid-twelfth century, all Welsh rulers were usually designated as kings but thereafter the greater rulers began to use the title of prince (*princeps*) and lesser ones employed that of lord (*dominus*). For the Welsh nomenclature used by the court poets, see Rhian M. Andrews, 'The Nomenclature of Kingship in Welsh Court Poetry 1100–1300; Part I: The Terms', *Studia Celtica*, 44 (2010), 79–109 and 'The Nomenclature of Kingship in Welsh Court Poetry 1100–1300; Part II: The Rulers', *Studia Celtica*, 45 (2011), 53–82.
2 The career of Owain Glyn Dŵr of course lies outside the scope of the present work; see, however, p. 153.
3 For detailed discussion and analysis, see Stephenson, *Political Power in Medieval Gwynedd*.
4 See discussion at pp. xxxii–xxxiii.
5 Of the relatively few poems directed at Llywelyn, two composed by Hywel Foel are less praise poems than demands for the release of Owain ap Gruffudd, held in captivity by Llywelyn after the

battle of Bryn Derwin in 1255, while other, more conventual (albeit passionately expressed) praise poems were mainly *marwnadau* (elegies).

6   In the cases of the descendants of members of the ministerial aristocracy, it does seem that it is important to trace their descent through female as well as male lines: their eminence appears to have derived both from their maternal as well as their paternal inheritances. Thus, the fact that the mother of Sir Rhys ap Gruffudd (d. 1356), one of the mightiest of the administrative magnates of the fourteenth century, was Nest, daughter of Gwrwared ap Gwilym of Cemais, son of the hugely important administrative magnate Gwilym ap Gwrwared, may have been an important element in his career.

7   See Ben Guy, *Medieval Welsh Genealogy*, especially p. 215 and n. 282.

8   This was presumably because though descendants of all three brothers held by privileged tenure, it was named after that one of them who was the most famous. For Ednyfed's brothers Goronwy and Heilyn, see Stephenson, *Political Power in Medieval Gwynedd*, pp. 102–4, 212–13, 215.

9   As well as the poems of Einion in *Cyfres Beirdd y Tywysogyon*, Volume I, see my suggestion that he may quite possibly have been the author of the prophetic poem associated with Meugan recently 'recovered' and edited by Marged Haycock in *CMCS* 81 (Summer 2021), 1–41. That suggestion is made in my 'The prophetic poem attributed to Meugan: notes on dating and possible authorship', *CMCS* 82 (Winter 2021), 41–51, where the date of the poem is fixed at late August or early September 1212.

10 *BT, Pen20 trans*, p. 120.

11 See note 7 above.

12 Guy, *Medieval Welsh Genealogy*, p. 214.

13 Guy, *Medieval Welsh Genealogy*, p. 215: 'Although he is never explicitly called *distain* in surviving sources, he was one of Llywelyn's leading courtiers from around 1217 to 1223 when he witnessed a number of documents'. I am inclined to place the beginning of Einion's importance at Llywelyn's court some years before 1217. It is possible that he had already begun to withdraw from the court by that date, in what became a commitment to a monastic life.

14 Descendants of Maredudd ab Iorwerth held lands by privileged tenure, as did the descendants of Iarddur ap Cynddelw, and of Iorwerth ap Gwrgunon: see Stephenson, *Political Power in Medieval Gwynedd*, pp. 110–15.

15 For Gwilym's career, see David Stephenson, *Medieval Wales c.1050–1332* (Cardiff: University of Wales Press, 2019), pp. 81–2.

16 See pp. 102–4.

17 The above represents only a brief list of some of the more 'official' activities of Hywel ap Meurig and his descendants. For a fuller treatment, see David Stephenson, *Patronage and Power in the Medieval Welsh March: One Family's Story* (Cardiff: University of Wales Press, 2021).
18 I should like to thank Mo Lloyd for very fruitful discussion of Llys Ifor and of Ifor ap Gruffudd.
19 *Calendar of Patent Rolls, 1281–92*, p. 15; Davies (ed.), *Welsh Assize Roll*, pp. 311, 326, 330.
20 Francis Jones, 'The Subsidy of 1292', *Bulletin of the Board of Celtic Studies*, 13 (1950), 229.
21 D. Stephenson, 'New light on a dark deed', *Archaeologia Cambrensis*, 166 (2017), 243–52; cf n. 20 above.
22 D. Stephenson, *Medieval Powys: Kingdom, Principality and Lordships, 1132–1293* (Woodbridge: Boydell Press, 2016).
23 *AWR* 464.
24 *AWR* 467 etc.
25 *AWR* 473 n, and Crouch, *Image of Aristocracy*, p. 122.
26 See the interesting comments of Davies, *The Age of Conquest*, pp. 126–7.
27 Stephenson, *Medieval Wales*, pp. 41–5.
28 D. Stephenson, 'The early physicians of Myddfai in context', in Robin Barlow (ed.), *Transactions of the Physicians of Myddfai Society, 2011–2017* (2018), pp. 61–8.

Chapter 1

1 R. R. Davies, *Conquest, Coexistence and Change, Wales 1063–1415* (Oxford: Oxford University Press, 1987), p. 380. This book was reissued as *The Age of Conquest* in 2000, with the same pagination to the text but with an updated bibliography. The military occupation was based on the remarkable and largely unprecedented programme of massive castle-building instituted by Edward after 1277 and continued after 1283 and 1295: the royal castles of the first wave of building at Flint, Rhuddlan, Aberystwyth, Builth, those of the second wave at Conwy, Caernarfon, Harlech, supplemented by refurbished native fortifications at Castell y Bere, Cricieth and Dolwyddelan, and the third wave constituted by Beaumaris, bear witness to Edward's expenditure of money, skill and energy on a remarkable work of encirclement of the heartland of Llywelyn ap Gruffudd's principality. The royal enterprise was augmented by baronial castles either built anew or developed from existing structures such as those at Holt, Dolforwyn, Ruthin, Denbigh and Pool (modern Powis). The admin-

istrative and legal settlement was based principally on the 1284 Statute of Rhuddlan, for discussion of which see Llinos B. Smith, 'The statute of Wales, 1284', *WHR*, 10 (1980–1), 127–54.

2   Davies, *Conquest, Coexistence and Change*, p. 385.
3   Davies, *Conquest, Coexistence and Change*, pp. 370, 386–7.
4   David Walker, *Medieval Wales* (Cambridge: Cambridge University Press, 1990), p. 157.
5   A. D. Carr, *Medieval Wales* (London: Macmillan, 1995), p. 88.
6   David Stephenson, *Medieval Wales c.1050–1332: Centuries of Ambiguity* (Cardiff: University of Wales Press, 2019), pp. 125–6.
7   Stephenson, *Medieval Wales*, p. 130.
8   For an examination of the nature and impact of the 1294–5 risings, see David Stephenson, 'The Malice and Rebellion of Certain Welshmen … The Welsh Risings of 1294–95', in A. Jobson, H. Kersey and G. McKelvie (eds), *Rebellion in Medieval Europe c.1000–1500* (Woodbridge, Boydell and Brewer, 2025.), pp. 133–48.
9   See my translation of the memoranda, derived from an Abergavenny chronicle, in 'The continuation of Brut y Tywysogyon in NLW, MS Peniarth 20 Revisited', in Ben Guy, Georgia Henley, Owain Wyn Jones and Rebecca Thomas (eds), *The Chronicles of Wales and the March* (Turnhout: Brepols, 2020), p. 158.
10 *Calendar of Close Rolls, 1288–1296*, p. 493.
11 Natalie Fryde (ed.), *List of Welsh Entries in the Memoranda Rolls, 1282–1343* (Cardiff: University of Wales Press, 1974), p. xv says that he was 'still imprisoned in Newcastle on Tyne in 1301', but without giving a reference.
12 G. Rex Smith, 'The Penmachno Letter Patent and the Welsh uprising of 1294–95', *Cambrian Medieval Celtic Studies*, 58 (2009), 49–67 at p. 63 n. 95 comments that Madog 'appears to have had VIP status' in the Tower.
13 H. Ellis (ed.), *Registrum vulgariter nuncupatum, 'the Record of Caernarvon'* (London: Record Commission, 1838), p. 45 shows Hywel ap Madog ap Llywelyn holding Lledwigan by a remarkably privileged tenure.
14 Morgan will be the subject of a detailed investigation in the following chapter, and will thus be treated only briefly here.
15 *Annales de Wigornia*, p. 526. On 7th June Edward wrote (*Calendar of Ancient Correspondence*, p. 208) to his brother Edmund to announce that he had received Morgan to his peace 'whereby he hopes that his business will soon be finished in those parts'.
16 The Worcester annals, once again the source of a detailed account, report that Cynan was examined by the king himself. It appears that an attempt to fool the king as opposed to invoking his mercy, as well

Notes

as manifest ingratitude to the king by rebelling when he had extended his favour and protection, were actions likely to provoke savage punishment.

17 *Calendar of Patent Rolls 1292–1301*, pp. 144–5. The lands of John de Hastings included both the lordship of Cilgerran and of Abergavenny. It is quite possible that Meurig ap Dafydd and his followers may have been beneficiaries of admission to the king's peace. The fact that the grant to John de Hastings is marked 'vacated because surrendered and cancelled' should not obscure the king's intention in issuing it.
18 *Calendar of Patent Rolls 1292–1301*, p. 165.
19 *Calendar of Patent Rolls 1292–1301*, p. 223. Thomas Danvers (elsewhere Anvers) was sheriff of Anglesey at this period (W. H. Waters, *The Edwardian Settlement of North Wales* (Cardiff: University of Wales Press, 1935), p. 172). He may have been included in the deputation to give it greater credibility with the king.
20 *Calendar of Close Rolls 1296–1302*, p. 75.
21 *Calendar of Patent Rolls 1307–13*, p. 239. See also Chapter 5, p. 139.
22 *Calendar of Patent Rolls 1292–1301*, pp. 290–1.
23 *Calendar of Close Rolls, 1296–1302*, p. 107.
24 J. Beverley Smith, 'Edward II and the Allegiance of Wales', *Welsh History Review*, 8 (1976–7), 139–71 at p. 142 n. 16 for a reference to a record in British Library Additional MS 7965 that Morgan was sent to Wales *pro quibusdam negociis regis secretis per preceptum ipsius regis speciale* (for certain secret business of the king, by the special order of the king himself).
25 The letter is preserved in the National Archives, and is calendared fully in J. G. Edwards (ed.), *Calendar of Ancient Correspondence concerning Wales* (Cardiff: University of Wales Press, 1935), p. 101. It is there dated to 1321–2, but is to be assigned to 1297: see the discussion by Beverley Smith referenced in note 24 above.
26 See David Pilling, *Edward I and Wales 1254–1307* (Barnsley: Pen and Sword, 2021), pp. 202–4. The early stages of the recruitment process can be traced in the Patent Roll entries for 17 May 1297:
> Order to all Welshmen of South Wales, to give credence to Thomas de Bossal and Master Gilbert de Arderne, in the matters which the king has entrusted to them. The like to all Welshmen of North Wales, to give credence to John de Havering, justice of those parts, and William de Cycon, constable of Aberconwy castle. The like to all Welshmen of Glamorgan, to give credence to Walter Hakelut, Morgan ap Maredudd and Dayid le Graunt. The like to all Welshmen of Powys, to give credence to William de la Pole and John de Borham (*Calendar of Patent Rolls, 1292-1301*, p. 249).

The presence amongst the recruiters of Welshmen – certainly Morgan ap Maredudd and William de la Pole (William ap Gruffudd, lord of Mawddwy) is an interesting sign of the development of a Welsh class of office-holders under English kings.

27 This is a fairly loose translation of a passage in *Annales Prioratus de Wigornia*, edited by H. R. Luard, in Volume IV of *Annales Monastici* (London, Rolls Series, 1869), p. 520.

28 *Calendar of Patent Rolls, 1292–1301*, p. 499.

29 Hywel was thus placed in charge of the development of Edward's castle at Builth, the strategic position of which in central Wales was crucial. See Stephenson, *Patronage and Power*, p. 22. An important point about Builth castle was that its central position in Wales enabled the king, via its custodian, to project power into many regions not otherwise dominated by a royal castle. A proper study of this castle is needed.

30 Stephenson, *Political Power in Medieval Gwynedd*, pp. 213–14, 218.

31 Carr, *The Gentry of North Wales*, p. 39.

32 See Stephenson, *Political Power*, pp. 112–14.

33 Davies, *Age of Conquest*, p. 370.

34 In recording the appointment, the copy in J. G. Edwards (ed.), *Littere Wallie* (Cardiff: University of Wales Press, 1940), p. 184 records the recipient as Philip ap Hywel ap Meurig, whereas the record in the Welsh Roll (*Calendar of Various Chancery Rolls*, p. 324) confuses the situation by giving his name as Philip ab Owain ap Meurig.

35 *Records of the Wardrobe and Household*, p. 478.

36 Francis Jones, 'The Subsidy of 1292', *Bulletin of the Board of Celtic Studies*, 13 (1948–50), p. 211.

37 Griffiths, *Principality of Wales I*, p. 279, states that on 9 December 1309 the justiciar, Roger Mortimer (of Chirk) wrote to the chancellor to delay Goronwy's removal from office because it might endanger peace. This is, however, a misidentification: see *Calendar of Inquisitions, Miscellaneous*, II, pp. 18–19, where it is clear that the men whose retention in their present offices Mortimer was seeking were Dafydd Bongam and Dafydd Fychan, as above.

38 Dafydd ap Moriz had a significant military record and was involved in the suppression of Rhys ap Maredudd's rising in 1287: *Records of the Wardrobe and Household*, pp. 486–9, 492, where he is recorded as prominent in a troop of Welsh light cavalry.

39 *Calendar of Fine Rolls, Edward I, 1272–1307*, p. 423. Philip's rent was £113 6s 8d per year.

40 Stephenson, *Patronage and Power*, p. 36.

41 Waters, *Edwardian Settlement*, p. 173.

42 Stephenson, *Medieval Powys*, pp. 212–13.

Notes

43 *Calendar of Chancery Warrants 1244–1326*, p. 64.
44 Keith Williams-Jones, *The Merioneth Lay Subsidy Roll, 1292–3* (Cardiff: University of Wales Press, 1976), p. 82 n. 3.
45 E. B. Fryde (ed.), *Book of Prests of the King's Wardrobe, 1294–5*, pp. 58–9, 135.
46 See Williams-Jones, *Merioneth Lay Subsidy Roll*, p. 82 n. 1.
47 *Edward of Carnarvon 1284–1307* (Manchester University Press, 1946), p. 97 n. 5. The passage quoted is omitted from *Calendar of Patent Rolls, 1313–17*, pp. 433–4. It is just a little ambiguous, as it can be translated as 'Ordinances made by our counsel and that of our aforesaid father' or 'Ordinances made by our Council and that of our aforesaid father'. Johnstone's comment remains entirely valid, however.
48 *Record of Caernarvon*, p. 214. The two Welsh commissioners were sons of Hywel ap Meurig: Philip ap Hywel and his brother Master Rees ap Hywel. Both are discussed in Chapter 2.

Chapter 2

1 The careers of Philip and Rees have been examined in some detail by David Stephenson, *Patronage and Power in the Medieval Welsh March: One Family's Story* (Cardiff: University of Wales Press, 2021). Much of their activity is therefore summarised in the present discussion, which focuses on those aspects of their work that serve to clarify their role in the elite group of Welsh administrators and military figures.
2 Unless he is to be identified as the William ap Hywel who acted as deputy constable of Dinefwr castle in 1310–12, William is absent from the records of the years after 1295. He was, however, the father of another of the elite figures examined in this chapter, Sir Philip Clanvowe.
3 He does not seem to have been involved, as Philip and William were, as an executor of his father's will.
4 His absence from the administrative records of several years after 1287 quite possibly reflects time spent in study. He had attained the status of Master (in Arts?) by the start of the next century.
5 See p. xxvi and pp. 29–32.
6 *Calendar of Patent Rolls, 1292–1301*, p. 598; *Calendar of Inquisitions, Miscellaneous, 1307–49*, no. 68; *Rotuli Scottie*, I, pp. 85, 156.
7 Hilda Johnstone (ed.), *Letters of Edward Prince of Wales, 1304–1305* (Cambridge: Cambridge University Press, 1931), p. 141. See also *Record of Caernarvon*, p. 214.

8   Stephenson, *Patronage and Power*, pp. 25–6. Ralph Griffiths, *Principality of Wales I*, p. 97 states that Rees 'organised the defence of south Wales in the face of the threatened Irish [sic] invasion of 1315', but it does seem that he, like his colleagues, was at work in the north as well.
9   See ibid., p. 34, n. 44.
10 See Stephenson, *Patronage and Power*, pp. 58–9, 112.
11 Roy Martin Haines, *King Edward II* (Montreal: McGill-Queen's University Press, 2003), p. 122, suggests that subsequently to 1316 Rees had 'taken service with Mortimer of Wigmore and, more particularly, with [the earl of] Hereford'. But it is probable that Rees was in Hereford's service long before that.
12 *Calendar of Ancient Correspondence concerning Wales*, pp. 219–20.
13 *Calendar of Close Rolls, 1318–23*, p. 285.
14 Griffiths, *Principality of Wales*, p. 102.
15 *Calendar of Patent Rolls, 1327–30*, p. 72.
16 Fryde, *List of Welsh Entries in the Memoranda Rolls*, p. 71.
17 Stephenson, *Patronage and Power*, cf. pp. 28, 32, 41, 70.
18 The Maelienydd episode took place in June, and the Brecon events in July/August. Philip's involvement at Hereford occurred in mid-July.
19 Stephenson, *Patronage and Power*, p. 35. In 1297, he is recorded as parson of the churches of Moccas (Hereford) and of Llanbister (Maelienydd, diocese of St Davids).
20 *Record of Caernarvon*, p. 214.
21 See p. 20.
22 Such was his work, together with William le Butler of Wem, in investigating complaints made by the burgesses of Montgomery that the townsmen of Chirbury had set up a market 'to the injury of the market and fairs of Montgomery': *Calendar of Patent Rolls 1313–17*, p. 318: orders of 21 April 1315.
23 *Calendar of Close Rolls, 1313–18*, p. 253: orders of 24 October 1315.
24 Philip had replaced one of the original men sent to try to settle matters in the lordship of Builth, William Bagot, on 28 December 1315: *Calendar of Patent Rolls, 1313–17*, p. 322. (This corrects a reference in Stephenson, *Patronage and Power* at p. 47 n. 30.)
25 *Calendar of Close Rolls, 1313–18*, p. 270. This last order was issued on 25 February 1316.
26 *Calendar of Patent Rolls, 1313–17*, p. 491.
27 *Calendar of Close Rolls, 1318–23*, p. 582.
28 Stephenson, *Patronage and Power*, pp. 44–5.
29 See pp. 47–50.
30 Pryce, *Acts of Welsh Rulers*, no. 457.
31 *Glamorgan County History III*, p. 60.

Notes

32 The Turberville case is examined by J. G. Edwards, 'The Treason of Thomas Turberville, in R. W. Hunt, W. A. Pantin and R. W. Southern (eds), *Studies in Medieval History Presented to F. M. Powicke* (Oxford: Clarendon Press, 1948), pp. 296–309.
33 *Calendar of Patent Rolls, 1292–1301*, p. 249; *Calendar of Close Rolls, 1296–1302*, p. 79.
34 Edwards (ed.), *Calendar of Ancient Correspondence concerning Wales*, p. 101 (incorrectly dated to 1321–2). The king's object in this Brecon episode is surely revealed in letters patent issued on 13 July 1297, granting power to Walter Hacklutel and Moran ap Maredudd to hear complaints of the people of the earl of Hereford in Brycheiniog against the earl and his ministers, to defend and maintain until justice be done those complaining and to admit to the king's peace those persons whom the earl has ejected from their lands and to reinstate them. The royal resolve to interfere in the lordship of Brecon is clear, and the letters give a strong hint of elements at least of Morgan's mission: *Calendar of Patent Rolls, 1292–1301*, p. 293.
35 For Philip ap Hywel's role in these events, see J. G. Edwards (ed.), *Calendar of Ancient Correspondence concerning Wales* (Cardiff: University of Wales Press, 1935), p. 24.
36 Stephenson, *Medieval Wales*, p. 146. The use of a phrase like 'secret agent' to describe Morgan is not guesswork: his mission in Wales in 1297 was described as furthering 'certain secret business of the king's by the special order of the king himself'. BL Additional MS 7965 f.25.
37 See p. 46.
38 *Calendar of Close Rolls, 1296–1302*, p. 208; cf Chapman, *Welsh Soldiers*, p. 29 n. 82.
39 Constance Bullock-Davies, *Menestrellorum Multitudo* (Cardiff: University of Wales Press, 1978), p. 186.
40 *Record of Caernarvon*, p. 186.
41 *Calendar of Close Rolls, 1302–7*, pp. 446–7.
42 *Calendar of Close Rolls, 1302–7*, p. 505.
43 See pp. 44–6.
44 See J. Beverley Smith, 'The Rebellion of Llywelyn Bren' in *Glamorgan County History III*, pp. 82–3.
45 See especially Morgan's role in joining Master Rees ap Hywel and Stephen de la More in raising 2,500 men in South Wales in July 1316; Morgan was then to lead the assembled men to York, en route to Scotland: *Rotuli Scotiae*, I, p. 156; *Calendar of Patent Rolls, 1313–17*, p. 539.
46 *Calendar of Inquisitions Post Mortem, 1327–36*, pp. 346–7.
47 See Stephenson, *Medieval Powys*, pp. xxi, 118.

48 Bartrum, *Welsh Genealogies*, I, p. 31, Bleddyn ap Cynfyn 4; III, p. 447, Gruffudd ap Cynan, 5.
49 *Calendar of Patent Rolls, 1307–13*, p. 405.
50 Michael Rogers, 'The Welsh Marcher Lordship of Bromfield and Yale 1282–1485' (unpublished PhD thesis, University College of Wales, Aberystwyth, 1992), p. 64.
51 *Calendar of Close Rolls, 1319–23*, p. 521.
52 Rogers, 'The Welsh Marcher Lordship of Bromfield and Yale', p. 327.
53 Rogers, 'The Welsh Marcher Lordship', p. 327.
54 *BT, Pen20 trans*, p. 126.
55 See David Stephenson, 'The continuation of *Brut y Tywysogyon* in NLW, MS Peniarth 20 Revisited', in Ben Guy, Georgia Henley, Owain Wyn Jones and Rebecca Thomas (eds), *The Chronicles of Medieval Wales and the March* (Turnhout: Brepols, 2020), pp. 155–68, esp. pp. 166–7. It should be added that what is by far the longest entry in the continuation, that for 1321–2, also coincides with a period when Madog was very active, both militarily and in changing his allegiance from the baronial to the royalist side.
56 Gresham, *Medieval Stone Carving in North Wales*, pp. 184–6.
57 Gresham, *Medieval Stone Carving*, pp. 184–6.
58 On the careers of these men, see Stephenson, *Political Power in Medieval Gwynedd*, pp. 207–9, 214–15, 218.
59 Gruffudd was engaged in action against the rebellion in north Wales of 1294–5, recorded in TNA E101/5/18, and noticed in Fryde, *Book of Prests*, pp. 165–7; later instances are recorded at *Calendar of Patent Rolls, 1292–1301*, p. 335 (returning with troops from Flanders, 1298); p. 342–3 (leading foot soldiers to a muster at Carlisle from north Wales, April 1298); p. 598 (leading foot soldiers to Carlisle for a Scottish campaign, 1301); ibid., *1301-7*, pp. 435, 529 (leading 300 and 500 troops to Scotland, 1306, 1307); *Calendar of Patent Rolls, 1307–13*, p. 82 (leading troops to Scotland, 1308); Carr, *The Gentry of North Wales*, p. 57 (led 2,000 troops from north Wales on Scottish campaign (Bannockburn) 1314; *Rotuli Scotiae*, p. 197 (raising men from north Wales for service in Scotland, 1319); *Calendar of Patent Rolls, 1321–4*, p. 35 (levying forces for the king, February 1322); p. 73 (arraying 2,200 men in North Wales for service against Scots and Contrariants, February 1322); p. 98 (taking men to Scotland, April 1322); Natalie Fryde, 'Welsh troops in the Scottish campaign of 1322', *BBCS*, 26 (1974–5), pp. 83–6 (Gruffudd's participation in the Scottish campaign in which his son Gruffudd was killed); *Calendar of Patent Rolls, 1324–7*, p. 325 (assembling troops in north Wales, September 1326). Additional references are found in *Calendar of Close Rolls, 1302–7*, pp. 446–7 (leading troops to Scotland to join Prince Edward against the Scots, May 1306); *Calendar of Close Rolls, 1313–18*, p. 367 (leading

Notes

forty men to the king at Newcastle for a campaign against the Scots, October 1316); *Calendar of Close Rolls, 1318–23*, p. 421 (taking troops to the king from North Wales, February 1321). These references are by no means exhaustive, but give a good idea of Sir Gruffudd's frequent involvement in campaigns.

60   Being appointed first in 1302, he was preceded as a sheriff by one Welshman Gruffudd ap Dafydd in Merionethshire, appointed in 1300.
61   Gruffudd held the shrievalties as follows:
Caernarfonshire: 1302–5; 1308–10
Anglesey: 1305–6
Merionethshire: 1314–17; 1321–7.
62   See p. 34.
63   We have seen that in the nearby lordship of Bromfield and Yale, Lancaster's Receiver, Madog ap Llywelyn, had raised troops and was leading them to join the king's forces. The curious case of Sir Gruffudd's encouragement of the attack on Dyffryn Clwyd on 11 March of 1322, just a few days before the battle of Boroughbridge on 16 March, in which men of Merioneth were prominent and numerous, is examined in *History of Merioneth II: The Middle Ages*, pp. 73–4; cf Chapman, *Welsh Soldiers*, p. 48.
64   *Calendar of Close Rolls, 1318–23*, pp. 415, 577.
65   *Calendar of Patent Rolls, 1321–24*, p. 335.
66   *Calendar of Patent Rolls, 1324–27*, p. 325.
67   Davies, *Age of Conquest*, p. 387.
68   J. G. Edwards, 'Sir Gruffydd Llwyd', *English Historical Review*, 120/30 (1915), 589–601.
69   'Sir Gruffudd Llwyd', *ODNB*.
70   R. C. Christie (ed.), *Annales Cestrienses* (Lancashire and Cheshire Record Society), p. 118.
71   Printed by Edwards, 'Sir Gruffydd Llwyd', p. 600.
72   Smith, 'Edward II and the Allegiance of Wales', pp. 165–7.
73   Smith, 'Edward II', p. 167.
74   Smith, 'Edward II', p. 154.
75   The most thorough examination of these letters to date is by J. Beverley Smith, 'Gruffydd Llwyd and the Celtic Alliance, 1315–18', *Bulletin of the Board of Celtic Studies*, 26 (1974–6), 463–78.
76   Smith, 'Gruffydd Llwyd and the Celtic Alliance', p. 478.
77   Smith, 'Edward II and the Allegiance of Wales', p. 156.
78   This was also the stance taken by R. R. Davies in his 1994 presidential address to the Royal Historical Society: 'The Peoples of Britain and Ireland 1100–1400. II Names, Boundaries and Regnal Solidarities', *Transactions of the Royal Historical Society* (1995), 1–20, at p. 3.

79 Adam Chapman, *Welsh Soldiers, 1282–1422* (Woodbridge: Boydell and Brewer, 2015), p. 43.
80 See p. 31.
81 Edwards, 'Treason of Thomas Turberville'. See also Stephenson, *Medieval Wales*, p. 146.
82 It is also noteworthy that the poet Gwilym Ddu o Arfon was prepared to compose two very significant poems lamenting Gruffudd's imprisonment in 1316–18. These were composed at different times in his captivity and demonstrate that some of Gruffudd's supporters were prepared to stand by him in his ordeal. See N. G. Costigan (Bosco), R. Iestyn Daniel and Dafydd Johnston (eds), *Gwaith Gruffudd ap Dafydd ap Tudur, Gwilym Ddu o Arfon, Trahaearn Brydydd Mawr ac Iorwerth Beli* (Aberystwyth, 1995), pp. 52–60. The poems of Gwilym Ddu are edited by Dr Daniel.
83 Edwards (ed.), *Calendar of Ancient Correspondence concerning Wales*, pp. 247–8.
84 For William ap Hywel, see pp. xl, 29.
85 There is a very helpful discussion by Richard Morgan, 'An extent of the lordship of Hay', *Brycheiniog*, 28 (1995–6), 15–21, at p. 20.
86 *Calendar of Patent Rolls, 1321–24*, p. 18.
87 *Calendar of Patent Rolls, 1321–24*, p. 77.
88 *Calendar of Close Rolls, 1318–23*, pp. 430, 433.
89 Griffiths, *Principality of Wales I*, p. 103; *Calendar of Fine Rolls, 1319–27*, pp.172, 234.
90 *Calendar of Patent Rolls, 1334–38*, p. 20; *Calendar of Inquisitions, Miscellaneous*, II, p. 346; *Rotuli Scottie*, I, pp. 289, 314, 365. In 1336, Owen of Montgomery was replaced by Rhys ap Gruffudd, but Philip Clanvowe remained in the post: *Rotuli Scottie*, I, p. 427.
91 *Calendar of Inquisitions, Miscellaneous*, II, p. 350.
92 *Calendar of Inquisitions, Miscellaneous*, II, p. 364.
93 *Calendar of Patent Rolls, 1338–40*, p. 284.
94 *Calendar of Patent Rolls, 1338–40*, p. 278.
95 TNA, SC6, 1221/3 m. 8; /4 m.4.
96 Griffiths, *Principality of Wales I*, p. 103.
97 *Calendar of Patent Rolls, 1338–40*, p. 135.
98 *Calendar of Patent Rolls, 1338–40*, p. 502; *Calendar of Patent Rolls, 1340–43*, p. 155; *Calendar of Fine Rolls, 1337–47*, p. 391.
99 *Calendar of Patent Rolls, 1345–48*, p. 301.
100 *Black Prince's Register*, I, p. 32.
101 *Black Prince's Register*, I, pp. 4–5.
102 *Black Prince's Register*, I, p. 45.
103 See Stephenson, *Patronage and Power*, ch. 6.
104 Stephenson, *Patronage and Power*, pp. 76, 79 n. 46.
105 Stephenson, *Patronage and Power*, p. 32.

106 Stephenson, *Medieval Wales*, p. 81.
107 Griffiths, *Principality of Wales I*, p. 99.
108 *Calendar of Patent Rolls, 1317–21*, pp. 493, 502; cf complaints that Rhys had been one of the magnates who had imposed English law in parts of the southern principality against the grant of Edward I and the wishes of the Welsh community. It is difficult to fix the date of the complaint, dated by William Rees, *Calendar of Ancient Petitions*, pp. 245–7 to 1322.
109 *Calendar of Close Rolls, 1318–23*, p. 464.
110 *Parliamentary Writs of Summons*, p. 546.
111 Griffiths, *Principality of Wales I*, p. 100.
112 *Gwaith Einion Offeiriad*, ed. R. Geraint Gruffudd and Rhiannon Ifans (Aberystwyth, 1997), pp. 7–21.
113 *Gwaith Llywelyn Brydydd Hoddnant, Dafydd ap Gwilym, Hillyn ac Eraill*, ed. Ann Parry Owen (Aberystwyth, 1996), pp. 134–5.
114 *Calendar of Patent Rolls, 1321–24*, p. 335.
115 *www.gasconrolls.org/edition/calendars/C61_36/document.html#it036_18_13f_259*. In this transcript Rhys ap Gruffudd's name is recorded as Gruffudd: in the quotation given here it has been silently restored to 'Rhys'.
116 See Griffiths, *Principality of Wales I*, p. 195, and cf p. 194.
117 His name appears before that of Philip Clanvowe.
118 *www.gasconrolls.org/edition/calendars/C61_49/document.html#it049_11_24f_215*. References in the calendar of this document to 'Ap Gruffudd' have been silently emended to 'Rhys'.
119 See ibid., doc. 421.
120 *Calendar of Ancient Correspondence*, p. 190.
121 *Calendar of Ancient Correspondence*, p. 193.
122 Griffiths, *Principality of Wales I*, p. 101.
123 Griffiths, *Principality of Wales I*, p. 101.
124 The date of his knighthood is something of a mystery. The *Dictionary of Welsh Biography* entry, by Thomas Jones Pierce, notes that Rhys's knighthood was conferred 'between June and November 1346'. But in the *Calendar of Close Rolls 1333–37*, pp. 73 and 128 for 1333 he is clearly and explicitly noticed as a knight.

Chapter 3
1 N. Denholm-Young (ed.), *Vita Edwardi Secundi* (London: Nelson, 1957), p. 66.
2 *Calendar of Close Rolls 1313–18*, p. 161. At some point soon after the death of Earl Gilbert, Llywelyn gave up at least some of his offices, in one of which he was succeeded by one of his sons.

3   *Vita Edwardi Secundi*, p. 66.
4   Davies, 'Bohun and Lancaster Lordships', p. 422 n. 65.
5   *Calendar of Patent Rolls, 1327–30*, p. 66.
6   *Glamorgan County History III*, p. 596 n. 261.
7   *Vita Edwardi Secundi*, p. 68.
8   Clark, *Cartae*, IV, 1172–3.
9   Clark, *Cartae*, III, 1158. All the other knights have Anglo-Norman names.
10 R. Iestyn Daniel (ed.), *Gwaith Casnodyn* (Aberystwyth: Canolfan Uwchefrydiau Cymreig a Cheltaidd Prifysgol Cymru, 1999), poem 2, *Marwnad Madog Fychan o Dir Iarll*, at l. 169.
11 *Glamorgan County History III*, pp. 83–4.
12 *Glamorgan County History III*, pp. 82–3.
13 *Gwaith Casnodyn*, poem 2, ll. 19–22, 61–2.
14 *Calendar of Patent Rolls, 1313-17*, p. 567; ibid., *1317–21*, p. 51.
15 *Calendar of Patent Rolls, 1313–17*, p. 582. The baronial forces had captured Newport castle on 8th May, and Cardiff castle on 9th May.
16 That his authority extended into Afan (Aveneslonde) is perhaps explained by the possibility that Leisan d'Avene, lord of Afan (for whom see below) was incapacitated and that his son John was as yet still a minor. Alternatively, it may suggest that Leisan had gone over to the invaders.
17 Clark, *Cartae*, III, 1158.
18 *Gwaith Casnodyn*, 2, ll. 53–4, 175–6.
19 His son Owain was mentioned in his elegy by Casnodyn, and appears too in record sources.
20 Davies, *Lordship and Society*, p. 89, suggests that the lords of Afan had adopted the new form of their name in the thirteenth century, as 'a token of their new submissive status'. This is a possible reading, but it is also possible that they were simply fitting into the predominantly Anglo-Norman names of the lords of Glamorgan, the intention being not to demonstrate subservience but to facilitate advancement, a process facilitated by the marriage of Morgan Fychan, sixth lord, to a daughter of Walter de Sully, while Leisan ap Morgan Fychan also married a Sully. It was presumably through these marriages that Leisan's successor John d'Avene was able to include Sully amongst his lordships: see below, and n. 31.
21 *Calendar of Close Rolls, 1313–18*, pp. 161–2, 406.
22 *Glamorgan County History III*, p. 82.
23 *Calendar of Fine Rolls, 1319–27*, p. 100
24 *Calendar of Fine Rolls, 1319–27*, p. 189.
25 *Calendar of Patent Rolls, 1324–24*, p. 73.
26 Certainly not 1314, as given by Ralph Griffiths in *Glamorgan County History III*, p. 341.

Notes

27 Bartrum, *Welsh Genealogies A.D. 300–1400*, III, Iestyn 5.
28 See Clark, *Cartae*, IV, pp. 1218, 1224, 1226, 1231, 1244–5, 1252, 1254–5 for charters in which John d'Avene appears as witness or grantor, usually described as a knight, in the late 1330s and early 1340s. His son Thomas is increasingly prominent.
29 *Calendar of Inquisitions Post Mortem*, XI, 1347–52, pp. 333, 338.
30 *Glamorgan County History III*, p. 82.
31 See, for examples, *Calendar of Ancient Correspondence concerning Wales*, p. 260, and *Calendar of Patent Rolls, 1317–21*, p. 73.
32 *Glamorgan County History III*, p. 86.
33 Clark, *Cartae*, VI, p. 2362.
34 See *inter alia* Clark, *Cartae*, IV, p. 1231 for Llywelyn ap Cynwrig as a witness (immediately after Sir John D'Avene) to a grant relating to land in Penmarc in 1339.
35 See pp. 66–7, 119–20 for references to Dafydd ap Meurig.
36 See Bartrum, *Welsh Genealogies*, Iestyn.
37 R. R. Davies, 'Bohun and Lancaster Lordships', p. 387.
38 *Calendar of Inquisitions Post Mortem*, IX, no. 118, p. 121.
39 It is assumed here that the Yevan ap Reys fitz Maistre Reys of the royal order to arrest some key opponents in the land of Brecon is a mistake for Yevan ap Maistre Reys or some such naming formula. See Stephenson, *Patronage and Power*, pp. 47–8, n. 40.
40 Stephenson, *Patronage and Power*, p. 60.
41 Stephenson, *Patronage and Power*, p. 60.
42 Stephenson, *Patronage and Power*, p. 60.
43 Stephenson, *Patronage and Power*, p. 60.
44 Stephenson, *Patronage and Power*, p. 61.
45 Stephenson, *Patronage and Power*, p. 61.
46 See the discussion in Stephenson, *Patronage and Power*, pp. 62–3, and see Philip ap Rees's Inquisition Post Mortem, in *Calendar of Inquisitions Post Mortem*, XII, no. 313, p. 286.
47 J. G. Edwards (ed.), *Littere Wallie* (Cardiff: University of Wales Press, 1935), pp. 28–9, 33–4.
48 *Calendar of Patent Rolls, 1292–1301*, p. 565.
49 Davies, *Lordship and Society*, p. 225 n. 45.
50 See for example Davies, *Lordship and Society*, p. 70.
51 See p. 119.
52 Interestingly, Hywel ap Hywel appears herein as a knight in Glamorgan contexts in 1329–31, while Adam Chapman, *Welsh Soldiers in the Later Middle Ages*, p. 62, points to Hywel ap Hywel of Brecon as a commissioner of array in 1338, and designated as a knight as was the Glamorgan man of that name.
53 *Calendar of Fine Rolls, 1319–27*, p. 84.

54 *Calendar of Fine Rolls, 1319–27*, p. 156, for the fine and its cancellation. It is explained at p. 154 that the fines (which included that of Hywel ap Hywel) were cancelled in the first parliament of Edward III on the grounds that the baronial quarrel with Despenser was a just one. A letter recording the quittance of the fine is on the Memoranda Roll for 1 March 1327: see Natalie Fryde (ed.), *List of Welsh Entries in the Memoranda Rolls, 1282–1343* (Cardiff: University of Wales Press, 1974), p. 68. For Philip ap Hywel, see pp. 24–9.
55 *Calendar of Fine Rolls, 1319–27*, Appendix, pp. 123–7.
56 *Calendar of Fine Rolls, 1319–27*, p. 125.
57 *Calendar of Patent Rolls, 1321–24*, p. 18.
58 *Calendar of Patent Rolls, 1321–24*, p. 73.
59 *Calendar of Close Rolls, 1318–23*, p. 420; *Calendar of Patent Rolls, 1321–24*, p. 77, where Meurig is one of those, who include Master Rees ap Hywel, his brother Philip, William, brother of Meurig son of Rees, Philip de Clanvowe, and Yevan ap 'Reys fitz' Maistre Reys (for whom, see note 38 above), all of whom were subject to a royal order to Robert de Morby to arrest them. It is to be noted that all of those mentioned above held dynastic names of descendants of Hywel ap Meurig.
60 *Calendar of Close Rolls, 1318–23*, p. 428. For William, see the previous note.
61 *Calendar of Close Rolls, 1318–23*, p. 206.
62 *Calendar of Close Rolls, 1318–23*, p. 167.
63 *Calendar of Close Rolls, 1318–23*, p. 206.
64 Davies, 'Bohun and Lancaster Lordships', pp. 394–5.
65 Thereby possibly maintaining the dynastic connection with Builth. See *Calendar of Patent Rolls, 1338–40*, p. 284.
66 The exception to this statement is the conflict between John Charlton and Sir Gruffudd Fychan de la Pole for control of the lordship, discussed below.
67 Edwards (ed.), *Littere Wallie*, pp. 42–3.
68 B. F. Byerly and C. R. Byerly (eds), *Records of the Wardrobe and Household, 1286–1289* (London: HMSO, 1986), pp. 424–34 *passim*.
69 For a recent account of the battle of Maes Moydog, which effectively brought Madog ap Llywelyn's rebellion to an end, and which involved both Madog ap Meilir and Madog ab Einion, see P. G. Barton, 'The Battle of Maes Moydog', *Montgomeryshire Collections*, 106 (2018), 33–42, especially pp. 39–40.
70 Barton, 'The Battle of Maes Moydog', pp. 39–40.
71 *Calendar of Patent Rolls, 1292–1301*, p. 163.
72 *Calendar of Patent Rolls, 1313–17*, p. 23.
73 See R. Iestyn Daniel (ed.), *Gwaith Dafydd Bach ap Madog Wladaidd, 'Sypyn Cyfeiliog'* (Aberystwyth: Centre for Advanced Welsh and Celtic Studies, 1998) pp. 13-14. See also John Davies, 'Christmas at

Notes

the court of Dafydd ap Cadwaladr at Bachelldre near Montgomery in the mid-fourteenth century', *Montgomeryshire Collections*, 109 (2021), 23–32.
74   *Calendar of Close Rolls, 1318–23*, p. 520.
75   Davies, 'Christmas at the court of Dafydd ap Cadwaladr', pp. 25–6.
76   See John Davies, 'Madog's raid: the Welsh attack on the Vale of Montgomery, 6 April, 1332', *Montgomeryshire Collections*, 106 (2018), 43–53, at p. 50.
77   Grant G. Simpson and James D. Galbraith, *Calendar of Documents relating to Scotland, Vol. 5 Supplementary, 1108–1516* (Scottish Record Office), p. 505 no. 3538. I owe this reference to the kindness of John Davies.
78   Simpson and Galbraith, *Calendar of Documents relating to Scotland*.
79   Including Madog ap Meilir (q.v.).
80   The standard discussions are Richard Morgan, 'The Barony of Powys, 1275–1360', *Welsh History Review*, 10 (1980), 1–42 and David Stephenson, 'Crisis and continuity in a fourteenth-century Welsh lordship: the struggle for Powys, 1312–32', *Cambrian Medieval Celtic Studies*, 66 (2013), 57–78.
81   Morgan, 'Barony of Powys', pp. 11 and 15.
82   Stephenson, 'Crisis and continuity', p. 63 n. 32.
83   Stephenson, 'Crisis and continuity', p. 61.
84   Constance Bullock-Davies, *Menestrellorum Multitudo* (Cardiff: University of Wales Press, 1978), p. 187, recording the knighting of *Griffinus filius Grifini de la Pole*.
85   Dinas, effectively a part of Mechain, had been bought by Gruffudd in the later 1290s from Roger Springhose, former sheriff of Shropshire and a long-standing friend of Gruffudd Fychan's father.
86   Stephenson, 'Crisis and continuity', p. 63 and n. 29.
87   Stephenson, 'Crisis and continuity', p. 62.
88   See Stephenson, *Medieval Powys*, pp. 153, 156, 175, 195, 244.
89   The evidence for institutional development within the barony of Powys is very slight during the fourteenth century but just enough survives to give us significant glimpses. See Morgan, 'Barony of Powys', pp. 1–42, and Stephenson, 'Crisis and continuity', pp. 57–78.
90   Stephenson, 'Crisis and Continuity', p. 70.
91   *Calendar of Patent Rolls, 1321–24*, pp. 157–8.
92   See for the Cyfeiliog Inquisition Post Mortem, G. T. O. Bridgeman, 'The Princes of Upper Powys', *Montgomeryshire Collections*, 1 (1868), 5–194, at p. 144.
93   See Stephenson, 'The Middle Ages in the pages of *Montgomeryshire Collections*', *Montgomeryshire Collections*, 100 (2012), 67–85, at pp. 69–70.

94 See Llinos Beverley Smith, 'The Arundel charters to the lordship of Chirk in the fourteenth century', *Bulletin of the Board of Celtic Studies*, 22 (1969) 153–66, at p. 162, where he heads the lay witnesses to the charter of 1324. At p. 159 n. 1, Dr Smith suggests that 'it is quite possible that he held office in the lordship of Chirk at this date' – though given that he appears as *Griffino domino de Glyndouerdo*, and that several office-holders appear with their offices specified, this is perhaps unlikely; it is perhaps more probable that he appears as a neighbouring magnate.
95 Gresham, *Medieval Stone Carving in North Wales* (Cardiff: University of Wales Press, 1968), pp. 153–5.
96 Pictured in Gresham, *Medieval Stone Carving*, at p. 154.
97 Davies, *Lordship and Society*, p. 224 n. 41.
98 *Calendar of Patent Rolls, 1313–17*, p. 21.
99 *Calendar of Inquisitions, Miscellaneous, 1307–49*, no. 507.
100 *Calendar of Close Rolls, 1330–33*, p. 84.
101 Paul Vinogradoff and Frank Morgan (eds), *Survey of the Honour of Denbigh, 1334* (London: British Academy, 1914), p. 57.
102 Vinogradoff and Morgan (eds), *Survey of the Honour of Denbigh, 1334*, p. 57.
103 Davies, *Lordship and Society*, p. 418.
104 Korngiebel, 'English Colonial Ethnic Discrimination', p. 19.
105 Davies, *Lordship and Society*, p. 418.
106 Korngiebel, 'English Colonial Ethnic Discrimination', p. 19.
107 Korngiebel, 'English Colonial Ethnic Discrimination', p. 19.
108 *Calendar of Patent Rolls, 1313–17*, p. 178. It is, however, interesting that Llywelyn's brothers, Maredudd and Hywel, were listed before him in the witness-list.
109 *Calendar of Patent Rolls, 1321–24*, p. 74.
110 Korngiebel, 'English Colonial Ethnic Discrimination', p. 20.
111 T. P. Ellis (ed.), *The First Extent of Bromfield and Yale AD 1315* (London: Hon. Soc. Cymmrodorion, 1924).
112 *First Extent*, p. 81.
113 Perhaps an error by the compiler of the *Extent* if the Llywelyn (Fychan) ap Llywelyn ap Maredudd is the same person.
114 Llywelyn appears as Llywelyn Fychan in the genealogical tracts (see Bartrum, *Welsh Genealogies*, IV, Sandde Hardd 2) but is generally Llywelyn of Bromfield in ecclesiastical records (see, for example, Pearson, *Fasti Ecclesiae Anglicanae 1066–1300: Volume 9, the Welsh Cathedrals (Bangor, Llandaff, St Asaph, St Davids)*, p. 36.
115 Llywelyn ab Ynyr appears first amongst witnesses to a deed executed by the rulers of northern Powys in 1247, and appears as a witness to a grant of Gruffudd ap Madog, lord of Bromfield to Emma, his

Notes

wife in 1268–69, and to a grant to Emma by her sons in 1270: Pryce, *Acts of Welsh Rulers*, nos. 513, 516, 526.
116 Pryce, *Acts of Welsh Rulers*, 529.
117 Gresham, *Medieval Stone Carving in North Wales*, pp. 182–5, dated to c.1320.
118 Gresham, *Medieval Stone Carving in North Wales*, pp. 152–3, dated to early fourteenth century. Gresham notes that on the grounds of probable date this could be the stone of Sir Gruffudd Llwyd (discussed in Chapter 2 above (at pp. 38–47) but we can dismiss this suggestion – which Gresham advances very tentatively – on the ground that Sir Gruffudd had little involvement with the north-east of Wales, and we have a much better candidate in the Gruffudd Llwyd recorded in both of the Survey entries for Bodidris and Gelligynan.
119 For whom, see p. 116.
120 *Calendar of Patent Rolls, 1321–24*, p. 74; Bartrum, *Welsh Genealogies*, IV, Sandde Hardd 4.
121 Carr, *Gentry of North Wales*, p. 51.
122 For his place at the centre of a network of relationships connecting his near kin with prominence in the church, see Carr, *Gentry of North Wales*, p. 65.
123 Tudur's acquisitions are well described by Carr, *Gentry of North Wales*, pp. 82–3, where it is noted that his first recorded one was in 1316, in Halkyn, and that between 1326 and 1366 there survive (and some are lost) eighty-six deeds to which Tudur was a party, of which the great majority date to the period before the Black Death; around 40% are conveyances by means of *tir pryd*.
124 For Madog ap Llywelyn ap Gruffudd, see pp. 35–8.
125 Carr, *Gentry of North Wales*, p. 51.
126 Carr, *Gentry of North Wales*, p. 52.
127 Carr, *Gentry of North Wales*, p. 51.
128 Carr, *Gentry of North Wales*, p. 65.
129 Carr, *Gentry of North Wales*, pp. 60, 65.
130 For Master Ystrwyth's career, see Stephenson, *Political Power in Medieval Gwynedd*, pp. 224–5.
131 *Calendar of Close Rolls, 1318–23*, p. 619.
132 *Calendar of Close Rolls, 1318–23*, p. 619.
133 Roberts, *Aspects of Welsh History*, pp. 161–2.
134 Carr, *Gentry of North Wales*, pp. 62, 124. *Calendar of Ancient Correspondence*, p. 228.
135 Stephenson, *Political Power in Medieval Gwynedd*, pp. 208–9; BT, Pen20 trans., p. 115.
136 Roberts, *Aspects of Welsh History*, p. 186.

137 For context, see G. Rex Smith, 'The Penmachno Letter Patent and the Welsh Uprising of 1294/95', *Cambrian Medieval Celtic Studies*, 58 (2009), 49–67.
138 *Record of Caernarvon*, p. 215.
139 Roberts, *Aspects of Welsh History*, p. 188.
140 In the event Hywel ap Gruffudd was unable to prosecute his case due to illness, and it was allowed to lapse.
141 *Rotuli Scotiae*, I, p. 156. The possibility that Sir Gruffudd Llwyd may have been involved in a complex manoeuvre is raised in discussion of Sir Gruffudd's career in chapter 2 (pp. 44–6 above).
142 *Calendar of Close Rolls, 1313–18*, p. 367. The discussion in Roberts, *Aspects of Welsh History*, p. 188, hardly tallies with the Close Roll reference given at his note 4 and given here. But Roberts's identification of Hywel ap Gruffudd as 'the semi-legendary Hywel y Pedolau' seems entirely credible.
143 *Calendar of Fine Rolls, 1307–1319*, p. 361; *Calendar of Fine Rolls, 1319–27*, p. 1.
144 *Calendar of Inquisitions, Miscellaneous, 1307–49*, no. 404.
145 Roberts, *Aspects of Welsh History*, p. 190.
146 W. Illingworth (ed.), *Placita de Quo Warranto* (Record Commission, 1818), p. 818.
147 Of course, the family's status as 'Wyrion Eden' was a good starting point.
148 *Calendar of Ancient Correspondence concerning* Wales, pp. 228–32.
149 Roberts, *Aspects of Welsh History*, p. 195.
150 Roberts, *Aspects of Welsh History*, p. 195.
151 Griffiths, *Principality of Wales*, I, pp. 103, 105.
152 See above, at pp. 51–6, the section of chapter 2 devoted to a survey of Rhys's career. All work on Sir Rhys ap Gruffudd owes a great debt to Ralph Griffiths, *Principality of Wales*, pp. 99–102 and references therein.
153 Bartrum, *Welsh Genealogies*, I, Bleddyn ap Cynfyn 26; IV, Marchudd 12.
154 Roberts, *Aspects of Welsh History*, pp. 191–2.
155 *Record of Caernarvon*, pp. 150–1.
156 See Carr, *The Gentry of North Wales*, p. 148, for Hywel, together with another cleric, Ithel ap Roppert, purchasing from the prince the right to sell the lucrative marriage of Generys, the sole heiress of Madog ap Goronwy Fychan, grandson of Goronwy ab Ednyfed Fychan.
157 Carr, *The Gentry of North Wales*, p. 146.
158 Rees, *Calendar of Ancient Petitions*, pp. 505, 514.
159 Stephenson, *Political Power in Medieval Gwynedd*, pp. 238–9.
160 Rees, *Calendar of Ancient Petitions*, p. 209.
161 Carr, *The Gentry of North Wales*, p. 32.

Notes

162 Carr, *The Gentry of North Wales*, p. 32.
163 Carr, *The Gentry of North Wales*, p. 32.
164 Carr, *The Gentry of North Wales*, p. 32.
165 Carr, 'Edeirnion', p. 148.
166 Carr, 'Edeirnion', p. 148.
167 Carr, 'Edeirnion', p. 148.
168 *Book of Prests*, pp. 163, 169, 186, where he is noted as *Griffinus dominus de Hendor*.
169 *Book of Prests*, pp. 58–9, 135.
170 Waters, *Edwardian Settlement of North Wales*, p. 173; Carr, 'Edeirnion', p. 148.
171 *Calendar of Patent Rolls, 1317–21*, p. 243, where Madog is granted the offices during pleasure; he in turn was followed by his cousins Gruffudd and Rhys, sons of Madog ap Dafydd.
172 *Calendar of Close Rolls, 1313–18*, p. 367.
173 *Calendar of Patent rolls, 1321–24*, p. 73 (wrongly given as p. 373 in Carr, 'Edeirnion', p. 148).
174 William Rees (ed.), *Calendar of Ancient Petitions relating to Wales* (Cardiff: University of Wales Press, 1975), p. 73, which also reports the king's acceptance of Madog's petition, for his good service. Powys was currently in the hands of Edward II as a result of the forfeiture of its lord, John Charlton, who had been aligned with Thomas of Lancaster against the king.
175 *Rotuli Scotiae*, p. 311.
176 Carr, 'Edeirnion', p. 149, makes the interesting observation that 'it must be more than coincidence that Dafydd ap Madog married an heiress from the Launceston area'.
177 Bartrum, *Welsh Genealogies*, I, Bleddyn ap Cynfyn 48.
178 *BT, Pen20 trans.*, p. 121, *sub*1292. For the development of the Peniarth 20 'continuation' of the *Brut* down to 1332, see David Stephenson, 'The continuation of *Brut y Tywysogyon* in NLW MS Peniarth 20', in Guy, Henley, Jones and Thomas (eds), *The Chronicles of Medieval Wales and the March* (Turnhout: Brepols, 2020), pp. 155–68.
179 Gresham, *Medieval Stone Carving in North Wales*, p. 192; the genealogy is taken from J. E. Griffith, *Pedigrees of Anglesey and Caernarvonshire Families* (Horncastle, 1914).
180 *Record of Caernarvon*, p. 220.
181 Keith Williams-Jones, *Merioneth Lay Subsidy Roll, 1292–3*, p. lxxxviii, notes that Ynyr Fychan 'was assessed at *only* [my italics] 8s 6½d in 1292–3'. This must be seen first in the context of Thomas Jones-Pierce's norm of 6s 8d for 'leading uchelwyr' (ibid.) and secondly as a possible reflection of Ynyr's local influence – in this case an ability to secure a low valuation.

182 *Rotuli Parliamentorum*, I, p. 397, where he is noted as Ynyr Fychan ab Ynyr ap Meurig de Merioneth.
183 Carr, *Gentry of North Wales*, p. 257.
184 Carr, *Gentry of North Wales*, p. 257.
185 The armour is interesting, as Gresham observes that, together with an effigy of an unnamed knight at Tywyn, also Merionethshire, it marks the first appearance of plate armour in north Wales. The very fine carving of the almost intact shield and the armour suggests a figure of some wealth. That and the fame of some of its members suggests that this was the leading family of the commote of Tal-y-bont.
186 *Iolo Goch ac Eraill* (1937), pp. 107 and 356.
187 Carr, *Gentry of North Wales*, p. 119.
188 Carr, *Gentry of North Wales*, p. 120.
189 *Calendar of Close Rolls, 1313–18*, p. 367. Glyn Roberts's discussion of this episode will not easily support his suggestion (in *Aspects of Welsh History*, p. 188) that the entry relates to the battle of Bannockburn.
190 The following list of sheriffs is heavily dependent on the initial researches of Waters, *The Edwardian Settlement of North Wales*, pp. 172–4.
191 See above, pp. 42–6, for Gruffudd's periods of imprisonment within these years.
192 Not dated by Waters, but described in *Calendar of Fine Rolls 1327–37*, p. 394 as 'late sheriff of Anglesey' and reference is made to his accounting from Michaelmas 6 Edward III until the following Michaelmas – which suggests 1332–3.
193 See Bartrum, *Welsh Genealogies*, I, p. 156, *sub* Cilmin 5. This identification assumes that Einion was by no means young when he acted as sheriff. For Ystwyth/Instructus as archpriest of Caer Gybi in north-west Anglesey, see Stephenson, *Political Power in Medieval Gwynedd*, p. 225.
194 See pp. 14–15 above.
195 Stephenson, *Political Power in Medieval Gwynedd*, pp. 296, 366, 370–1, 376, 379, 385.
196 *Archaeologia Cambrensis Supplement*, 1877, p. clx, *sub Fidelitas Baronum*.
197 Rhys's baronial estates were relatively small lands in West Wales, especially Llansadwrn. Cf. Chapman, *Welsh Soldiers in the Later Middle Ages*, pp. 161–4.
198 Griffiths, *Principality of Wales*, I, pp. 366, 371; cf *Calendar of Close Rolls, 1333–37*, p. 337.
199 Bartrum, *Welsh Genealogies*, II, Eidio 5.
200 Idris Ll. Foster, 'The Book of the Anchorite', *Proceedings of the British Academy*, 36 (1950), 197–226.
201 Griffiths, *Principality of Wales*, I, pp. 296, 385.

Notes

202 *Littere Wallie*, p. 40.
203 Jones, 'The Subsidy of 1292', *Bulletin of the Board of Celtic Studies*, 13 (1950), p. 221.
204 Stephenson, *Patronage and Power in the Medieval Welsh March*, pp. 22–4.
205 Rhys, *Ministers' Accounts for West Wales 1277–1306*, p. 401.
206 See Griffiths, *Principality of Wales*, I, pp. 358–9, 362. The suggestion made by Griffiths, ibid., p. 358, that Gruffudd Crach might be identified as the Gruffydd Goch, a former rebel whose property was restored to him in November 1316, is perhaps unlikely.
207 Griffiths, *Principality of Wales*, I, pp. 109, 270. See, for his involvement in the commission of 1350, Griffiths p. 109, and cf. *Calendar of Patent Rolls, 1348–50*, pp. 589–90. Griffiths, ibid., suggests that he may be identified as the deputy-steward of the Mortimer lordship of Narberth in 1357–8.
208 Griffiths, *Principality of Wales*, I, p. 473.
209 *Calendar of Inquisitions, Miscellaneous*, II, p. 292.
210 On this outstanding figure, see Stephenson, *Medieval Wales*, pp. 79, 81–2.
211 Thomas Parry (ed.), *Gwaith Dafydd ap Gwilym* (Cardiff: University of Wales Press, 1952), p. xxvi.
212 *Calendar of Fine Rolls, 1319–27*, p. 385; ibid., *1327–37*, p. 67.
213 Griffiths, *Principality of Wales*, I, p. 208.
214 *Calendar of Fine Rolls, 1327–37*, p. 433.
215 *Calendar of Ancient Correspondence concerning Wales*, p. 237.
216 *Archaeologia Cambrensis Supplement*, 1877, p. clviii.
217 *Archaeologia Cambrensis Supplement*, 1877, p. clviii.
218 For detailed discussion of their location, see Parry (ed.), *Gwaith Dafydd ap Gwilym*, p. xxviii.
219 Parry (ed.), *Gwaith Dafydd ap Gwilym*, pp. 31–8.
220 'He who kills shall be killed', at ll. 98 and 107–8.
221 Parry (ed.), *Gwaith Dafydd ap Gwilym*, p. xxx, where Parry adds to Evans's suggestion that it is possible that some disagreement had arisen between Llywelyn and the new lord of Emlyn, and that it was the latter who killed him.
222 See Chapter 5.

Chapter 4

1 For a possible case, see pp. 62–3 regarding Hywel ap Hywel.
2 Davies, *Lordship and Society*, p. 226.
3 To those long-established communities of agriculturalists in the Englishries of the Middle and south-eastern March we must add, by the later thirteenth century, settlers brought in after the Edwardian conquest – as in the well-known case of those brought in under

lordly direction or encouragement in the lordship of Denbigh. See D. Huw Owen, 'The Englishry of Denbigh: an English colony in Medieval Wales', *Transactions of the Honourable Society of Cymmrodorion* (1974–5), pp. 57–76.

4 Further work on the impact of the Black Death in Wales is needed, but we can safely follow the estimate of Dr Stevens that probably over a third of the population died as a result of the famine of 1315–22 and the plague of 1349: Matthew Frank Stevens, *The Economy of Medieval Wales, 1067–1536* (Cardiff: University of Wales Press, 2019), pp. 82–4, 87–90, 110–12.

5 The reference to adult males reflects the standard used, however approximately, by the medieval recruiters whose instructions sometimes referred to males from 16 to 60 years of age. It should be emphasised that medieval population figures are something of a minefield: estimates of the pre-Black Death population of England have varied from c.3.7 million to closer to 7 million.

6 See Chapman, *Welsh Soldiers*, p. 228.

7 For examples, see the following: Owain Gwynedd (Pryce, *Acts of Welsh Rulers*, no. 196, dated as 'probably November 1165 – early March 1166'); the Lord Rhys (ibid., nos 26, 28, dated as November 1165 – April 1197); Dafydd ab Owain Gwynedd (ibid., no. 200); Llywelyn ab Iorwerth (ibid., nos 213–74, *passim*), Dafydd ap Llywelyn (ibid., nos 292, 294, 296, 298–9, 307–8) and Llywelyn ap Gruffudd (ibid., nos 328, 353–430, *passim*).

8 *BT, Pen 20 trans.*, p. 68.

9 Stephenson, *Medieval Wales*, pp. 106–7.

10 Pryce, *Acts of Welsh Rulers*, pp. 399–400. The words of the agreement were that Llywelyn would act *ut ballivus domini regis*. For an instance in which Llywelyn was called upon to act as a royal official see his intervention in the politics of South Wales to force Rhys Gryg, a son of the Lord Rhys, to hand over lordships to the Marchers from who they had been taken, and to perform homage to the king, in 1220. For the complexities of the situation that developed in his relationship with Rhys Gryg in this context, see Stephenson, *Medieval Wales*, pp. 109–12.

11 William de Braose senior was brought low, chased out of his lands, and eventually forced into exile in France, where he died in 1211; his wife Matilda and eldest son William were taken into royal custody and, apparently, starved to death in prison in 1210.

12 Nowhere more so than in his *Lordship and Society in the March of Wales, 1284–1400* (Oxford, 1978).

13 Davies, *Lordship and Society*, p. 227.

14 For Gruffudd Fychan de la Pole, see herein p. 77; and for Llywelyn Bren, see p. 61.

15 For Rhys ap Gruffudd's escapes from the realm of England and Wales, see herein pp. 53–4; or for Philip ap Hywel's narrow escape after a period

Notes

of imprisonment, see herein p. 27. It is also worth remembering that it is sometimes difficult, and even unhelpful, to differentiate too clearly between rebellion and loyalty. Morgan ap Maredudd is frequently described as a rebel in 1294–5, whereas he claimed that he was not acting in Glamorgan against the king, but only against the earl of Gloucester – the implication being that his actions were in the royal interest – a claim apparently fully accepted by Edward I. While not identical, a related issue appears in the cases of Sir Gruffudd Llwyd and Sir Rhys ap Gruffudd in 1326–7: they could be cast by those surrounding Edward, the heir to Edward II's kingdom, as dangerous subversives whereas they would have claimed that they were merely acting as loyal subjects of Edward II.

16 Davies, 'Bohun and Lancaster Lordships', p. 120.
17 See, for just a few out of many examples, the references in the poems of Dafydd ap Gwilym in praise of Llywelyn ap Gwilym: see Thomas Parry (ed.), *Gwaith Dafydd ap Gwilym* (Cardiff: University of Wales Press, 1952), pp. 31–9: *Moliant/Mawl Llywelyn ap Gwilym*, ll. 29–31; and *Marwnad Llywelyn ap Gwilym*, ll. 57–60.
18 Key references are P. C. Bartrum, *Welsh Genealogies, AD 300–1400* (Cardiff: University of Wales Press, 1974), Vol. 4, Marchudd, pp. 4, 14.
19 See ibid., Vol. 1, Rhys ap Tewdwr, p. 4.
20 See Stephenson, 'The continuation of Brut y Tywysogyon in NLW, MS Peniarth 20', in Guy et al. (eds), *The chronicles of Medieval Wales and the March*, at pp. 164–8, for discussion of Madog ap Llywelyn.
21 Unless he is to be identified as the William ap Hywel who acted as deputy constable of Dinefwr 1310–12: Griffiths, *Principality of Wales I*, p. 244.
22 On this appointment, see *Calendar of Patent Rolls, 1327–30*, p. 66.
23 See, for examples, Madog Gloddaeth, who married Morfydd, a daughter of Sir Gruffudd Llwyd: Carr, *Gentry of North Wales*, p. 146, while we have noted the marriage of Tudur, one of the ambitious sons of Ithel Fychan of Flintshire, to Erddylad, daughter of Madog ap Llywelyn, a dominant figure in Bromfield and Yale (see above, p. 124).
24 *Calendar of Patent Rolls, 1321–24*, pp. 73–4, 77.
25 *Calendar of Patent Rolls, 1321–24*, p. 77.
26 See Stephenson, *Patronage and Power in the Medieval Welsh March*, Appendix, pp. 123–7.
27 For discussion, see Stephenson, *Patronage and Power in the Medieval Welsh March*, pp. 47–8 n. 40 where it is argued that this is an error for 'Ieuan fil Master Rees'.
28 Morby's custody of the lordship of Brecon follows the death of Earl Humphrey de Bohun, lord of Brecon, 'against the peace' at the battle of Boroughbridge in 1322. De Bohun's lands were taken into the king's hands and not released to Humphrey's heir, John, the 5th earl of Hereford, until after the fall of the Despensers in 1326.

29 Lleucu and her sons by Llywelyn appear to have been released from royal custody after Llywelyn's execution; they were given refuge in the lordship of Brecon by Humphrey de Bohun.
30 *Calendar of Patent Rolls, 1321–24*, p. 105
31 *Calendar of Patent Rolls, 1321–24*, p. 77.
32 Recruitment in the principality lands was mainly begun with the appointment on 28 September of Rhys ap Gruffudd to assemble all the men of West Wales and South Wales to go against the invaders. Sir Gruffudd Llwyd received a similar appointment with regard to North Wales on the same day.
33 For his lands in both Gower and Haverford, see Griffiths, *Principality of Wales I*, p. 104. He would go on, in the 1330s, to act as deputy justiciar of South Wales (ibid.).
34 *Calendar of Close Rolls, 1318–23*, p. 421.
35 This figure includes joint leadership by both English and Welsh officials when the latter are men identified as significant in Chapters 2 and 3. It should of course be stressed that at 'grass-roots' level the cooperation of Welsh officials or community leaders was necessary for successful raising of troops.
36 The calculation of leaders does not of course include discussion of the identity of centenars (commanders of a hundred men) or other subordinate officers such as vintenars (commanders of a troop of twenty men) for which figures are in significant degree lacking.
37 See pp. 17–18.
38 For Meurig and William, see pp. 71–2, 124.
39 The chancery rolls contain place-dates so that this progress can be monitored closely.
40 Chapman, *Welsh Soldiers in the Later Middle Ages*, p. 219.

Chapter 5

1 See Stephenson, *Patronage and Power*, pp. 62–3.
2 The figures are based on those given for individual campaigns in tables 4 and 5 in Appendix 1 of Chapman, *Welsh Soldiers*, pp. 228–9. Into the first period, 1297–1322, come those of 1297–8, 1298, 1300, 1301, 1307, 1319, 1322; the second period, 1334–46, includes those of 1334–5, 1335, 1336, 1338–9, 1342–3, 1345, 1346.
3 Chapman, *Welsh Soldiers*, p. 218.
4 For Llywelyn ap Gwilym, pp. 103, and 179, n.17.
5 For more details of this killing, see pp. 103–4 above.
6 Smith and Smith (eds), *History of Merioneth II: The Middle Ages*, pp. 76–7.
7 See Smith and Smith (eds), *History of Merioneth II*, p. 80 and n. 133, quoting *Calendar of Close Rolls, 1369–74*, p. 158.

Notes

8   Edwards (ed.), *Calendar of Ancient Correspondence concerning Wales*, p. 231.
9   Edwards (ed.), *Calendar of Ancient Correspondence*, p. 231.
10 Edwards (ed.), *Calendar of Ancient Correspondence*, pp. 231–2.
11 It seems likely that one of these was the source of the information in this letter.
12 *Calendar of Ancient Correspondence*, pp. 233–4.
13 *Calendar of Ancient Correspondence*, p. 233.
14 *Calendar of Ancient Correspondence*, pp. 230–1.
15 *Calendar of Ancient Correspondence*, p. 231.
16 *Calendar of Ancient Correspondence*, pp. 231–2.
17 *Calendar of Ancient Correspondence*, pp. 229–30.
18 The quotations in this and the following paragraph are all taken from Trumwyn's report of late May, 1345: *Calendar of Ancient Correspondence*, pp. 247–8.
19 A glance at those who were implicated, or believed to be implicated, in the Shaldeford murder may be thought to strengthen this possibility. See John de Pirye's report, which follows immediately, and below, *Calendar of Ancient Correspondence*, 232–3.
20 The troops may have been thinking of their experience or that of their families, of the days of leadership by men such as Sir Morgan ap Maredudd, or Madog ap Llywelyn, or of paymasters like Philip and Master Rees, sons of Hywel ap Meurig, all of whom had served with, and died before, Sir Gruffudd Llwyd.
21 *Calendar of Ancient Correspondence*, pp. 232–3.
22 *Black Prince's Register*, I, p. 160.
23 *Black Prince's Register*, I, p. 108; sessions were therefore hurriedly arranged, though in the event they were postponed on news that the justice was returning to deal with the upsurge in violence: ibid., p. 113.
24 *Black Prince's Register*, I, pp. 159–60. The ordinance in question, for which see *Record of Caernarvon*, pp. 131–2, had previously been ignored in specific cases; see, for examples, Kenfig, Builth, Cardigan and Newcastle Emlyn, in Griffiths, *Principality of Wales*, p. 284.
25 Matthew Frank Stevens, *The Economy of Medieval Wales 1067–1536* (Cardiff: University of Wales Press, 2019), p. 84.
26 Stevens, *The Economy of Medieval Wales*, p. 86.
27 Stevens, *The Economy of Medieval Wales*, p. 87.
28 Stevens, *The Economy of Medieval Wales*, pp. 89–90.
29 Stevens, *The Economy of Medieval Wales*, p. 90.
30 Roberts, *Aspects of Welsh History*, p. 195.
31 Williams, *The Welsh Church*, p. 80.
32 See, for example, Williams, *The Welsh Church*, p. 123.
33 *Calendar of Patent Rolls, 1345–48*, pp. 292–3.
34 *Calendar of Patent Rolls, 1345–48*, p. 344.

35 Even in the two cases – those of bishops Brian (1349–52) and Houghton (1361–89) – their elections in Glanmor Williams's words were made 'not on account of their local associations but chiefly because of their usefulness to the king' (Williams, *The Welsh Church*, p. 122).
36 Williams, *The Welsh Church*, p. 127. For Ithel's elegy, see *Gwaith Iolo Goch*, pp. 98–100.
37 The situation at Bangor in 1366 is instructive: the vacancy of the see in that year gave the Black Prince an opportunity to advance his servant, Thomas Dalby, but Pope Urban V ordered the archbishop of Bordeaux to 'inform himself, within two months, by means of persons in his city and province, many of whom speak Welsh' whether Dalby was competent enough in that language to be able to preach in it. The report must have been negative, as Gervase de Castro, a Dominican, and assuredly a Welshman, became bishop of Bangor. Thomas Dalby remained the prince's constable of Bordeaux. (Williams, *The Welsh Church*, p. 126.)
38 *Black Prince's Register*, I, p. 47; there were similar instructions relating to appointments of royal clerks in the same year to the bishop of Bangor regarding the churches of Llanbeblig and Aberffraw, ibid., pp. 119, 138; and to the bishop of St Asaph regarding the church of Northop, ibid., p. 118.
39 For the different geographic elements in Flintshire, see map 1 above.
40 *Black Prince's Register*, I, p. 49.
41 *Black Prince's Register*, I, p. 72, and repeated on 8 June, p. 84.
42 *Black Prince's Register*, I, p. 125.
43 *Black Prince's Register*, I, p. 155.
44 *Calendar of Chester Recognisance Rolls*, in *Thirty Sixth Annual Report of the Deputy Keeper of the Public Records* (1875), p. 427.
45 *Black Prince's Register*, III, p. 46.
46 *Black Prince's Register*, III, p. 14.
47 *Black Prince's Register*, III, p. 14.
48 *Black Prince's Register*, III, p. 184.
49 *Black Prince's Register*, III, pp. 318–22.
50 *Black Prince's Register*, III, p. 319.
51 *Black Prince's Register*, III, p. 320.
52 *Black Prince's Register*, III, pp. 321–2.
53 *Black Prince's Register*, III, p. 322.
54 *Black Prince's Register*, III, pp. 359–60.
55 Carr, *The Gentry of North Wales*, p. 130.
56 He is sometimes described as Sir Rhys ap Gruffudd II (see, for example, Griffiths, *Principality of Wales I*, pp. 262–3. His name, replicating that of his father, makes nonsense of the normal Welsh patronymic system, under which he should have been known as Rhys Fychan ap Rhys ap Gruffudd.

Bibliography

Primary sources (manuscript)

Trinity College, Dublin MS 212.
TNA E101/3/11.
TNA E101/5/18.
TNA, SC6, 1221/3 m. 8; /4 m.4.

Primary sources (printed)

'An Extent of the lordship of Hay', ed. Richard Morgan, *Brycheiniog*, 28 (1995–6), 15–21.
Annales Cestrienses, ed. R. C. Christie (Lancashire and Cheshire Record Society, 1887).
The Book of Prests of the King's Wardrobe for 1294–5, ed. E. B. Fryde (Oxford, 1962).
Brut y Tywysogyon or the chronicle of the Princes, Peniarth MS 20 Version, ed. and trans. T. Jones (Cardiff, 1952).
Calendar of Ancient Correspondence concerning Wales, ed. J. G. Edwards (Cardiff, 1935).
Calendar of Ancient Petitions relating to Wales, ed. W. Rees (Cardiff, 1975).
Calendar of Chancery Warrants 1244–1326 (London, 1927).
Calendar of Close Rolls, 1272–1422, 35 volumes (London, 1900–32).
Calendar of Documents relating to Scotland, Vol. 5 Supplementary, 1108–1516, ed. G. G. Simpson and J. D. Galbraith (London, 1881).
Calendar of Fine Rolls, 1272–1422, 14 volumes (London, 1911–34).
Calendar of Inquisitions, Miscellaneous, Henry III–22 Edward III, 2 volumes (London, 1916).
Calendar of Inquisitions Post Mortem, 1300–1377, volumes 4–13 (London, 1913–54).
Calendar of Patent Rolls, 1292–1377, 23 volumes (London, 1891–1916).

Calendar of Various Chancery Rolls, 1277–1326 [includes the Welsh Rolls] (London, 1912).
Cartae et alia Munimenta quae ad dominium de Glamorgancia pertinent, 6 vols, 2nd edition, ed. G. T. Clark (Cardiff, 1910).
Chronicles of the Reigns of Edward I and Edward II, ed. W. Stubbs, vol. 2 (London, 1883).
'Early Accounts relating to North Wales temp. Edward I', ed. J. Griffiths, *Bulletin of the Board of Celtic Studies*, 16 (1955), 109–34.
The Extent of Chirkland, 1391–93, ed. G. Peredur Jones (Liverpool, 1933).
The First Extent of Bromfield and Yale AD 1315, ed. T. P. Ellis (London: Hon. Soc. Cymmrodorion, 1924).
Flintshire Ministers' Accounts 1301–1328, ed. A. Jones (Flintshire Historical Society, 1913).
Flintshire Ministers' Accounts 1358–1353, ed. D. L. Evans (Flintshire Historical Society, 1929).
Gwaith Bleddyn Ddu, ed. R. I. Daniel (Aberystwyth, 1994).
Gwaith Casnodyn, ed. R. I. Daniel (Aberystwyth, 1999).
Gwaith Dafydd ap Gwilym, ed. T. Parry (Cardiff: University of Wales Press, 1952).
Gwaith Dafydd Bach ap Madog Wladaidd 'Sypyn Cyfeiliog' a Llywelyn ab y Moel, ed. R. I. Daniel (Aberystwyth: Centre for Advanced Welsh and Celtic Studies, 1998).
Gwaith Einion Offeiriad a Dafydd Ddu o Hiraddug, ed. R. G. Gruffydd and R. Ifans (Aberystwyth, 1997).
Gwaith Gruffudd ap Dafydd ap Tudur, Gwilym Ddu o Arfon, Trahaearn Brydydd Mawr ac Iorwerth Beli, ed. N. G. Costigan (Bosco), R. I. Daniel and D. Johnston (Aberystwyth, 1995).
Gwaith Iolo Goch, ed. D. R. Johnston (Cardiff, 1985).
Gwaith Llywelyn Brydydd Hoddnant, Dafydd ap Gwilym, Hillyn ac Eraill, ed. A. P. Owen (Aberystwyth, 1996).
Letters of Edward Prince of Wales, 1304–1305, ed. H. Johnstone (Cambridge: University Press, 1931).
The Life of Edward the Second, ed. W. Childs (Oxford, 2005).
List of Welsh Entries in the Memoranda Rolls, 1282–1343, ed. N. Fryde (Cardiff: University of Wales Press, 1974).
Littere Wallie, ed. J. G. Edwards (Cardiff, 1935).
The Merioneth Lay Subsidy Roll, 1292–3, ed. K. Williams-Jones (Cardiff: University of Wales Press, 1976).
Ministers' Accounts for West Wales (1277–1306), ed. M. Rhys (London, 1936).
Original Documents printed as a supplement to the Archaeologia Cambrensis, 1877 (London, 1877).
Placita de Quo Warranto, ed. W. Illingworth (Record Commission, 1818), p. 818.

Records of the Wardrobe and Household, 1286–1289, ed. B. F. Byerly and C. R. Byerly (London: HMSO, 1986).
Register of Edward the Black Prince, ed. M. C. B. Dawes, 4 volumes (London, 1930–3).
Registrum vulgariter nuncupatum 'the Record of Caernarvon', ed. H. Ellis (London: Record Commission, 1838).
Rotuli Parliamentorum, 7 volumes (London: Record Commission, 1783–1832).
Rotuli Scotiae, ed. D. Macpherson et al., 2 volumes (London, 1814–19).
South Wales and Monmouth Record Society Publications vol. 3, ed. H. J. Randall and W. Rees (1954).
Survey of the Honour of Denbigh 1334, ed. P. Vinogradoff and F. Morgan (London: British Academy, 1914).
Vita Edwardi Secundi, ed. N. Denholm-Young (London, 1957).
The Welsh Assize Roll, 1277–8, ed. J. C. Davies (1940).
Welsh Genealogies A.D. 300–1400, ed. P. C. Bartrum, 8 volumes (Cardiff, 1974).

Material on the internet

This category of primary sources includes the quite outstanding website Medieval Source Material on the Internet. The material includes a huge number of documents, some in English translation, some in the original languages mostly Latin, and these are constantly augmented. It incorporates the website of The Anglo-American Legal Tradition, a project to digitise mainly unpublished records in the National Archives, which currently holds over six million images of mainly medieval English documents. They are all freely available, like the other material on Medieval Source Material on the Internet, though they require both linguistic and paleographic skills.

Also of great help is the very extensive site British History Online. Some categories of sources available here can only be accessed on payment of a modest fee. Also worth exploring is the very large collection of chronicles and related texts held by archive.org, another free site – which is always grateful for donations.

Secondary sources
** indicates a work of considerable importance*

Andrews, R. M., 'The Nomenclature of Kingship in Welsh Court Poetry 1100–1300; Part I: The Terms', *Studia Celtica*, 44 (2010), 79–109.
—— 'The Nomenclature of Kingship in Welsh Court Poetry 1100–1300; Part II: The Rulers', *Studia Celtica*, 45 (2011), 53–82.

Barrell, A. D. M. and Davies, R. R., 'Land, Lineage and Revolt in North-East Wales, 1243–1441: a Case Study, *Cambrian Medieval Celtic Studies*, 29 (1995), 27–51.

Barton, P. G., 'The military career of William de la Pole, 1293–1304: an inherited role', *Montgomeryshire Collections*, 105 (2017), 7–15.

—— 'The Battle of Maes Moydog', *Montgomeryshire Collections*, 106 (2018), 33–42.

Bridgeman, G. T. O., 'The Princes of Upper Powys', *Montgomeryshire Collections*, 1 (1868), 5–194.

Bullock-Davies, C., *Menestrellorum Multitudo* (Cardiff: University of Wales Press, 1978).

Carr, A. D., 'The barons of Edeyrnion 1282–1485', *Journal of the Merioneth History and Record Society*, 4 (1961), 187–93, 298–301).

—— 'An Aristocracy in decline: the native Welsh lords after the Edwardian conquest', *Welsh History Review*, 5 (1970), 103-29.*

—— 'Rhys ap Roppert', *Transactions of the Denbighshire Historical Society*, 25 (1976), 155–70.

—— *Owen of Wales: the end of the house of Gwynedd* (Cardiff, 1991).

—— *Medieval Wales* (London: Macmillan, 1995).

—— 'Edeirnion', in J. B. Smith and LL. B. Smith (eds), *A History of Merioneth II: The Middle Ages* (2001).

—— 'Lineage, Power and Land in Medieval Flintshire: the descendants of Ithel Fychan', *Flintshire Historical Society Journal*, 36 (2003), 59–81.*

—— *Medieval Anglesey* (2nd edn, Llangefni, 2011).

—— *The Gentry of North Wales in the Later Middle Ages* (Cardiff, 2017).*

Chapman, A., *Welsh Soldiers in the Later Middle Ages 1282–1422* (Woodbridge: Boydell and Brewer, 2015).*

Crouch, D., *The Image of Aristocracy in Britain, 1100–1300* (London, 1992).

Davies, J., 'Madog's raid: the Welsh attack on the Vale of Montgomery, 6 April, 1332', *Montgomeryshire Collections*, 106 (2018), 43–53.

—— 'Christmas at the court of Dafydd ap Cadwaladr at Bachelldre near Montgomery in the mid-fourteenth century', *Montgomeryshire Collections*, 109 (2021), 23–32.

Davies, R. R., 'Colonial Wales', *Past and Present*, 65 (1974), 3–23.*

—— 'Race Relations in Post-Conquest Wales', *Transactions of the Honourable Society of Cymmrodorion* (1974–5), 32–56.*

—— *Lordship and Society in the March of Wales, 1284–1400* (Oxford, 1978).*

—— 'The Peoples of Britain and Ireland 1100–1400. II Names, Boundaries and Regnal Solidarities', *Transactions of the Royal Historical Society* (1995), 1–20.

—— *The Age of Conquest: Wales 1063–1415* (Oxford, 2000) (Originally published with the same text as *Conquest, Coexistence and Change: Wales 1063–1415* (Oxford, 1987); the reissue includes an updated Bibliography).*

Bibliography

Edwards, J. G., 'Sir Gruffydd Llwyd', *English Historical Review*, 120/30 (1915), 589–601.
—— 'The Treason of Thomas Turberville', in R. W. Hunt, W. A. Pantin and R. W. Southern (eds), *Studies in Medieval History Presented to F. M. Powicke* (Oxford: Clarendon Press, 1948), pp. 296–309.
Evans, D. L., 'Some Notes on the History of the Principality of Wales in the time of the Black Prince', *Transactions of the Honourable Society of Cymmrodorion* (1925–6), 25–110.
Fryde, N. M., 'Welsh Troops in the Scottish Campaign of 1322', *Bulletin of the Board of Celtic Studies*, 26 (1974–5), 82–9.
Fryde, N., *The tyranny and fall of Edward II, 1321–1326* (Cambridge, 1979).
Gittos, B. and Gittos, M., 'Gresham revisited: a fresh look at the medieval monuments of north Wales', *Archaeologia Cambrensis*, 161 (2012), 357–88.
Gresham, C., *Medieval Stone Carving in North Wales: Sepulchral Slabs and Effigies of the Thirteenth and Fourteenth Centuries* (Cardiff: University of Wales Press, 1968).*
Griffith, J. E., *Pedigrees of Anglesey and Caernarvonshire Families* (Horncastle, 1914).
Griffiths, R. A., *The Principality of Wales in the Later Middle Ages: The Structure and Personnel of Government. I. South Wales 1277–1536* (Cardiff, 1972).*
—— *Conquerors and Conquered in Medieval Wales* (Stroud, 1994).
Guy, B., *Medieval Welsh Genealogy* (Woodbridge, 2020).
Haines, R. M., *King Edward II* (Montreal: McGill-Queen's University Press, 2003).
Holmes, G. A., *The Estates of the Higher Nobility in Fourteenth-Century England* (Cambridge, 1957).
Jack, R. I., 'Welsh and English in the Medieval Lordship of Ruthin', *Transactions of the Denbighshire Historical Society*, 18 (1969), 23–49.
Jones, B., *Fasti Ecclesiae Anglicanae 1300–1541: Volume 11, the Welsh Dioceses (Bangor, Llandaff, St Asaph, St Davids)* (London, 1965).
Jones, C. O., *Llywelyn Bren* (Llanrwst, 2006).
Jones, F., 'The Subsidy of 1292', *Bulletin of the Board of Celtic Studies*, 13 (1948–50), 210–30.
Korngiebel, D. M., 'English Colonial Ethnic Discrimination in the Lordship of Dyffryn Clwyd: Segregation and Integration, 1282–c.1340', *Welsh History Review*, 23 (2006), 1–24.
Lewis, H., Roberts, T. and Williams, I. (eds), *Cywyddau Iolo Goch ac Eraill, 1350–1450* (Cardiff, 1937).
Morgan, R., 'The Barony of Powys, 1275–1360', *Welsh History Review*, 10 (1980), 1–42.
—— 'An extent of the lordship of Hay', *Brycheiniog*, 28 (1995–6), 15–21.

Owen, D. H., 'The Englishry of Denbigh: an English colony in Medieval Wales', *Transactions of the Honourable Society of Cymmrodorion* (1974–5), 57–76.
Pilling, D., *Edward I and Wales 1254–1307* (Barnsley: Pen and Sword, 2021).
Pryce, H. (ed.), *The Acts of Welsh Rulers 1120–1283* (Cardiff, 2005).
Rees, W., 'The Black Death in Wales', *Transactions of the Royal Historical Society*, 4th series, 3 (1920), 115–35.
Roberts, G., *Aspects of Welsh History* (Cardiff, 1969).*
Schofield, P. R., 'Wales and the Great Famine of the Early Fourteenth Century', *Welsh History Review*, 29 (2018), 143–67.
Siddons, M. P., *The Development of Welsh Heraldry II* (Aberystwyth, 1993).
Smith, J. B., 'Gruffudd Llwyd and the Celtic Alliance', *Bulletin of the Board of Celtic Studies*, 26 (1974–6), 463–78.
—— 'Edward II and the Allegiance of Wales', *Welsh History Review*, 8 (1976–7), 139–71.*
—— 'Marcher Regality. Quo Warranto Proceedings relating to Cantrefselyf in Lordship of Brecon, 1349', *Bulletin of the Board of Celtic Studies*, 28 (1978–80), 267–88.
—— 'Sir Gruffudd Llwyd', *Oxford Dictionary of National Biography* (2004).
Smith, L. B., 'The Arundel charters to the lordship of Chirk in the fourteenth century', *Bulletin of the Board of Celtic Studies*, 22 (1969), 153–66.
—— 'The statute of Wales, 1284', *Welsh History Review*, 10 (1980–1), 127–54.
Smith, G. R., 'The Penmachno Letter Patent and the Welsh Uprising of 1294–95', *Cambrian Medieval Celtic Studies*, 58 (2009), 49–67.
Stephenson, D., 'The Middle Ages in the pages of *Montgomeryshire Collections*', *Montgomeryshire Collections*, 100 (2012), 67–85.
—— 'Crisis and continuity in a fourteenth-century Welsh lordship: the struggle for Powys, 1312–32', *Cambrian Medieval Celtic Studies*, 66 (2013), 57–78.
—— *Political Power in Medieval Gwynedd: Governance and the Welsh Princes* (Cardiff, 2014). Previously published as *The Governance of Gwynedd* (Cardiff, 1984). The new edition has an expanded introductory chapter.
—— *Medieval Powys: Kingdom, Principality and Lordships, 1132–1293* (Woodbridge, 2016).
—— 'New light on a dark deed', *Archaeologia Cambrensis*, 166 (2017), 243–52.
—— 'The early physicians of Myddfai in context', in Robin Barlow (ed.), *Transactions of the Physicians of Myddfai Society, 2011–2017* (2018), pp. 61–8.

—— *Medieval Wales c.1050–1332: Centuries of Ambiguity* (Cardiff: University of Wales Press, 2019).*
—— 'The continuation of *Brut y Tywysogyon* in NLW, MS Peniarth 20 Revisited', in B. Guy, G. Henley, O. W. Jones and R. Thomas (eds), *The Chronicles of Medieval Wales and the March* (Turnhout: Brepols, 2020).
—— *Patronage and Power in the Medieval Welsh March: One Family's Story* (Cardiff: University of Wales Press, 2021).*
—— 'The Malice and Rebellion of Certain Welshmen ... The Welsh Risings of 1294–95', in A. Jobson, H. Kersey and G. McKelvie (eds), *Rebellion in Medieval Europe c.1000–1500* (forthcoming).
Stevens, M. F., *Urban Assimilation in Post-conquest Wales: Ethnicity, Gender and Economy in Ruthin, 1282–1348* (Cardiff: 2010).
—— *The Economy of Medieval Wales, 1067–1536* (Cardiff: University of Wales Press, 2019).*
Walker, D., *Medieval Wales* (Cambridge: Cambridge University Press, 1990).
Waters, W. H., *The Edwardian Settlement of North Wales in its Administrative and Legal Aspects (1284–1343)* (Cardiff: University of Wales Press, 1935).
—— *The Edwardian Settlement of West Wales, 1277–1343* (Abergele: 2000).
Williams, G., *The Welsh Church from Conquest to Reformation* (2nd edn, Cardiff, 1976).

County histories

These are of varying usefulness in the present context but all will repay study, even if only to demonstrate how important themes are sometimes missed out:
Cardiganshire: *Cardiganshire County History: Volume 2. Medieval and Early Modern Cardiganshire*, ed. G. H. Jenkins, R. Suggett and E. M. White (Cardiff, 2019).
Carmarthenshire: *A History of Carmarthenshire I: From Prehistoric Times to the Act of Union*, ed. J. E. Lloyd (Cardiff, 1935).
Glamorgan: *Glamorgan County History III: The Middle Ages*, ed. T. B. Pugh (Cardiff, 1971).*
Gwent: *The Gwent County History II: The Age of the Marcher Lords c.1070–1536*, ed. R. A. Griffiths, T. Hopkins and R. Howell (Cardiff, 2008).
Merioneth: *History of Merioneth II: The Middle Ages*, ed. J. B. Smith and L. B. Smith (Cardiff, 2001).*
Pembrokeshire: *Pembrokeshire County History II: Medieval Pembrokeshire* (Haverfordwest: 2002).

Unpublished theses

Davies, R. R., 'The Bohun and Lancaster Lordships in Wales in the Fourteenth and Early Fifteenth Centuries (unpublished D. Phil thesis, University of Oxford, 1965).*

Rogers, M., 'The Welsh Marcher lordship of Bromfield and Yale, 1282–1485' (unpublished PhD thesis, University College of Wales, Aberystwyth, 1992).

Biebrach, R., 'Memorialisation and the Gentry of Glamorgan 1250–1550' (unpublished PhD thesis, Swansea University, 2010). (This thesis, and a subsequent book, R. Biebrach, *Church Monuments in South Wales, c.1200–1547* (Woodbridge, 2017) serve, in the present context, to contrast the areas of the south studied, marked by a significant lack of funerary memorials to Welsh figures, with the situation in the north, for which see the entry for Colin Grisham's work.)

Index

Aberconwy
　abbot of 5
　castle 5
　constable 159 n.26
　treaty of xxxviii, 94, 100
Abergavenny
　lordship xxxix, 35, 69, 70, 119
　rising in 3, 5
Administrative aristocracy in Wales xxvii, xxviii, xxxi, 1, 36, 38, 60
Age of the Princes xxiv, 95, 109
Ales ferch Ithel Fychan 88

Bamburgh Castle 3–4
Bangor (Bishop of) 34, 39, 46, 88, 141, 143–4, 182 nn.37–8
Bangor, Dominican friary 90–1
Bannockburn, Battle of 25, 39, 41, 61, 164 n.59
Bere, Richard de la 103–4, 130
Berwyn mountains xxv
bishops in Wales 26, 141–4, 181 n.35
Black Death in Wales, impact of 86, 102, 105, 128, 137–9, 145, 178 n.4
Black Prince 47, 50, 55–6, 68, 89, 92, 94, 99, 101, 103, 129, 139–40, 144–8
　see also Edward
Bohun, Humphrey de, 3rd earl (d. 1298) xxvi, xxxviii, 9, 2, 32
Bohun, Humphrey de, 4th earl (d. 1322) 20, 25, 27, 41, 48, 62, 67, 70–2,

Bohun, Humphrey de, 6th earl (d. 1361) 68, 128, 179 n.29
Boroughbridge, battle of (1322) 27, 36, 48, 70, 82, 89, 165 n.63
Bromfield and Yale, lordship 35–7, 59, 84, 86
Bronllys castle and lordship 23
Bruce, Edward the, invasion of Ireland 25, 39–40, 44–6, 78
Bruce, Robert the 25, 33–4, 39, 91
Brut y Tywysogyon, continuation of 28, 37, 59, 95, 107, 158 n.9
Builth (Buellt), castle and Lordship of xxvii, xxxvi, xxxvii, xxxix, xl, 4, 13, 15, 23–4, 26, 41, 47, 49, 54–5, 68, 73, 100, 105, 157 n.1, 160 n.29, 162 n.24

Calais 145
Carr, A. D. x, 13, 94
Charlton, John, lord of Powys xxiv, 27, 77, 79–80, 175 n.174
Clanvowe, Sir John (d. 1349) 47–50, 99, 128
Clare, lord of Glamorgan *see* Gilbert the Red (d. 1295); Gilbert the Last (d. 1314)
Clement, Geoffrey, deputy justiciar, South Wales xxvii
Clement, Robert, brother of Geoffrey 119, 121
Clipstone Tower 34, 39, 46
Cycon, William de, constable of Aberconwy 4, 42, 159 n.26
Cynllaith xxiv–xxv, 81

Cynan ap Maredudd (rebel leader) 4
 death of 158–9 n.16 `
Cynwrig ap Gruffudd, sheriff of Anglesey (1332–33) 97–9
Cynwrig ap Llywarch 82–3
Cynwrig Sais (Northop) x, 86–8, 117, 122, 145

Dafydd ap Cadwaladr 75, 128, 170–1 n.173
Dafydd ab Einion Fychan ab Einion xxxii
Dafydd ap Gwilym xxxv, 103, 130, 177 n.221, 179 n.17
 descent of xxxv
Dafydd ap Hywel ap Dafydd 14–15, 99, 160 n.37
 see also Dafydd Bongam
Dafydd ap Llywelyn ap Philip 99
Dafydd ap Madog ap Gruffudd 95, 175 n.176
Dafydd ap Meurig (Morganwg? Meisgyn and Glynrhondda) 66–7, 119–20, 160 n.37
Dafydd Bongam, steward of Cantref Mawr (1303–9) 14–15, 99, 160 n.37
Dafydd Fychan 15
Danvers, Thomas 5, 159 n.19
Davies, R. R. ix, 156, 165
Dindaethwy, commote of (office of *rhaglaw* of) 90, 93
distain, office of xxviii–xxix, xxx, xxxii–xxxiv, xl–xli, 6, 38, 74, 79, 89, 156 n.13
Dryslwyn Castle, of Rhys ap Maredudd xxiii–xxiv, 13–14, 74

Edeirnion, barons of xiv, 15, 94–5, 98, 111–12, 174–5
Ednyfed Fychan xxix–xxxiii, xxxv, 38, 59–60, 112, 125, 145, 156 n.8
 see also Wyrion Eden
Edward I (d. 1307)
 Assessments of x, xi, 1–2, 139–40
 Edward's Interventions in Wales 3–17, 56
 The Edwardian Settlement xxvii
 Appointment of Welsh magnates to senior posts 12–17
 Treatment of Leaders of risings in (1294–5) 3–4
 Edward's developing conciliatory policy in Wales 3–17, 140
 Influence in principality of Wales after 1301, 16, 98
Edward of Caernarfon, as Prince of Wales (1301–7) 16, 20, 24, 33, 98
Edward II (1307–27) x, 21, 25, 27, 34, 36, 39–41, 45, 61, 78, 114, 122–3, 139–40
Edward III (1327–77), attitude to Wales 129–30, 139–40 *passim*
Edward the Black Prince, impact of rule of 50, 55, 129, 137, 143, 148, 181 n.37
Einion ab Ieuan, sheriff of Anglesey (1316–27) 88, 97–8
Einion ap Gwalchmai xxix, xxxii–xxxiii
Einion ap Madog xxxix–xl
Einion Fawr ap Gwilym 102
Einion Fychan ab Einion ap Gwalchmai xxxii
Einion Fychan ap Gwilym 103
Einion Sais ap Rhys xi, 68–9, 93
Elen, daughter of Thomas ap Llywelyn ab Owain xxv
Ellesmere, manor of 116
Erddylad, ferch Madog ap Llywelyn ap Gruffudd 86, 179 n.23
expertise, culture of, developing in the High Middle Ages across Wales, xlii–xliii

Flintshire 6, 85–8
 corruption and oppression in 145–52, *passim*

Gaveston, Piers 47, 48, 70, 75, 82

Index

Gilbert de Clare, earl of Gloucester, lord of Glamorgan (d. 1295) 4, 29–31, 61, 108, 179 n.15
Gilbert, last de Clare earl of Gloucester (d. 1314) 61
Glamorgan xxvi, 3–4, 10–11, 21, 29–32, 34–5, 51, 61–7, 69–71, 78, 108, 115, 118, 124, 128, 159 n.26, 178 n.15
Gloddaeth, Madog 93, 179 n.23
Goronwy ab Ednyfed 59, 89, 111, 174 n.156
Goronwy ab Einion xl
Goronwy ap Tudur (d. 1331) 59, 91–2, 128
Goronwy Goch, steward of Cantref Mawr 14, 99
Grave slabs, inscribed 37, 59–60, 82–3
Gruffudd ab Ednyfed 38, 51, 99, 110
Gruffudd ab Owain, sheriff of Anglesey (1306–9) 97
Gruffudd ap Dafydd, lord of Hendwr 15–16, 94–5, 98, 111, 165 n.60
Gruffudd ap Gruffudd 80
Gruffudd ap Gwên xl, 74, 79–80
Gruffudd ap Gwenwynwyn xxiii–xxiv, xxvi, 1, 75–7
Gruffudd ap Gwilym 103
Gruffudd ap Llywelyn 109
Gruffudd ap Llywelyn, Gelligynan 84–5
Gruffudd ap Madog (Glyndyfrdwy, Cynllaith) 81
Gruffudd ap Rhys (Sir Gruffudd Llwyd)
   noble and princely pedigree of 38
   military activity of, especially for Edward II 38–9, 39–46, 123
   administrative services to Edward I–Edward III 39, 98
   known as 'a man of the Court' 43, 47, 135
   periods of imprisonment 42–6
   assessment of 33, 38, 46
Gruffudd Fychan (d. 1289) xxiv–xxv, 81
Gruffudd Fychan de la Pole 76–7, 109, 128, 170 n.166
Gruffudd Grach/Crach 101
Gruffudd Llwyd (Gelligynan) 84–5
Gwenllian, daughter of Lord Rhys xxx–xxxi, 38, 110,
Gwerful ferch Madog ap Dafydd, mother of Hywel ap Goronwy 92, 95
Gwilym ab Einion 102
Gwilym ap Gruffudd ap Gwenwynwyn (de la Pole) 75–6
Gwilym ap Gwrwared, lineage xxxv
   offices held by xxxv–xxxvi
   descendants of 51, 102, 112, 156 n.6
Gwyn ab Ednywain xxix, xxxiii
Gwynllŵg, ministerial dynasty of xl, 29, 110

Hastings, John lord of Abergavenny and Cilgerran 5, 159 n.17
Havering, John de, justice of North Wales 5, 42–3, 159 n.26
Hendwr 15, 91–2, 94–5, 111, 115
Henry II 107
Henry III xxx, xxxvi, xxxix, 18, 36, 107
Hope and Hopedale 6, 139
Huntingdon, John of 130–1
Hywel ab Einion Sais 69
Hywel ap Cynwrig 5
Hywel ap Goronwy ap Tudur Hen 132–3, 136
Hywel ap Gruffudd (Hywel 'y Pedolau') 91, 96, 174 nn.140, 142
Hywel ap Hywel (Brecon) 63, 69–71
Hywel ap Hywel (Glamorgan) 62–3, 69–71

Hywel ap Madog ap Llywelyn 158 n.13
Hywel ap Meurig xxxvi, 13, 19–20

Ieuan ap Sir Gruffudd 89
Ieuan ap Hywel, sheriff of Merionethshire (1306–9) 98
Ieuan ap Madog Fychan 101–2
Ieuan ap Moelwyn, 100–1
Ieuan ap Rees (Middle March) 67, 112, 117
Ieuan Wyn, Poursuivant d'amour, son of Rhys ap Roppert 152
Ifor ap Gruffudd (Elfael) xxxvii–xxxviii
Iolo Goch xxv, 92, 143
Iorwerth ap Llywarch 82–3
Iorwerth ap Rhirid 88
Ithel Fychan x, 86–8, 179 n.23
Ithel Person 86–7
Ithel ap Cynwrig Sais x, 146, 148, 150

John ap Llywelyn 101
John d'Avene 65, 168 n.20, 169 nn.28, 34

Kennington 16, 24, 90

Launceston (Cornwall), Castle of 92–3, 95, 175 n.176
Leisan d'Avene 6, 63–76, 116, 128
Lestrange, Eubolo xxv, 82
Lleucu, wife of Llywelyn Bren 62, 65, 117, 180 n.29
Llywelyn ab Iorwerth (Prince, d. 1240) xxiii, xxix–xxx, xxxii–xxxiii, xlii, 38, 89, 97, 107, 178 n.7
Llywelyn ab Ynyr, Llywelyn of Bromfield, bishop of St Asaph 84–5, 141, 172 n.115
Llywelyn ap Cynwrig ap Hywel 65–6
Llywelyn ap Gruffudd, Prince of Gwynedd (1246–82) xxiii, xxx, xxxiv, xxxvii, xxxix, 1, 29, 35
Llywelyn ap Gwilym 103–4, 130, 179 n.17

Llywelyn ap Llywelyn ap Maredudd, Bodidris 85
Llywelyn ap Madog, Dyffryn Clwyd 84, 116, 128
Llywelyn ap Philip 99
Llywelyn Bren 21, 34, 40, 51, 61–5, 109, 111–12, 117–18

Madog ab Einion 74, 170 n.69
Madog ap Dafydd 95, 175 n.171
Madog ap Gruffudd ap Dafydd 95
Madog ap Gruffudd ap Madog 81
Madog ap Llywelyn ap Gruffudd 35–8, 59, 86, 108, 110
Madog ap Llywelyn of Meirionnydd xxv, 3, 6, 16
Madog ap Maredudd, ruler of Powys (1132–60) xxiii–xxiv, xlii, 16, 35, 81, 110
Madog ap Meilir 73–5, 170 n.169
Madog Fychan, Tir Iarll 63, 65–6, 119, 128
Madog Llwyd 97
Maelgwn ap Rhys xxvi, 3–4
Maelienydd 7–9, 11, 24, 124, 162 n.18
Malore, Peter 6
Maredudd ap Llywelyn 84–5
Mauny, Walter de 130
Mechain 74, 77, 171 n.85
Meurig ab Ynyr Fychan 96
Meurig ap Dafydd 3, 159 n.17
Meurig ap Rees ap Meurig 71, 73, 115, 117–18, 122, 124, 128
Morgan ap Maredudd (Sir)
  background 3–4, 29–30, 110
  involvement in undercover work for the king 9, 29–32, 46
  administrative and military work 20, 25, 32–3, 63
  eminence 33, 99, 110
Roger Mortimer of Chirk 44, 52, 76
Mortimer, Edmund of Wigmore (d. 1304) 7–9, 24
Mortimer, Roger of Wigmore (d. 1282) 19

Index

Mortimer, Roger of Wigmore, 1st earl of March (d.1330) 22, 25, 27–8, 41, 48, 52, 66, 118, 123

Newcastle Emlyn 15, 102–3, 181 n.24
Newcastle on Tyne 3

Owain ap Gruffudd ap Gwên 80
Owain ap Gruffudd ap Gwenwynwyn xxiv, 74, 77, 79
Owain Lawgoch xxvi, 152

Pederton, Walter de, 20, 24–5
Penteulu, office of xxix, 76, 95
Philip ap Goronwy xli
Philip ap Hywel
    multiple stewardships in 1290s 24, 32
    Philip as a royal officer and adviser 15, 24–6, 160 n.34, 161 n.48, 163 n.35
    opponent of Hugh Despenser the Younger 28, 41, 48, 70
    supports the baronial faction 27–8
    arrested but released 109
    ecclesiastical eminence 24, 28
Philip ap Rees (Philip de Bronllys) 68, 112
Pool (Welshpool) Castle and lordship xxiv, 27, 41, 77, 157
population of Wales, early fourteenth century 105–6
Powys, lordship of xxiii–xxv, xl, 73–9, 95, 98, 115
Praers, William de 87–8, 151
Prid (Welsh mortgage) 86
'Prince', designation of in fourteenth century 155 n.1

Rees ap Hywel (Master) 19–22, 25, 31–48, 67–8, 71–2, 108–10, 117, 124, 127–8, 161 n.48, 163 n.45, 170 n.59
Rhodri ap Gruffudd xxvi
Rhuddlan 131, 133

Rhys ap Gruffudd (Yr Arglwydd Rhys), ruler of Deheubarth (d. 1197) 107, 110
Rhys ap Gruffudd (Sir)
    background and pedigree 51, 99, 110, 113, 145, 156 n.6
    royal service, administrative and military 52–5, 115–19, 166 n.90
    failed attempts to save Edward II 53, 109
    re-emergence as a leading administrator for Edward III 55
    reputation for oppression 55–6, 128
Rhys ap Gruffudd the younger (Sir) 112, 152, 182 n.56
Rhys ap Maredudd, xxiii, 13–14, 74, 102
Rhys ap Meurig xli
Rhys ap Roppert x, 87–8, 112, 145–52
Roberts, Glyn x, xiv, 139, 176 n.189

St Davids, bishop of 5, 49, 141–3
Seals, possession of xliii, 59
Sepulchral effigies 59–60
Shaldeford, Henry de 92–5, 131–5, 181 n.19
Smith, J. Beverley x, 65
Stafford, Richard de 132–3
Strata Florida, abbey of 12
Sybil, wife of Llywelyn ap Gruffudd ap Gwenwynwyn xxiv

Tower of London xxvii, 3–4, 22–3, 27, 41, 52, 62–3, 125, 127
Trefddisteiniaid xxxii
troops 16, 19, 20, 24–5, 32–4, 38, 41, 43, 47–9, 51–5, 66, 68–70, 73–6, 85, 93–6, 106, 109, 112, 114–16, 118, 121–5, 129, 135, 142, 164, 165 nn.59, 63, 180 n.35
Trumwyn, Roger 45, 76, 79–80, 133
Tudur ab Ednyfed xxxii, xl
Tudur ab Ithel 86, 88

Tudur ap Goronwy (d. 1311) 5–6, 89
Tudur ap Goronwy ap Tudur Hen 92

Violence in Welsh political life 93, 103–4, 130, 181 n.23

Welsh soldiers xxxix, 52–4, 74, 164 n.59
  declining use of 129
  see also troops
West Wales 6

William ap Gruffudd ap Gwenwynwyn xxvi, 74, 76, 160 n.26
William ap Hywel ap Meurig 47, 161, 179 n.21
Wives, mothers, of English origin 113
Wyrion Eden xxxi, 87, 136, 145

Ynyr Fychan 95–6, 111, 175 nn.181–2
Ystrwyth (Instructus), Master 89, 98, 173 n.130